Clara Inés Peña de Carrillo

Adaptive and Assisted Educational Hypermedia

Clara Inés Peña de Carrillo

Adaptive and Assisted Educational Hypermedia

Conceptual Model and Technological Solution
using Intelligent Agents

VDM Verlag Dr. Müller

Imprint

Bibliographic information by the German National Library: The German National Library lists this publication at the German National Bibliography; detailed bibliographic information is available on the Internet at http://dnb.d-nb.de.
   Any brand names and product names mentioned in this book are subject to trademark, brand or patent protection and are trademarks or registered trademarks of their respective holders. The use of brand names, product names, common names, trade names, product descriptions etc. even without a particular marking in this works is in no way to be construed to mean that such names may be regarded as unrestricted in respect of trademark and brand protection legislation and could thus be used by anyone.

Cover image: www.purestockx.com

Publisher:
VDM Verlag Dr. Müller Aktiengesellschaft & Co. KG, Dudweiler Landstr. 125 a, 66123 Saarbrücken, Germany,
Phone +49 681 9100-698, Fax +49 681 9100-988,
Email: info@vdm-verlag.de

Produced in USA and UK by:
Lightning Source Inc., La Vergne, Tennessee, USA
Lightning Source UK Ltd., Milton Keynes, UK
BookSurge LLC, 5341 Dorchester Road, Suite 16, North Charleston, SC 29418, USA

ISBN: 978-3-639-00402-1

Acknowledgements

At a moment like this, I find this to be the most difficult section to write. I cannot find the words to express my thanks to so many people who have offered unconditional help during this long road of suffering and joy I decided to follow to carry out this enthusiastic research work.

First of all, thank you God since I would not have done anything without you.

To Gilberto and my teenagers ("mis chinitos") Paulo Nicolás and Paula Alejandra, because without their sacrifice and support in the good and in the bad, this work would never have begun. I am sorry for not being available for family plans since I was always doing research.

To doctors José Luis Marzo and Peplluis de la Rosa, for believing in me and allowing me to develop with interest and dedication the topic of this work which has pleased me so much.

To doctors Ramón Fabregat and Teo Jové, from the BCDS research group at the Universitat de Girona, for the opportunity to work on the **Unitat de Suport a la Docència Virtual** (USDV) and to serve the university community through the USD (Unitats de Suport a la Docencia) platform, providing materials to support traditional instruction.

To the members of the European projects GALECIA and AGENTCITIES, in which I had the opportunity to participate, and whose contribution was vital for the scientific support of this book.

To all my undergraduate students and the multidisciplinary experts from the Universidad Industrial de Santander and the Universitat de Girona who in one or another way have supported me in the implementation of the ideas proposed in this work.

Finally, in spite of not being persons but as if they were, thanks to mateo (my dog before) and runy (my actual dog) for their silent company during the long hours of writing.

TABLE OF CONTENTS

PART 2: MASPLANG E-LEARNING ENVIRONMENT:
Adaptive Presentation, Adaptive Navigation and Affective
Behavior in an E-Learning Hypermedia System with

1. LIST OF FIGURES

LIST OF TABLES

General Introduction

General Introduction

The potential of the Internet for creating online learning environments to support education has been amply demonstrated [Fet 1998, Har 1999 and Yaz 2002]. The web as a learning aid is bringing us closer than we ever thought possible to making tele-learning a practical reality. Learning via the web may enable every person to acquire knowledge of all kinds, at all levels, at any time and in any place, following their own pace.

The need to link pedagogy to the prevailing technological infrastructure was highlighted by Mergendoller [Men 1996] and Roschelle [Ros 1999]. However, they emphasized the need for additional new frameworks for online learning. To meet this requirement, several researchers have offered different solutions. Bonk offered frameworks for learner-centered web instruction in [Bon 1998], and in [Bon 2001] he wrote about the integration of the web in instruction and the role of the online instructor, while Cummings in [Cum 2002] detailed the types and forms of interaction made possible by the growth of the web.

Although web technology has allowed teachers to use multimedia in the presentation of teaching materials, most web-based learning environments are nothing more than a set of static electronic pages. Creating interactive (i.e., more interesting) online courses and tutorials means using a combination of hypertext and multimedia (hypermedia) while a number of aspects need to be dealt with before the true potential of web-based learning environments can be exploited [Nik 1999]. These aspects include adaptivity, a broader range of educational material and access to course material which, at present, remains slow.

In a general sense, a web-based learning environment should interact with the students, adapt to their needs, assist the students during learning, support teacher-student and student-student interaction and, finally, be user-friendly to the authors of the material.

Adaptivity is the ability to be aware of a user's behavior, to take his or her level of knowledge into account, and so provide the user with the right kind of instructional material [Bar 1999]. As stated by Hoschka [Hos 1996], "adaptation" is an important issue in the research of learning environments, since it can lead to better learning in such systems. However, before an effective and efficient adaptation in learning systems is possible, many issues must be addressed [Mil 1996]. This means developing a student model which captures student interaction with the system in order to extract information about their competence level for various domain concepts and tasks.

A promising technology that could be applied to web-based learning is Intelligent Software Agent environments. The development of Intelligent Software Agents is still in its early stages, however in this scenario, a web agent can be thought of as a software package that helps guide the user. Agents could be used to support online education, by assisting, tutoring and monitoring students throughout their learning process.

The purpose of this work is to show that intelligent agents in web-based learning environments may be used to improve the guidance given to the user, while increasing user motivation and the adaptivity of course materials.

The main goal, for which an approach and a methodology are suggested in this work, concerns two important aspects: (i) choosing the right instructional strategy based on learning styles and (ii) providing access to didactic materials adapted to learning styles and levels of knowledge.

Within the context of this work, learning is defined as the process of internal change which under various conditions results in the acquisition of an internal representation of a notion (knowledge) or an attitude. This internal process cannot be measured directly, but it can be measured through the external observable demonstrations that constitute the behavior related to the object of knowledge. Finally, this change is a result of the experience or training by the web and has a durability which depends on factors such as motivation and compromise [Hui 1999].

The contribution of the new Information and Communication Technology (ICT) to the construction of a new educational society is presented here. This text considers multimedia, hypertext, agent technology and adaptivity in building a learning environment that takes into account the following 'actors':

- The teacher. The educator is more than a mere dispenser of knowledge; he/she is henceforth a «facilitator», a mediator between the knowledge and the learner.
- The construction of a differentiated pedagogy. This becomes a necessity through the convergence of the cognitive system of the educator and that of the learner in this new environment.
- The knowledge. The contents are not frozen, but in evolution. This means that the learning processes are not simple reproduction mechanisms; on the contrary, they use real approaches and training.

This work assumes that the teacher should consider the cognitive styles of students in order to deliver adaptive education. In this sense, the system aims to construct a warehouse of courses in which each set of concepts, or ideas is affected by certain parameters chosen by the author's methodological criteria. These parameters can be classified into two groups: the first, which gives importance to the content (accumulation of knowledge – rigid pedagogy); and the second, which cedes a place to the chosen processes (construction of the knowledge, mediation, etc. – flexible pedagogy). The latter is considered the heart of the MASPLANG (MultiAgent System PLANG[1]), an adaptive multiagent hypermedia system for education purposes, in particular ODL[2], which is proposed here.

This book is divided into two main parts: the first describes, in four chapters, the current state of the art. That is, it provides a complete exploration of the fundamentals of Computer Mediated Education, Intelligent Tutoring Systems, Adaptive Hypermedia, Software Agent Technology and this work proposal.

In Chapter 1, we describe the limits of teaching, knowledge, traditional teaching and the integration of the computer into teaching, with its advantages and disadvantages.

In Chapter 2, we discuss hypermedia and adaptive hypermedia in education.

---

[1] PLANG: project supported by the Spanish Research Council (CICYT) TEL 98-0408-C02-01 and TEL99-0976. Its name belongs from the Spanish sentence '**PLA**taforma de **N**ueva **G**eneración'.
[2] ODL: Open and Distance Learning

In Chapter 3 we provide an introduction to Intelligent Agent Technology, considering its characteristics, classification and applications in web-based learning environments and multiagent architectures.

Chapter 4, represent this work proposal. A web-based hypermedia learning environment will be formulated. This environment takes into account learning styles and the state of student knowledge to provide access to suitable educational materials, using a multiagent architecture to provide adaptivity, assistance and motivation by means of information and interface agents. With this methodology, enhanced learner tutorship, assistantship and motivation will be demonstrated.

The second part of this work contains three chapters concerned with the conceptual model; the design, development and implementation of the method; and the results of the experimentation and evaluation of the prototype. This part extends the proposal presented in Chapter 4.

In Chapter 5, we set down the method by formalizing the conceptual model of an adaptive hypermedia system for education, i.e. Chapter 5 contains the conceptual model of the MASPLANG.

In Chapter 6, we describe the design, development and implementation issues of the MASPLANG multiagent architecture in achieving adaptive presentation and adaptive navigation.

In Chapter 7, we present the results of experimentation and evaluation, showing the important role of testing, evaluating, developing and experimenting in developing the MASPLANG prototype.

We end with our general conclusions and suggestions for future work. Finally, information such as the bibliography of references, the appendices and the author's publications bring the text to a close.

This work was carried out within the BCDS (Broadband Communications and Distributed Systems) research group at the University of Girona.

Part 1

State of the Art

Education, Adaptive Hypermedia and Multiagent Systems

Introduction Part 1

Future technologies such as computer-mediated communications, intelligent tutoring systems, intelligent agents and virtual reality are maturing and converging to create "virtual classrooms." Intelligent agents in particular can act as cognitive tools for human learning [Bay 1999], managing large amounts of information, serving as a pedagogical expert, and creating programming environments for the learner.

In this section, a wide panoramic state of the art, which is the base for this work, is presented. The reviewed topics are: the influence of cognitive theories in education, the use of new technologies in Virtual Education, Intelligent Tutoring Systems (ITS) (including the educational hypermedia systems and their adaptivity in considering the student level of knowledge and preferences), and Intelligent Agent technology.

The development of an educational tool based on Information and Communication Technologies and which is suitable to offer the learners an adaptive and personalized working environment is possible with the conjunction of the following four major areas as stated by Laroussi in [Lar 2001]:

- Knowledge Engineering
- Cognitive Psychology
- The Human-Machine Interface
- Artificial Intelligence (IA)

Knowledge Engineering concerns the set of methods used by knowledge-based systems to allow the modeling of knowledge by using adaptive didactic materials and facilitating the user's training.

Cognitive Psychology is concerned with advances in the study of memory, perception, problem solving and thinking, among other areas. Understanding the learner's psychology is indispensable in maximizing the probability of training success and its influence in adaptive education.

The **Human-Machine Interface** permits didactic materials in a pleasant and attractive environment to be created for the learner's comfort. (It is concerned with the generation of ergonomic learning tools.) This science must also be considered to make the introduction of teaching information easy for teachers.

The contribution of **Artificial Intelligence** resides in the techniques used to integrate the different sciences mentioned above in order to offer virtual education by means of adaptive hypermedia. Specifically, Intelligent Agent Technology allows learning to be defined and coordinated in a personalized and motivated educational environment.

Chapter 1.   Information, Knowledge and Education

1.1   Society of Knowledge

One can define knowledge as "the capacity to act", as the potential to "start something going" [Cog 1998]. Thus, scientific or technical knowledge is primarily nothing other than the ability to act. The privileged status of scientific and technical knowledge in modern society is derived not from the fact that scientific discoveries are generally considered to be credible, objective, in conformity with reality, or even indisputable, but from the fact that this form of knowledge, more than any other, incessantly creates new opportunities for action.

Some of the challenges of knowledge, education and learning in this age are the ability to be more familiar and comfortable with abstract concepts and uncertain situations. Nowadays, much of the academic environment shows the already-made problems to the students and asks them to solve such problems. The reality of the growing corpus of global information and knowledge is that problems are rarely well defined. It requires those people trying to make valuable use of that knowledge to watch out for problems, gather the necessary information, and make decisions and choices based on complex and uncertain realities. Consequently, people have to process more information, handle social developments and critical situations, and make more decisions. Knowledge is a conscious application and classification of either information or its meaning-related assessment.

There are new technologies and new techniques generated by the information revolution that allow the creation of new knowledge and the dissemination of data, information and knowledge. Some of these technologies are: the Internet, the World Wide Web, the CD-ROM, audio, video and other electronic media forms. These new technologies allow academic practitioners to assist students in gaining the skills and abilities required to acquire and utilize knowledge contained in various forms.

Using advanced Information and Communications Technologies (ICT), a new system of knowledge education and learning breaks the boundaries of space and time, helping the professors and students through a wide range of synchronous and asynchronous activities. Synchronous activities include real-time lectures (featuring audio, presentations, web sites, and even video), quizzes and group discussions; all can occur with the instructor at the same location as the learner or even at a different location. Asynchronous activities include stored lectures (in audio and video) and other course material that can be accessed at nearly anytime and in anyplace.

A Distance Education system must support, as much as possible, the problems caused by the physical distance between teacher, student, and classmates. The classic approach of education as knowledge transmission has been changing into a model of practical experimentation and interaction that promotes changes in concepts and student strategies until he/she reaches proficiency. In this context, teachers perform the role of significative assistant instead of information provider. This requires more efficient mechanisms of adaptivity and assistance in problem-solving processes. The system must perform the teacher's role as much as possible, building a robust student model for each user that would enable: adapting the curriculum to each user; helping him/her to navigate through course activities; giving support in task accomplishment and in exercises and problem solving; and providing help resources anytime they are needed.

There are significant contrasts between knowledge, education and learning. "Education is generally seen as a formal process of instruction, based on a theory of teaching, to impart formal knowledge (to one or more students)" [Cog 1998]. However, the process of learning can occur with or without formal institutional education. "Knowledge accumulation and accumulation of skills will occur increasingly outside the traditional institutions of formal education. Learning in the workplace and through collaborations will become more commonplace" [Cog 1998].

1.2   Knowledge Area Components

Working in the knowledge area, it is important to distinguish between two specialized people that are clearly differentiated in the knowledge and learning society: the *knowledge manager*, who establishes the direction of the knowledge process, and the **knowledge engineer**, who develops the means to accomplish that direction (see Figure 1).

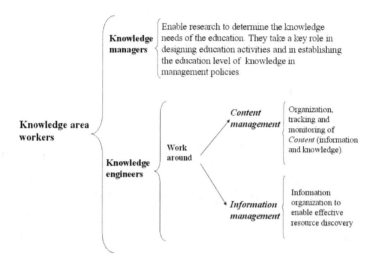

Figure 1. Knowledge area workers

Knowledge Management (KM) is a multi-disciplinary approach to achieve organizational objectives by making the best use of knowledge [see KM]. It focuses on processes such as acquiring, creating and sharing knowledge and the cultural and technical foundations that support those objectives. However, KM standards, are in the process of being developed and may cover a wide range of practices. Typically, KM involves an alignment of organizational objectives with the knowledge processes such as acquisition, workflow and sharing. **Knowledge managers** should enable research to determine the knowledge needed to make decisions and the corresponding actions.

Knowledge engineers work around areas of information representation (*Content Management*), encoding methodologies, data repositories (*Information Management*), work flow management, GroupWare technologies, etc. These people would most likely be researching technologies needed to meet the enterprise's knowledge management needs. They should also be establishing the processes of examining knowledge requests, assembled information, and requester-returned knowledge.

Content may broadly be understood as including both information and (storable) knowledge. Content can be represented in various formats, such as images, animation, movies and print. The three main components of content are:

- The *format*: related to natural language or visual format;
- The *organization*: content should be logically organized, for example, introduction, sections, conclusion; and
- The *presentation*: the way of presenting the content to the user.

Content Management refers to a range of procedures such as the packaging of content chunks, the tracking of its use and reuse, the formats used, and the issues of localization and internationalization. The use of chunks of content for particular purposes relies on the knowledge and the effective organization of content. *Content Management* systems, then, have been developed to organize, track and monitor content. Current *Content Management* systems are also designed to display information under specified categories, enable the user to save search results and provide inbuilt alert mechanisms.

Effective **Information Management** is the organization of information to enable effective resource discovery. Effective *Information Management* is related to standards on thesauri, subject headings, information management schemes (such as metadata, see [MET] and [MARC]), cataloguing rules and classification schemes. All these standards contribute to enabling the description of resources/information in a consistent manner. Describing similar resources in such a manner allows us to achieve precision in searching results. Information management standards include aspects such as subject headings, taxonomies, and protocols for storing and retrieval.

1.3   Cognitive Theory in Education

Cognition can be defined as "the act or process of knowing"; or more specifically, "an intellectual process which transforms perception or ideas into knowledge" [Web 1913]. Cognition was crucial in the development of psychology as a scientific discipline. The establishment of Wilhelm Wundt's laboratory in 1879 to study human thought processes is often used as the beginning of modern psychology. Cognitive psychology is one of the major psychological approaches and can be contrasted with a behavioral view (focused on observable behavior), a psychoanalytic view (focused on the unconscious), and a humanistic view (focused on personal growth and interpersonal relationships).

There are a variety of perspectives and emphases within cognitive psychology that are currently impacting educators' concerns about how to improve the teaching/learning process. For instance, the *Information Processing* approach focuses on the study of the structure and function of mental processing within specific contexts or environments [Rau 1995]. Benjamin Bloom and his colleagues developed the *Taxonomy of the Cognitive Domain* [Blo 1956] as a way to classify the variety of educational objectives related to what and how people know.

Researchers in the area of intelligence study how human beings learn from experience, reason well, remember important information, and adapt to the environment. Jean Piaget's theory [Pia 1969] of *cognitive development* describes the process and stages by which human beings develop the capacity to engage in abstract symbolic thought, one of the distinguishing features of human activity. Piaget's theory is often contrasted with the views of Jerome Bruner [Bru 1960] and Lev Vygotsky [Vyg 1978].

Several different areas of inquiry provide an opportunity to test out these different theories. For example, in the area of critical thinking researchers study how to apply cognitive processes to evaluate arguments (propositions) and make decisions. On the other hand, in the area of creative thinking, researchers study how to generate ideas and alternatives that do not fit the "rule." These two areas are often contrasted as the difference between *convergent thinking* (a thinking pattern used when one wants to summarize and evaluate ideas) and *divergent thinking* (a thinking pattern used to expand or develop new ideas). A similar comparison can be found between left-brain and right-brain orientations in the literature on brain lateralization dominance [Iac 1993].

Metacognition is another cognition area that arises from different perspectives and is the study of how knowledge is developed over one's own cognitive system. There are several study methods developed from cognitive psychology. They provide guidance on how to get the most from a textbook or distance/online course. The most popular is SQ3R or its derivatives as proposed by Robinson in [Rob 1970].

SQ3R

SQ3R is named after the acronym of the actions taken in learning: Survey, Question and Read, Recite and Review (SQRRR).

- Survey -- Read chapter outlines, chapter headings, recaps, objectives, etc.
- Question -- Formulate questions you believe will be addressed in reading.
- Read -- Read material quickly, carefully, actively; try to answer previously formulated questions.
- Recite -- Explain aloud to yourself or another person what you have read; use study guide; answer questions at end of chapter.
- Review -- Go back over knowledge learned; use study guide; reread recaps, reviews, or end-of-chapter summaries.

SQ4R

Based on the research on how important *elaboration* is to the learning process, a 4th R was added for reflection or recording:

- First three SQ3R actions.
- Reflect -- Write in journal, make notes, or simply wonder about material.
- Last two SQ3R actions.

These areas provide information about how to be most effective and efficient during the process of learning.

1.3.1   Taxonomy of the Cognitive Domain

Beginning in 1948, a group of educators undertook the task of classifying education goals and objectives. The intent was to develop a classification system for three domains: the cognitive, the affective, and the psychomotor. Work on the cognitive domain was completed in 1956 and is commonly referred to as *Bloom's*

Taxonomy of the Cognitive Domain. The major idea of the taxonomy is that educators may organize knowledge following a complexity hierarchy from lesser to more complex concepts. The taxonomy is presented in Table 1 with sample verbs for each level.

Table 1.   Bloom's taxonomy review (adapted from [Blo 1956])

LEVEL	DEFINITION	SAMPLE VERBS
KNOWLEDGE	Student recalls or recognizes information, ideas, and principles in the approximate form in which they were learned.	Write, List, Label, Name, State, Define
COMPREHENSION	Student translates, comprehends, or interprets information based on prior learning.	Explain, Summarize, Paraphrase, Describe, Illustrate
APPLICATION	Student selects, transfers and uses data and principles to complete a problem or task with a minimum of direction.	Use, Compute, Solve Demonstrate, Apply, Construct
ANALYSIS	Student distinguishes, classifies and relates the assumptions, hypotheses, evidence, or the structure of a statement or question.	Analyze, Categorize, Compare, Contrast, Separate
SYNTHESIS	Student originates, integrates and combines ideas into a new product, plan or proposal.	Create, Design, Hypothesize Invent, Develop
EVALUATION	Student appraises, assesses, or critiques on a basis of specific standards and criteria.	Judge, Recommend, Critique, Justify

This classification permits teachers to introduce a pedagogical decision rule in their teaching material, based on student abilities, to determine the student's state of knowledge and adapt learning materials. This adaptation may be either to introduce new concepts or to do further training on weak concepts.

1.3.2   Cognitive/learning Styles

Cognitive style refers to the preferred way an individual processes information. Unlike individual differences in abilities [Gar 1983], [Gui 1967], [Ste 1983] which describe peak performance, style describes a person's typical mode of thinking, remembering or problem solving. Furthermore, styles are usually considered to be bipolar dimensions (i.e., Visual/Verbal) whereas abilities are unipolar (ranging from zero to a maximum value, i.e., 2 more visual, 1 visual, 0 neutral). Having more of an ability is usually considered beneficial while having a particular cognitive style simply denotes a tendency to behave in a certain manner. Cognitive style is usually described as a personal dimension which influences attitudes, values, and social interaction.

A number of cognitive styles has been identified and studied over the years. *Field independence* versus *field dependence* [Gra 1996] is probably the most well known style. It refers to a tendency to approach the environment in an analytical, as opposed to a global, fashion. At a perceptual level, field independent people are able to distinguish figures as discrete from their backgrounds compared to field dependent individuals who experience events in an undifferentiated way. Studies have identified a number of connections between this cognitive style and the corresponding learning style (see [Mes 1976]). For example, field independent individuals are likely to learn more effectively under conditions of intrinsic motivation (e.g., self-study) and are less influenced by social reinforcement.

Other cognitive styles that have been identified are:

- *Scanning* - differences in the extent and intensity of attention resulting in variations in the vividness of experience and the span of awareness.
- *Leveling* versus *sharpening* - individual variations in remembering that pertain to the distinctiveness of memories and the tendency to merge similar events.
- *Reflection* versus *impulsivity* - individual consistencies in the speed and adequacy with which alternative hypotheses are formed and responses are made.
- *Conceptual differentiation* - differences in the tendency to categorize perceived similarities among stimuli in terms of separate concepts or dimensions.

On the other hand, *learning styles* specifically deal with characteristic styles of learning. Kolb in [Kol 1984] proposes a theory of experiential learning that involves four principal dimensions:

- Concrete Experiences (CE)
- Reflective Observation (RO)
- Abstract Conceptualization (AC)
- Active Experimentation (AE)

The CE/AC and AE/RO dimensions are polar opposites as far as learning styles are concerned. In consequence, Kolb postulates four types of learners (*divergers, assimilators, convergers, and accommodators*) depending upon their situation with respect to these two dimensions. For example, an *accommodator* prefers concrete experiences and active experimentation (CE, AE).

Pask in [Pas 1975] has also described a learning style called *serialist* versus *holist*. *Serialists* prefer to learn in a sequential fashion, whereas *holists* prefer to learn in a hierarchal manner (i.e., top-down).

Theoretically, cognitive and learning styles may be used to predict the most effective instructional strategies or methods for a given individual learning task (since not all students learn in the same way then not all teachers should teach in the same way). Current research has not identified many robust relationships between cognitive and learning styles (see [Cro 1977].) However, the 4MAT framework [4MAT] has been widely applied in education and the learning styles framework helps to differentiate individual learning. The 4MAT framework is based on the work of Bernice McCarthy and suggests 4 learning modes (*Analytic, Imaginative, Common Sense, and Dynamic*), whereas the learning style framework developed by Dunn & Dunn [Dun 1999] seems to be useful in terms of creating teacher awareness of individual differences in learning. (See the result of experiences in the Learning-Styles Network website [LSN]).

In a Science Education and Computer Assisted Learning (CAL) scenario, the Felder and Silverman Learning Style Model (FSLSM) [Fel 2002] was developed based on theories of Jung (theory of psychological types [Jun 1921]) and Kolb (theory of experiential learning [Kol 1984]). This model originally had five dimensions: processing (active/reflective), perception (sensing/intuitive), input (visual/auditory), organization (inductive/deductive), and understanding (sequential/global). Later, this model was updated deleting the organization dimension to yield sixteen categories and renaming the input dimension named auditory as verbal. Next section describes in detail this model due to its application in this book.

Applications of learning styles in web-based educational systems may be observed in: RAPITS [Woo 1995], Arthur [Gil 1999], INSPIRE [Gri 2001],

CAMELEON [Lar 2001], AEC-ES [Tri 2002], iWeaver [Wol 2002] and ExplanAgent (a work in progress [Dan 2003]) between others.

Tips of the FSLSM learning style model

The FSLSM model is a synthesis of a huge research work. It was designed with dimensions made up of 4 contrary pairs that should be particularly relevant to Science Education and Computer Assisted Learning. This model distinguishes those four dichotomous dimensions to learning styles, as is shown in Table 2.

Table 2.   Dichotomies for the four levels of Felder's learning styles

DICHOTOMY	
Active	Reflective
Sensing	Intuitive
Visual	Verbal
Sequential	Global

The dichotomies were partially defined by considering the answers to the following four questions [Cur 1987]:

- How does the student process information?
- What type of information does the student preferentially perceive?
- Through which modality is sensory information most effectively perceived?
- How does the student progress toward understanding?

The answers given by the FSLSM model to the above questions were:

- Information can be processed by *active* tasks through engagement in physical activity or discussion OR through *reflection* or introspection.
- Basically students perceive information of two different kinds: External or *sensory* information, such as sights, sounds, physical sensations, OR internal or *intuitive* information, such as memories, ideas, insights, etc.
- Concerning the external information, students basically receive information by *visual* formats, e.g., pictures, diagrams, graphs, demonstrations etc. OR by *verbal* formats, e.g., sounds, written and spoken words, symbolic formulas, etc.

- Student progress towards understanding implies *sequential* procedures that necessitate a logical progression of small incremental steps, OR *global* understanding that requires a holistic view.

The description of an application of this model within the context of this work can be found in chapter 7.

1.4   Intelligent Tutoring Systems

1.4.1   Introduction

Discussions concerning computer use in education have rapidly passed through different phases. The first phase is centered on the need for "computer literacy," generally defined as computer awareness and computer programming. In the second phase of the computer literacy debate, the emphasis shifted to the role of the computer as a tool and as a method for solving problems. The third phase addresses issues related to computer applications in support of the curriculum.

Computers have been used in education for over 20 years. Computer-Based Training (CBT) and Computer Aided Instruction (CAI) were the first such systems deployed to teach using computers. In these kinds of systems, the instruction was not individualized to the learner needs. The learner abilities were not taken into account.

While both CBT and CAI may be somewhat effective in helping learners, they do not provide the same kind of individualized attention that the student would receive from a human tutor [Blo 1984]. A computer-based educational system, designed to provide such attention, must include tasks about the domain and the learner. This has prompted research in the field of Intelligent Tutoring Systems (ITS) and it has supposed a great challenge for researchers in educational technology and a support to testing cognitive theories [Nwa 1990].

1.4.2   ITS performance

The concept known as Intelligent Tutoring Systems (ITS) or Intelligent Computer-Aided Instruction (ICAI) has been pursued for more than three decades by researchers in Education, Psychology, and Artificial Intelligence (see

Figure 2). Nowadays, prototype and operational ITS provide practice-based instruction to support corporate training, college education, and military training. Additionally, the technology is now ready to support computer learning for the first time.

Figure 2.   ITS domain

The goal of an ITS is to provide the benefits of one-to-one instruction automatically and cost effectively. Like training simulations, ITS enable participants to practice their skills by carrying out tasks within highly interactive learning environments. However, ITS go beyond training simulations by answering user questions and providing individualized guidance. Unlike other computer-based training technologies, ITS systems assess each learner's actions within these interactive environments and develop a model of learner's knowledge, skills, and expertise. Based on the learner model, ITS can tailor instructional strategies, in terms of both the content and style, and provide explanations, hints, examples, demonstrations, and practice problems as needed.

ITS apply Artificial Intelligence techniques to the development of educational systems based on computers with the purpose of building systems able to adapt dynamically to the learning evolution. ITS also offer considerable flexibility in presentation of material and a greater ability to respond to idiosyncratic student needs. These systems achieve their "intelligence" by representing pedagogical decisions about how to teach as well as information about the learner. N. Major in [Maj 1995] states that an ITS should adapt to a particular student by varying "difficulty of material, presentation style, help offered, path taken, [and] generality of the material". He further states that the path through the courseware is calculated whilst the student is using the system (i.e., it is not pre-programmed).

However, an ITS will typically constrain the student to learning by a predetermined method or strategy (see [Rid 1989] and [Kin 1997]). ITS use a model of the student's knowledge (student model) so that the student is presented with new information only when he/she requires it. This is carried out in order to reinforce a point, to progress in the learning and/or to identify misconceptions and wrong-rules [Sle 1982]. Such systems have been criticized for constraining the student to solving a problem in a particular way [Rid 1989]. In most complex problem domains, there can be many methods to achieve a correct solution. Some people may find one particular method that suits their way of thinking better than others. It has been argued that students should be able to experiment with their own ideas and find methods that naturally suit them.

Elsom-Cook in [Els 1989] reviewed some Computer-Based Learning (CBL) and ITS packages, and graded them between two extremes: totally constrained and totally unconstrained. (Most systems were found to be near the totally constrained side.) He argued that ITS lie at the constraint end of this spectrum, whereas an electronic textbook type system would be unconstrained. He also argued that the perfect tutoring system should be able to "slide" between these two extremes according to the student's needs and the state of knowledge.

Therefore, a system could appear as a traditional ITS to a novice student or as a discovery learning hypermedia system to an advanced student. Hartley in [Har 1993] reinforces this point by stating that when there is a mismatch between strategies (of the learning system) and learning style (of the student), then performance is degraded. He also states that support for different styles and viewpoints of users is required.

Further research has shown that the learning process is improved when a student is allowed to follow pathways of their own choice, at their own pace, and is able to monitor their progress by instant feedback to questions [Kib 1990]. These ideas are similar to the idea of "cognitive scaffolding" (see [Hen 1999] and [Rob 1995]), whereby a learner is supported in their learning activity when he/she needs support. Nevertheless, the support is reduced as he/she becomes more capable and hence is empowered to go through learning in his/her style.

1.4.3 ITS components

Each ITS must have the following four model components (see Figure 3):

- Knowledge of domain (*domain model*)
- Knowledge of teaching strategies (*pedagogic model*)
- Knowledge of learner (*learner model*)
- *Communication model*

This basic outline of requirements has been around since 1973 when it was introduced by Derek H. Sleeman and J.R. Hartley [Har 1973]. The goal of every ITS is to effectively communicate to the student its embedded knowledge by using the communication model [Wen 1987].

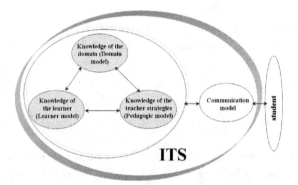

Figure 3.   The necessary base for an effective teaching in ITS

The *domain model* contains the knowledge of the matter to be trained and is usually pedagogically organized to facilitate the task of the pedagogic model. The knowledge represented in this module is used to determine what should be presented to the student and how to evaluate his/her actions and answers.

Through the *pedagogic model* the different teaching strategies are represented and the methods for controlling the session are implemented by means of the appropriate selection and sequencing of these strategies. This module takes charge of promoting the learning by designing, regulating and organizing the instruction that will be carried out for each student. It also is able to decide, using the information represented in the domain module and in the student model, the concepts which should be offered at each moment, how to present each concept, and when and how to interrupt the student.

The *learner model* represents the image of the system that has the knowledge which the student has acquired during the instruction process. It also incorporates other aspects of his/her behavior and knowledge with possible repercussions on his/her performances and learning, the type of student, favorite learning styles, motivation level, etc. The learner model evaluates each learner's performance to determine his/her knowledge, perceptual abilities, and reasoning skills. It stores specific information of each individual learner. At least, such a model tracks the way a student is performing on the material being taught. A possible addition can be recording misconceptions. Since the purpose of the learner model is to provide data for the pedagogical module of the system, all of the information gathered should be able to be used by the tutor [Arr 1998].

Interactions with the learner, including the dialogue and the screen layouts, are controlled by the *Communication model.*

1.4.4   Necessity of Intelligent Tutoring Systems

It is becoming evident that more efficient training systems are needed by all organizations undergoing rapid technological changes. Lecture-style training and traditional instructional systems are unable to keep up with the number of people who require training. New technologies are needed to reduce the increasing cost and burden of education and training.

On the other hand, effective multimedia intelligent systems often include substantial multimedia components, making these systems memory and computer intensive. Because educational computational resources are typically limited, cross-platform delivery is essential. In this case, a web-based solution could be the best.

Properly designed computer-based tutoring systems have proven highly effective as learning aids. ITS have been shown to teach twice as quickly as traditional classroom methods [Shu 1995] and to produce increased skill retention with fewer mistakes [Laj 1993]. Individualized instruction has proven extremely useful in improving the education of students [Blo 1984]. ITS can provide the individualized instruction that cannot be achieved in a lecture-style class.

ITS have been used to teach a variety of skills, from LISP programming [And 1985] to treating heart attack patients [Eli 1996]. For training people in technical fields, educational systems have been developed that provide realistic working environments [Laj 1992]. These systems include simulations of complex and dangerous machinery, thus providing opportunities to learn that otherwise would be not available.

Although ITS have proven highly effective for teaching, there are very few systems available over the WWW. The lack of instantaneous interaction between the tutor and the student has been an obstacle to the development of truly intelligent Web-based tutors.

1.4.5 Limitations of Intelligent Tutoring Systems

While ITS have been somewhat successful on a small scale, several problems must be overcome before they have widespread impact. Various authors (e.g., Wenger [Wen 1987], Psotka, Massey, and Mutter [Pso 1988] and Bloom [Blo 1995] among others) have discussed a wide range of limitations. Many of these challenges can be predictably factored by ITS component limitations. These may be associated with the expert system, the student model, the pedagogical component, and the interface. In this section a few brief fundamental shortcomings which may not be overcome simply through incremental improvements to various ITS components are considered (see Table 3.)

Table 3.   Limitations of ITS

LIMITATIONS	EXPLANATION
In educational technologies	ITS systems have been developed only for a few topic areas which are relatively simple, and perhaps of minor importance in emerging curricula. Effective ITS require virtual *omniscience* – a relatively complete mastery of the subject area they are to tutor, including an understanding of likely student misconceptions.
In teaching and pedagogical expertise	Most ITS have very impoverished pedagogical components. Such components often comprise a collection of rules that seem to work reasonably well in practice. There is no scientific encyclopedia of good tutoring heuristics to consult, yet principled theory of one-to-one tutoring might drive specific heuristics to follow. To improve the pedagogical capabilities of an ITS, one needs to enhance the rule-based coaching of students. This is needed to enrich the pedagogical knowledge base. The *drill-and-practice method* of teaching embedded in ITS, appears to be more suitable for tuning existing knowledge than for conceptual learning of substantial pieces of new knowledge [Ohl 1991]. This limitation partially reflects some limitations in the cognitive science that underpins ITS.
In authoring, architectures and delivery platforms	Bloom in [Blo 1995] identifies four problems in the Intelligent Tutoring paradigm: 1) *ITS authoring is complex*, requiring specialist domain authors. 2) *The "real world communities" (the end users) seem unwilling to accept the ITS paradigm*, mainly because they do not understand the technology and nothing is offered to the human teacher. 3) There is *very little reuse of ITS architectures across applications*. This argument corresponds with the criticisms of Kinshuk and Patel in [Kin 1997,] in that a new ITS is generally developed for each new domain of application. Bloom points out that in order to be named "generic," an ITS must have the ability to reuse the student model, the instructional model and the knowledge base inference mechanisms. 4) Most ITS require *specialist delivery platforms*, i.e., they may not suit the systems that the end-user may already have, although this is less likely to be the case today as computer systems are more powerful and cheaper.

1.5 Constructionism, Instructionism and AI in Education

It is known that most Computer Based Learning systems, such as *tutorial* systems, *drill-and-practice* programs, *simulations*, and *mindtool*, basically follow two pedagogical methods for teaching and learning [Jon 1996]:

- ***Instructionism:*** the learner is seen as a *passive* human being, who can absorb much information given by the instructor or instructional media, and translate it into his/her knowledge. A learning system responds acceptably with respect to some performance criteria within a time interval following a change in its environment.

- ***Constructionism:*** the learner *actively* constructs his/her knowledge by gathering information from his/her surroundings and combining it with his/her previous knowledge. Learning is a piecewise refinement of schema due to encoding and discovering new chunks of knowledge.

One of the weaknesses of the *Instructionism* method is that there are discrepancies between the concepts that the learners absorb and the contexts or situations where those concepts may be applied [DeC 1996]. In general, *Instructionism*-based systems can only cover a limited level of information processing.

On the other hand, *Constructionism*-based systems may provide learning environments where the learners interact not only with the tutorial system but also with many other tools and facilities to do their tasks or to solve their problems [Dil1993]. At their own wish, learners may also get some guidance or advice from a tutor, who can be human, or from other components of the system. In general, *Constructionism*-based systems allow learners to apply a learning style that is directed by their particular goals.

Even though *Constructionism* based systems promise a better understanding of learning materials to learners, they must acquire certain learning skills before this promise can be fulfilled. Learners must be able to define their own goals. Furthermore, they have to be able to direct, plan and monitor their learning activities. In short, learners must have a "self-directed learning" capability. Such a capability needs to be developed and a Computer Based Learning environment may be designed, in addition, to help them to understand the learning materials.

Constructivism and *Constructionism* are relatively new ideas in the field of learning. These ideas were presented by Papert in [Pap 1990] as alternatives to *Instructionism,* the dominant learning method. Papert described *Constructivism, Constructionism* and the difference between them as follows:

*"The word with the **v** expresses the theory that knowledge is built by the learner, not supplied by the teacher. The word with the **n** expresses the further idea that this happens felicitously when the learner is engaged in the construction of something external or at least shareable...a sand castle, a machine, a computer program, a book."*

Constructivism is therefore the theory where the new knowledge is reached by the understanding and appreciation in a context that one oneself builds. One makes ideas about the world, as opposed to getting ideas about it. When one encounters a new idea, one tries to relate to knowledge already acquired. Traditional teaching methods provide large amounts of knowledge for students to memorize, hoping that learning will come about, as opposed to actually encouraging students to think for themselves as they learn.

Constructionism is the practical manifestation of *Constructivism*. *Constructionism* actually involves two instances of construction in a student, the construction of ideas in the student's mind and the actual real world construction of personally meaningful objects [Kaf 1996]. A constructionist environment could therefore be imagined as [Wil 1996]:

"A place where learners work together and support each other's work as they use a variety of tools and information resources in their guided pursuit of learning goals and problem-solving activities."

In the heated debate between learning by construction versus instruction [Hof 1997], it is easy to overlook that the disagreement has an empirical base. The central disagreement concerns the person in the best position to make key decisions needed to promote learning. A knowledgeable teacher (automated or otherwise) would be essential to choose appropriate tasks, to provide rich and individualized feedback and to situate learning in authentic tasks. Students -- working with tools that act as intelligent cognitive amplifiers and in a supportive context that includes peers and mentors -- make these decisions themselves. The concern centers on the students' possibilities to generate better feedback for learning than that of a tutor in rich but passive environments, or if the students are in a better position to know what information they need for learning than the teacher is.

To clarify the above concerns, several research strategies are feasible. One pragmatic approach is to push the extreme alternatives as far as they would go. For ITS, this means watching the functions of human tutors that can be usefully automated and assessing the quality of student learning they engender. The central question is about the possibility of developing computer-based agents that are able to suggest interesting tasks at the edge of students' skills; or agents that are able to coach students and provide adequate feedback. If this were possible, the question turns into the development of agents for specific subjects and topics of learning, and also into the quality of learning, that is, the skills and depth of understanding.

By the same token, pushing the ILE alternative as far as it will go means developing increasingly effective empowering tools and technologies for learning, embedding them in congenial learning environments, and demonstrating the efficiency of largely self-guided or inquiry-based learning. At this point, the doubts turn to:

- How dramatically can such ILE magnify self-directed learning skills?
- How crucial for learning is the support of peers, mentors, and the broader culture of learning?
- What quality of learning do such highly student-controlled environments yield?
- Do students acquire ideas inefficiently because their searches too often just wander?
- Do they develop a deeper conceptual understanding of ideas and of inquiry itself?

Research in human tutoring [Lei 1989] [McA 1990] and the increasing popularity of mixed-initiative tutoring systems suggest that the best learning environments will be completely controlled neither by students nor by tutors. The most effective learning environments include a mix of direct teaching, more passive support for learning, together with substantial student choice. For example, in studies of inquiry-based tutoring by humans [Lew 1992] noticed that even teachers experienced in orchestrating student-centered inquiries, often interpolated bouts of lecture and tutor-directed coaching. Similarly, much work developing ILE and mixed-initiative systems recognizes the need for active support of learning (e.g., [Bro 1993], [Ros 1992]). However, active roles in learning are typically associated with mentors, co-workers and peers, who engage learners in rich dialogues. In these environments, the role of technology is largely to provide a useful collection of tools that can amplify, enhance, or even transform the nature of these dialogues where learning takes place.

The *constructionist* approach imposes an external reality onto the learner where the teacher presents the knowledge pre-determined by specified objectives. The *constructivistic* approach views learning as being constructed by a learner from his or her own perceptions and interpretations and of the external world. The learner is actively involved in the process by reflecting on information and creating his/her own learning environment and knowledge base. Teachers should change their role from instructor to facilitator.

From a methodological point of view, the relationship between *constructivism* and *instructionism* should not be based upon the format "either - or", but rather upon the "and - and" format. This means that a balance between those two approaches should be found. A multimedia program should ensure opportunities for both *constructivistic* and *instructionistic* activities. The focus of control should be imposed both on the system (*instructionism*) and on the learner (*constructivism*).

Meanwhile, as mixed-initiative systems begin to mature, more ambitious roles must be given to those technologies. An omniscient and highly-controlling ITS may be an inappropriate model for the use of technology in effective learning environments. However, as noted before, this is no longer the only alternative to relatively passive ILE. Instead, in the near future one can expect to see mixed-initiative systems that include not only tools which amplify the students' inquiry but also local intelligent agents which provide many of the active supports now supplied by peers and mentors. This work is focused in this direction. Intelligent agents are used to support learning -assisting, motivating and modeling the student to achieve adaptive education by considering learning styles.

Until the answers to the empirical questions outlined above arrive, the roles locally intelligent computer-based agents should play in learning and how dominant they will be remains unclear. Of course, to some extent, the appropriate active tutoring role of such agents will depend on the subjects to be learned, on the background experience of students and on their learning styles. For example, if one believes it is still valuable for students to learn symbol manipulation skills in algebra, an environment heavily populated with guiding agents -- approximating an ITS -- may be the most effective way to learn. If students are learning inquiry skills by themselves, then local intelligent agents may play very modest roles. Similarly, a novice student may learn best in environments that include agents which can model and coach formative skills [Col 1987].

Therefore, in some cases intelligent agents may play substantial teaching roles, and in other cases the role of intelligent agents would be modest. However, one might like these roles to be modest because one believes that such roles lead to the best student outcomes, not simply because one is technically unable to develop agents that are smart enough in certain areas. In other words, one would like to limit the role of intelligent agents in education by principled choice, instead of practical necessity. Today, it is believed that most errors in applications of AI in education, including ITS, come from technical limitations in modeling human pedagogical expertise, not from wrong principles.

In short, the main point is that the ideas from Artificial Intelligence and knowledge-based systems support neither *Instructionist* nor *Constructionist* views of teaching and learning wholeheartedly; rather, they can and will be used to implement a diverse set of methods of learning and teaching. However, well-designed intelligent agents may eventually exercise strong control over a learning interaction. It is a naive caricature to assume that future applications of AI in education will be subject to the same limitations that occurred in first-generation ITS.

Future mixed-initiative applications will not necessarily teach just through drill-and-practice or lecture. They will neither "program" students to behave like a rigid procedure, nor will they necessarily assume that each task has only one "right answer". As AI expands to provide models of subtle reasoning skills, new systems will not be limited to tutoring routine procedural skills. Similarly, intelligent systems, like good human tutors, will learn to confront the challenges of teaching without "knowing everything" about the topics that students learn. Moreover, although intelligent agents for learning will certainly transform the roles of teachers (and peers) in the classroom, they do not pretend to replace them.

1.6   Conclusions

In this chapter, basic concepts related to knowledge process generation by means of Information and Communication Technologies have been introduced. The integration of the computer as a tool for training processes and the influence of Cognitive Theory and Artificial Intelligence techniques in this process implementation have also been considered.

From a pedagogical point of view, two main methodologies to assist the student, *instructionism* and *constructivism,* were studied. As a result of this study, it has been concluded that the first methodology looks easier to implement, even if it does not efficiently support student learning of new knowledge. Constructivism seems to support the student much better in acquiring new knowledge, but it leaves some questions to be answered and presents more implementation problems. New teaching and learning research ought to overcome this dichotomy, let knowledge be available, meaningfully accompany student learning and be very friendly.

The combination of Intelligent Tutoring Systems (*instructionist* tendency) and Interactive Learning Environments (*constructivist* tendency) as a base from which generate adaptive learning environments (one of the goals of this work) is presented in chapter 2.

Chapter 2.   Hypermedia

2.1   Hypertext and Hypermedia

The term "hypertext" was described as "non-sequential writing" by Ted Nelson in his publication *Literary Machines* [Nel 1987]. Many subsequent writers have understood hypertext as to be a distinctly electronic technology that must involve a computer. For example, Janet Fiderio in [Fid 1988], writes:

"Hypertext, at its most basic level, is a DataBase Management System (DBMS) that lets you connect screens of information using associative links. At its most sophisticated level, hypertext is a software environment for collaborative work, communication, and knowledge acquisition. Hypertext products mimic the brain's ability to store and retrieve information by referential links for quick and intuitive access."

Hypertext, when well designed, enables people to read, author and comprehend information more effectively than traditional documents. People typically read documents from beginning to end, i.e., in a linear, sequential manner. Paper constrains authors to compose information in a linear format. Due to tradition and the need to print, many computerized documents are written in a linear format. However, hypertext frees readers and authors from this form of expression. Authors may structure information as a web of information chunks and interrelated links. For example, authors could place their main idea or an overview in an entry-point chunk with multiple links connecting logical next steps or related tangential information chunks. Presenting information as a web enables readers to access information in a way which is more appropriate for their purposes.

Hypertext concepts may supplement other computer applications. Applications themselves may provide links on screens and within documents to related information, and may implement hypermedia navigation, annotation and structural features to provide additional context and increase comprehension. Hypertext constructions may be predefined or they may be dynamically generated as an application is executed.

Some people consider the terms hypertext and hypermedia as synonymous, but hypertext refers to relating textual elements, while hypermedia encompasses relationships among elements of any media type. The concepts are identical, though hypertext is more difficult to implement in non-textual media (such as audio, video, etc.)

Hypertext + Multimedia = **Hypermedia**

Hypermedia ([Bus 1945], [Con 1987]) is not a new concept. It has been used in some approaches to document managing ([Ber 1992]), education ([Bel 1992], [Bru 1996b], [Fab 2000a]), and knowledge engineering ([Aks 1988], [Are 1992]).

In short, hypermedia is a way of building systems for information representation and management around a network of multimedia nodes connected together by typed links.

2.2   Hypermedia Structures

According to Laroussi in [Lar 2001] the terms hypertext and hypermedia could be defined using the following three points of view: Semantic, Structural and Functional.

From the **Semantic definition** point of view, hypertext is considered as an entity that is in turn composed of two more entities: a **set of documents** and **a knowledge structure**. The poorest representation of this second entity is a link written down inside the first entity, and this is what Nanard calls a "hard link" that joins two documents [Nan 1993]. The most elaborated representation of this knowledge can be generated by a complex system based on domain modeling and user modeling. According to the chosen modeling, the relationship between nodes can be expressed as functional relations or sequences to define a logical structure of documents.

Considering **Structural definition,** Balasubramanian in [Bal 1994] defines a hypertext as a system composed of **nodes** and **links**. The nodes may include textual information (hypertext), or multimedia information such as pictures, diagrams, animations, videos or computer programs (hypermedia). Nodes are joined by links.

A **node** is an integrated and self-sufficient unit of information; it is part of a complete hypertext document. The nodes can be considered as origin – the origin of the link (**reference nodes**) – or as destination – the destination of the link (**referred nodes**).

A **link** is an instruction that allows the user to move from the referenced node to the referred node, this is then, a way of traversing the information superhighway. There are different types of links and different actions may be performed from a link. These are stated below.

- A **reference link** may be used to replace the current node by the new node.
- A **note link** may be used to display the new node in a pop up window while keeping the current node in the main browser window.
- An **expansion link** can be used to reveal more information and to branch out in the original space of the link. The link can be reversed, leaving the original one.
- A **command link** enables an action to be performed, such as downloading a file, or running an executable file.
- An **anchor** is the visible element, word, phrase or picture that has to be selected to activate the link.

The links can be more or less complex; they can be **unidirectional** to allow going from one page to another, they can also be **marked** in order to specify the semantics of the link and, finally, they can be **disposed** all in one page; however, their roles may sometimes be defined by their position in the document, or by the semantics of the page (i.e., if the page is an index page, the links will enable the nominated pages). These links define the architecture of the system commonly known as hyperspace [WHATIS].

With respect to **Functional definition**, hypertext can be considered as a computer process that permits associating a minimal entity (i.e., a word, a portion of a picture or an icon) to another more extended entity (i.e., a paragraph, a picture or a page). Therefore, that mechanism allows the user to move freely in the hypertext. This property of hypertext gives the document interactivity characteristics that a user can take advantage of.

In [Con 1987], Conklin describes several types of hypermedia structure. The most common types use **referential** links that join two nodes in a non-hierarchical way, resulting in a largely unstructured domain. Referential links are commonly associated with selectable words within a document or as "hot spots" within a graphic. **Organizational** links may be used, additionally, to connect a node to its parent or child nodes; they are traversed via a separate mechanism from the node itself, either via a graphical browser or via a list of available links. **Keyword** links or **dynamic** links search for relevant keywords in the hypermedia current node.

Whether or not it is better to employ **non-structured** hypermedia (employing referential links), **hierarchical hypermedia** (organizational links) or a **mixture of both** is subject to an author's criteria. The proponents of unstructured hypermedia argue that its unstructured nature provides the richness and freedom associated with hypermedia. However, navigating in such structures exacerbates the well-known problem of cognitive loading [Low 1999] (see details in section II.5). A hierarchical structure is largely dependent on the ability of the defined hierarchy to match the requirements of the user.

A Hypermedia system has been described as a suitable medium for representing structural information (although not all hypermedia systems do). Currently, there is a growing number of systems with information organized on a computer in a structured hypermedia fashion. These systems organize and display information as a meaningful hierarchy instead of a potentially meaningless list of files and directories. Examples of these systems can be observed in:

HIPERBOLIC and SEMIOMAP [Tun 1999] which use Artificial Intelligence techniques to extract information that has been stored within each file so that it may be related to other files in a hierarchical manner. Information is then presented to the user in a structured hypermedia fashion by using a graphical browser interface.

NOTECARDS [Hart 1993] which uses referential and organizational links; although the authors point out that the most common links are organizational.

In PLANG [Fab 2000], a web-based hypermedia environment is used as fundamental support for this work proposal which is also based on organizational links. However, the domains employed by the authors in these systems were invariably computer science domains.

Other hypermedia systems such as MICROCOSM [Low 1999] and HYPER-G [Mau 1996] also offer structural and referential link types; however, STRATHTUTOR [Kib 1989] offers dynamic link types using pattern matching heuristics to calculate them.

If the above, or similar, systems replace existing browsers then the structured hypermedia paradigm would become familiar to the computer-using population. Moreover, the cognitive overhead associated with using hypermedia would be reduced.

2.3   Hypermedia Architectures

2.3.1   Introduction

Hypermedia systems are older and more intense than the World Wide Web. In fact, three hypermedia generations have been distinguished in the literature [Hal 1988]:

- The *first one* comprises hypertext systems based on mainframes. They offered support for multiple collaborative users but, at the same time, presented seriously limited navigational help and graphic interfaces were not supported.
- In the *second generation*, systems were based on workstations and personal computers for single users or small groups including advanced user interfaces. Multimedia information and graphical navigational help can be observed. Current hypermedia systems belong to this second generation, resulting in closed systems with storage mechanisms and no interpretability.
- In 1987 the *third generation* research began with the development of prototypes that included the conceptualization of hypermedia systems by means of abstract models. The HAM [Cam 1988], Trellis [Sto 1989] and Dexter [Hal 1990] reference models belong to this effort (see details in section II.3.4). At this stage, prototypes were created with the aim of supporting structuring mechanisms with composed nodes. The main objective of this last generation, with which present research is now concerned, is to achieve the incorporation of hypermedia features into software and information systems in order to provide users with an

associative way of accessing, analyzing and organizing information, i.e., the integration of hypermedia functionality [Bal 1994].

Hypermedia has been considered, from its beginning, as a technology with much educational potential. Certainly one of the earliest leaders in educational hypermedia application was Nelson [Nel 1971] [Nel 1972] [Nel 1987]. Nevertheless, the first article to describe hypertext technology, "as we may think" [Bus 1945], describes its potential educational benefits. There has been much recent attention paid to the educational applications of hypermedia systems in general, and most recently, of the World Wide Web [AACE1] [AACE2]. Some referenced literature contains many successful experiences in these areas [Bac 1996] [Mau 1997] [Bue 2001].

One of the primary reasons to see hypermedia as a useful technology for education is its explicit **support of structure**. Conventional data-oriented environments allow the handling of information. Hypermedia enables environments to handle structures among this information. It is clear that such structures, or associations among pieces of information, form an integral part of people's understanding. As a matter of fact, systems that treat structures as first class objects can potentially model and communicate people's understanding more accurately, so that hypermedia systems have great potential for education. A possible next issue to consider is about the optimal application principles underlying hypermedia technologies.

The essence of a hypertext system is the functionality of the structure manipulation that it serves. Obviously, hypermedia systems may also serve a wide variety of other functions (e.g., data storage). However, the services that hypermedia offers clearly form the essence of the hypermedia core. Thus, an open hypermedia system allows an open set of clients to access its structure functionality. Furthermore, most open hypermedia systems require little modification of existing applications to allow them to use hypermedia functions, while closed systems require greater modification of these applications.

Hypermedia systems have been closed systems with proprietary storage mechanisms and very little or no interoperability. A number of layered architectures, models or engines, and frameworks have been proposed and developed by researchers in an effort to make hypertext systems more generic and integrated into the desktop environment [Grø 1997] [Nür 1998]. Some application development tool kits have been provided to assist programmers in adding hypertext functionality to the existing systems. In order to make hypertext systems fully open and integrated, the following issues must be addressed [Mal 1991]: interoperability, programmability, node and link typing, distributed linking, concurrency control for multi-user access in a shared environment and operating systems support

Most of these requirements can be achieved using object-oriented techniques [Lan 1993].

2.3.2   Closed Hypermedia Architectures

A closed hypermedia system has two types of conceptual entities a **set of data storage engines** and the **hypermedia engine**. A data storage engine may be any kind of process that serves data (e.g., a file system, an HTTP daemon (httpd), an ftp daemon (ftpd), etc.) The hypermedia engine consists of three logical parts:

- The **frontend part,** that renders data, structures it for the user and interprets user interactions for the rest of the engine;
- The **link service part,** that translates user requests passed from the frontend into storage requests;
- The **storage mapping part,** which translates link service storing requests into external data storage engine requests. This part must map between the data abstractions of the external stores and the structure abstractions used by the rest of the hypermedia engine.

WWW browsers are by far the most ubiquitous examples of closed hypermedia systems, but many other examples may be found in the research literature [Len 1996] [Toc 1996]. The three parts of a hypermedia engine can be identified easily in WWW browsers. The **frontend** of such processes is an HTML rendering engine that understands mouse clicks on certain (anchored) text strings or images. The **link service** parses the URL provided in the anchor tag and generates a data retrieval request. This request then goes to the appropriate data storage engine. The **storage mapping part** of the browser translates the generic retrieval request of the link service into the protocol used by the appropriate data server. When the requested data is retrieved, it is passed to the frontend to be rendered.

2.3.3   Open Hypermedia Architectures

In an open hypermedia architecture there are five types of conceptual entities: **clients**, **structure servers**, **hyperbases**, **behaviors**, and **data storage engines**. **Clients** correspond to the frontend part of the hypermedia engine in closed systems. The main differences in open systems are that clients have their own processes, and that the interfaces to the structure servers are well-known (open) by other arbitrary clients who may use the services of the structure servers. The amount of modification necessary to integrate many common applications into contemporary OHS's has been shown to be relatively low [Dav 1992], [Dav 1994], [Sch 1994], [Whi 1997].

Structure servers correspond to the link service part of the hypermedia engine in closed systems. Each structure server works with different structure models and functionalities. Every OHS has a structure server with functionality equivalent to a link service in closed systems. However, some OHS's also serve other kinds of structure at this layer, such as composites (e.g., DHM [Grø 1994]) or information retrieval types of generic links (e.g., Microcosm [Dav 1992]). Moreover, some OHS's open this layer in the architecture (e.g., HOSS [Nür 1996] and HyperDisco [Wii 1996]). That is, different structure servers can be added to the system by providing a component-like (open) framework into which new structure server components may be placed.

Hyperbases correspond to the storage mapping part of the hypermedia engine in closed systems. Hyperbases are structure-aware storage engines. The advantage of separating this layer from structure servers becomes apparent when one considers the fact that OHS's contain multiple structure servers. By abstracting the structure/data mapping into a separate architectural layer, the mapping only needs to be allocated in one place. Changes or upgrades to this mapping functionality (e.g., the adding of version management, concurrency control, etc.) need only be implemented in one entity instead of an open set of structure servers.

Behaviors have no direct analog in closed hypermedia systems. These entities contain the computation carried out while getting through a link. Structure servers call behavior entities when they resolve link endpoints. Often, this computation is empty, and link endpoint resolution occurs in the normal way. However, the ability to specify arbitrary computation in this part of the system allows many interesting possibilities for structures with dynamic endpoints (i.e., endpoints that are determined only at the time of the traversal and may vary over time) and for treating structures as truly first-class objects in the system.

Data storage engines have the same conceptual function in open hypermedia systems as they do in closed ones.

In order to make hypertext systems fully portable, existing document standards such as ODA [ODA] and SGML [SGML] must be extended to support unstructured documents and their linking. International standards such as HyTime [HyTime] and MHEG [MHEG] are emerging to support hypertext functionality and multimedia information in applications.

2.3.4   Hypermedia Reference Models

From the third generation of hypermedia systems, different reference models have been proposed with the aim of converting them to open systems and integrating their functionality in any framework or application. These models describe every conceptual element that includes, from the point of view of their authors, a hypermedia model. Three of the most extended ways of understanding and modeling these systems are in the following: HAM, TRELLIS and DEXTER.

Hypertext Abstract Machine – HAM (1987)

HAM is a general purpose, transaction-based, multi-user server for a hypertext storage system. It was a first attempt to express a hypermedia system based on an abstract model. The HAM does not describe the full hypertext system, just the HAM objects and their applicable operations are defined. The HAM is at the top of the storage system, and it manages and provides the hypermedia information to the applications and user interfaces. This model defines five types of objects: *graphs, contexts, nodes, links* and *attributes*. The HAM also maintains a history of these objects which allows selective access through filtering mechanisms (by means of expressions based on object attributes and their values). Data access restriction mechanisms based on an Access Control List (ACL) are also included.

A *graph* is the highest level object and it contains one or more contexts. *Contexts* are subsets of *nodes* connected by *links* to a hyperdocument. *Attributes* can be attached to contexts, nodes, or links representing application-specific properties of objects or containing information that further describes an object. This model only describes two of these attributes: identifier and version based on the creation or updated time of an object.

The Trellis reference model (1989)

Richard Furuta and P. David Stotts [Sto 1989][Fur 1990] developed a hypertext reference model (*r-model*) based on Petri Nets, called the Trellis System. The *r-model* is separated into five logical levels. Within each level there are one or more representations of part or all of the hypertext. In contrast to the HAM, the defined levels represent levels of abstraction, not components of the system.

The first level presents the components *(structure, abstract contents, abstract buttons and abstract containers)* that are associated in the second level to form the hypertext.

In addition to traditional nodes (*abstract contents*) and links (*abstract buttons*), the Trellis system supports two more elements: *structure* and *containers*. The first merely describes a skeleton of the graph which provides *placeholders* that will be associated with the hypertext abstract contents and relationships. The containers are an abstraction of how the information pieces of the hypertext are aggregated and combined for display.

The relationship associations between the elements of the Abstract Component Level are made in the Abstract Hypertext Level. They can be content-structure, button-structure and container-structure associations. The Abstract Hypertext Level describes these associations but it does not describe how these associations will be displayed. The mapping between the abstract hypertext and windows is made in the Concrete Context Level. This indicates how a particular piece of information will be displayed, or the details of operations derived from a link navigation. Finally, the fourth and fifth levels specify the visible presentation of the document on a particular user interface.

In Trellis, the model, the separation between components and associations and between components and their implementation by Petri nets is achieved by a dynamic adaptation of the appearance and the behavior of the hyperdocument when it is navigated. According to Stotts and Furuta, a hypertext document has two layers: a fixed underlying information structure that is created by the hypermedia author and a flexible structure that is superimposed on the former and is tuned to each user's requirement.

The Dexter Model (1990)

The Dexter model is an attempt to capture, both formally and informally, the important abstractions found in a wide range of existing and proposed hypertext systems. The goal of the model is to provide a basis for comparing systems as well as for developing interchange and interoperability standards. The model is divided into three layers with glue in between.

The Dexter model is focused on the *storage layer*, which models the basic node/link network structure that is the essence of the hypertext. The *storage layer* describes a sort of "database" that is composed of a hierarchy of data-containing "components" (normally called *nodes*) which are interconnected by relational *links*. The *storage layer* focuses on the mechanisms by which the components and links are "glued together" to form hypertext networks. The components are treated in this layer as generic containers of data.

In the *within component layer* the model is concerned with the contents and structure of the components of the hypertext network. This layer is purposefully not elaborated within the Dexter model. The range of possible content/structure that can be included in a component is completely open. It would have no sense to define a generic model to explicitly cover all possible data types for such components. Instead, the Dexter model treats the within-component structure as being outside of the hypertext model per se. It only treats the glue between the storage layer and the *within-component layer*, a mechanism for addressing (or referring to) locations or items *within* the content of an individual component. This mechanism is called **anchoring**.

The *storage* and *within-component* layers treat hypertext as an essentially static data structure. However, hypertext systems provide users with tools to access view and manage the network structure. This functionality is captured by the **runtime layer** of the model. The Dexter model provides only a bare-bones model of the mechanism for presenting a hypertext to the user for viewing and editing. The range of possible tools is too broad and too diverse to allow a simple, generic model.

As in the case of anchoring, a critical aspect of the Dexter model is the interface between the *storage layer* and the *runtime layer*. However, this is accomplished using the notion of **presentation specifications**. These are mechanisms which present information of a component/network to the user. This information can be encoded into the hypertext network at the *storage layer*.

2.4   Hypermedia in Education

Hypertext and Hypermedia systems are increasingly used in educational environments even if their efficiency is not clear enough [Jon 1990]. The active participation of readers and authors is generally supposed to be the major advantage of hypertext systems (e.g., [Lan 1992]). There is some evidence from cognitive psychology that supports this assumption. A deep processing and elaboration usually leads to better comprehension than an information analysis at higher levels of processing. One way of reaching these deep processing levels is by "doing things" [May 1992]. However, an active involvement of learners does not mean letting them browse in a hypertext base aimlessly. Students must be encouraged to actively seek out information. This can only be achieved by giving well-defined tasks to students [Ham 1992].

The idea of education based on learning more than on teaching has intrigued cognitive psychologists and educators. They have studied the ways in which people learn in order to find the best ways of presenting knowledge which could be used in developing materials for individual interactive learning. It has been shown that it is easier to learn and remember material presented in graphical form, and when learning, it requires more activity on the students' behalf [Bar 1990]. Another way of learning is through goal-based scenarios. The teacher sets the learning goals and each student researches the subject in his or her own way, discussing it later with colleagues. In this way students are more mentally involved, which results in better understanding and learning of the material.

Some studies have shown that the use of hypermedia, besides improving student motivation, also improves students' ability to make their own cognitive connections, handle large amounts of information, use critical, relational thinking, participate in class discussions and their ability to read [Cos 1994].

According to Szuprowicz [Szu 1992], what makes the use of interactive multimedia courseware in education particularly attractive is the *"individualization of instruction, self-paced exploration of knowledge, experimental learning, and instant and effortless performance measurement."* This helps to develop new ways of thinking and drawing conclusions for the students who use interactive multimedia. The visible advantages of interactive multimedia depend on how the courseware is adapted by students. It has been expected that the use of interactive multimedia in schools will grow because of the above advantages, as well as because of the drop in the cost of hardware and multimedia software.

Pereira, de Oliveira and Vaz [Per 1991] maintain that a hypermedia system for education should contain three significant components, a **text database** (and other media), a **semantic network** which interrelates the database components and enough **tools** to allow the user to explore the database and the semantic network. The authors of hypermedia domains should generate only few closely interrelated links instead of linking to anything, so that the user may navigate using the "pseudo hierarchical structure" known as "cognitive scaffolding".

Jonassen and Grabinger [Jon 1990] suggested that a hypermedia system can be defined as a network of ideas. The linking structure of the ideas helps improve user comprehension of the node content. Such a structure is suitable for learning, due to the similarity between the associative structure of hypermedia and the associative structures existing in the human brain:

"The belief that hypertext can mimic human associative networks implies that an appropriate method for structuring hypertext is to mirror the semantic network of an experienced or knowledgeable performer or expert" [Jon 1993-2].

The knowledge structures are transferable from the hypermedia to the learner; however, simply browsing through a hypermedia system is not enough to produce any appreciable transference of structural knowledge. Moreover, it is necessary to provide exercises that explicitly test the learner's structural knowledge of the domain. Information may be considered as stored in the brain in an associative manner, thus information is linked together to form a network of knowledge. Such a structure is referred to as a "schema", and each one has a number of attributes that enable it to be linked to other knowledge structures. The process of learning is the acquisition of such information schema and arranging them into the learner's knowledge structures.

Jonassen [Jon 1993-2] stated that three processes allegedly govern learning: **accretion, restructuring** and **tuning.**

Accretion is the process of adding information to existing schemas, i.e. new content is added with links to other existing schemas.

Restructuring occurs when a schema has been expanded to a point where it is no longer viable. Additional schemas are then created from the existing schema and the new knowledge which allows the learner to access and interpret the existing knowledge in new ways.

Tuning is the process of making small adjustments to the schema while it is being used, i.e., with practice, the learner becomes better at using the knowledge.

A useful hypermedia structure would therefore be a representation of the knowledge schema of an expert. The learner attempts to map these structures onto their own, using the hypermedia. This transferral of structure, from the hypermedia to the learner, represents a challenge to hypermedia designers. It is necessary to set up an adequate structure so that the learner will have sufficient cues to incorporate the information into their own knowledge structures.

"The less structured the hypermedia is, the less likely users are to integrate what they have learned into their own knowledge structures, because the hypermedia facilitates only the acquisition part of learning" [Jon 1990].

The above discussion suggests therefore that structural information is paramount for an educational system.

2.5   Advantages and Drawbacks of Hypermedia

While hypermedia has become more popular and hypermedia systems have come into more widespread utilization, limitations and shortcomings of current hypermedia are becoming increasingly apparent [Hal 1988]. The simple basic hypermedia model lacks too much to support the organizing, structuring and accessing tasks required by many applications [Ham 1993].

2.5.1   Advantages

A hypermedia environment offers new possibilities for accessing large or complex information sources. Hypermedia has been considered as a progress in ergonomic applications because of its easy usage (the user does not have to learn an interaction language with the system or its different functionalities), easy conception, freedom to choose (the user clicks on a button according to a semantic or syntactic choice), etc.

Conklin in [Con 1987] sumarizes the following advantages of hypermedia:

- *Ease of tracing links:* machine support for link tracing means that all links are equally easy to follow forward or backward.
- *Ease of creating new references:* students may simply annotate someone else's document part with a comment or annotation while the referenced part remains unchanged.
- *Information structuring:* both hierarchical and non hierarchical organizations may be imposed on unstructured information; even multiple hierarchies may allow the same material to be organized in different ways.
- *Global views:* current browsers support easier access to large or complex information environments.
- *Customized documents:* segments can be threaded together in many ways, allowing the same document to serve multiple functions.

- *Modularity of information:* since the same document parts may be referenced from several places, ideas may be expressed with less overlap and duplication.

- *Consistency of information:* references are embedded in their document part, and if that is moved by the editor, or replaced by an alternative document part, the link information still provides direct access to the reference.

- *Task stacking:* the user may have several paths of inquiry active and displayed on the screen at the same time.

- *Collaboration:* several authors may cooperate to develop documents and tightly interwoven comments about the document. Apparently, the hypermedia model serves as an excellent (artificial) metaphor to represent a shared environment.

2.5.2   Drawbacks

There are two different classes of problems related to hypermedia: problems with the current implementations and problems with the whole hypermedia model.

Problems with the current implementations are mostly interface problems. These are merely technical shortcomings, expected to be solved sometime in the future. Typical dilemmas in this category include delays in the display of referenced material, lack of browsers or deficiencies in existing browsers, and so on.

Problems with the whole hypermedia model, according to a few influential authors in the field (e.g., Conklin [Con 1987], [Ram 1992] and Nielsen [Nie 1990]) are problems that may in fact ultimately limit the usefulness of hypermedia: **disorientation** and **cognitive overhead**.

Disorientation in Hypermedia Environments

The risk of disorientation while navigating the information space (also known as getting lost in hyperspace [Con 1987]), is one of the major usability problems with hypermedia systems. For example, studies by Nielsen [Nie 1990] showed that 56 percent of the readers of a document that was composed in one of the most popular commercial hypermedia systems (HyperCard) agreed fully or at least partly with the statement: "I was often confused about 'where I was' ".

Of course, a disorientation problem also occurs in traditional linear documents. But in a linear document a reader only has two options: he/she can search for the desired object further on or earlier in the document. The hypermedia model offers more freedom, more dimensions in which the reader may move, and hence a greater potential for him/her to become lost or disoriented. So along with the power to organize information in a much more complex way, students have to face the problem of having to keep track of where they are in the network and, even more difficult, how to get to some other place they know (or think they know) exists in the graph. In a large network, information may easily become hard to find or even become forgotten.

Hypermedia and Cognitive Overhead

Conklin also presents another fundamental problem of using hypertext: *the cognitive overhead*. It may be difficult for group members to become used to the additional mental overhead required to create and keep track of links. In general: the additional effort and concentration necessary to maintain several tasks or trails at one time may be experienced as an imposition.

This problem does not just occur in the process of constructing hyperdocuments, it also frequently happens while browsing hyperspace. A student is often presented with a large number of choices about which links to follow. At the moment he encounters a link, how can he decide the most worthwhile path? This must sound familiar to anyone who has ever used the Microsoft Windows [WIND] on-line help facility which is loaded with numerous hyperlinks.

Moreover, when the computer display is small, group members may see only a small part of the information at the same time. This means that they can easily lose track of how the current fragment is related to the immediately preceding or following media object, since this fragment is often invisible at this time. Nielsen calls this a problem with "context-in-the-small" as opposed to the "context-in-the-large" mentioned problem, the equivalent of "getting lost in hyperspace".

Solutions to Some Drawbacks

Many researchers ([Hal 1987], [Con 1987], [Tri 1988], [Ben 1994]) have proposed the use of default pathways within the hypermedia in order to support a user who is unable to decide where to go. The theory is that a novice user is able to follow a predefined path, but such user is free to break from it whenever he/she wishes. Such an approach has been criticized, most notably by Jonassen and Grabinger in [Jon 1990] for providing the unambitious, uninterested or lost learner with a path that they can blindly follow, thus ignoring the wealth of information elsewhere in the hypermedia database. The original idea for default paths, as indeed the original idea for hypermedia, is often attributed to Bush [Bus 1947]. However, Bush describes a system where a user builds up their own pathways as they discover relationships between concepts. On the other hand, the guided tours proposed by Trigg in [Tri 1988] are provided beforehand by the domain author. They therefore may not have any relationship to the student's current learning needs and consequently the tours seem wholly inappropriate for an educational system [Jon 1990], although they may be usable in non-educational systems.

Cognitive overhead is also induced by the complexity of the domain itself. When students use a hypermedia system, they must use trails from the domain to orientate themselves and to navigate further into the domain. Hence the cognitive loading problem is exacerbated when the hypermedia is being employed as a tutoring medium, since the student is not just navigating in order to find a particular piece of information but is actively attempting to learn the contents of parts of the domain. However, the structure of the hypermedia may be a key part in the learning activity, as it may provide context and examples. This structural information may therefore provide the learner with "cognitive scaffolding" onto which the learner may "attach" their newly learned material [Jon 1993-2].

One possible solution to avoid being lost in the hyperspace is the use of filters so that the reader is presented with a manageable level of detail, by removing nodes that are not likely to be of interest [Bru 1996]. Other techniques to solve the inconveniences of common hypermedia are discussed in the next section when adaptive systems are introduced.

2.6   Adaptive Hypermedia

2.6.1   Introduction

A hypermedia application offers much freedom to navigate through a large hyperspace. Adaptive Hypermedia (AH) offers (automatically generated) personalized content and navigation support, so that the choice between freedom and guidance may be made on an individual basis.

Adaptive hypermedia is a direction of research at the crossroads of hypertext (hypermedia) and user modeling. Adaptive hypermedia systems build a model of the goals, preferences and knowledge of the individual user and use this throughout the interaction to adapt the hypertext to the needs of that user [DeB 1999].

This section introduces the adaptivity approach as a feature to be considered when building success-adaptive hypermedia systems.

2.6.2   Types of Adaptation

A good learning system may need to provide a protected learning environment (by restrictions or warnings) to facilitate efficient learning for the students. From the human-computer interaction point of view, a careful examination is necessary with regard to adapting the learning environment to the learner's goal and capability in such protected situations [Opp 1997].

The concept of adaptation has been an important issue of research for learning systems in the last decade. The research has shown that the application of adaptation can provide a better learning environment in such systems but many research issues need to be fixed before an effective and efficient adaptation in learning systems is possible.

There have been many attempts to include user models and adaptation features in recent years. They have tried to improve the correspondence between user, task and system characteristics and consequently increase the user's efficiency. Two kinds of systems have been developed for supporting the user in his/her tasks: *adaptable and adaptive.*

Systems that allow the user to change certain system parameters (that is, parameters that can be modified on explicit user request) and adapt their behavior accordingly are called **adaptable**. Systems that adapt to the users automatically, based on the assumptions they make about user needs (psychological state, knowledge), are called **adaptive** [Opp 1994]. The whole spectrum of these two concepts is shown in the following figure that represents the idea proposed by Oppermann in [Opp 1997].

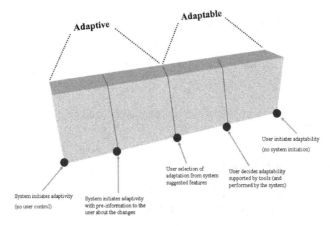

Figure 4.   Spectrum of the adaptation in computer systems

DeBra in [DeB 1999a] describes the types of adaptation mentioned above, as follows:

- In an *adaptable* hypermedia system the user can provide a profile (through a dialog or questionnaire). The system provides a version of the hypermedia application that better represents the selected profile. Settings may include certain presentation preferences (colors, media type, learning style, etc.) and user background (qualifications, knowledge about concepts, etc.). On the Web there are several such sites that use a questionnaire to tailor some part of the presentation to the user.

- *Adaptive* hypermedia systems monitor the user behavior and adapt the presentation accordingly. The evolution of the user preferences and knowledge may be deduced (partly) from page accesses. Sometimes the system may need questionnaires or tests to get more accurate information of the user's state of mind. Most of the adaptation, however, is based on the user's browsing actions, and possibly on the behavior of other users as well.

2.6.3   Adaptive Systems

Adaptive systems are systems which can alter aspects of their structure, functionality or interface, in order to accommodate the differing needs of individuals or group of users and the changing needs of users over time [Ben 1987].

Adaptive learning systems emphasize the following aspects:

- Systems that readily adapt the learning experience to the skills and needs of the learner.
- Systems that are flexible and scalable, that allow the content and courseware to be widely reusable and easily organized in different ways at different instructional levels.
- Systems that provide content development tools that function across a broad range of platforms, easily used by domain experts who are not programmers — systems which are adaptable to the educators as well as to the learners.

Adaptivity Determinants

The set of adaptivity determinants adopted in currently implemented systems is large and diverse. In most approaches it seems that there is a common set of characteristics that are considered essential. This set includes:

- User characteristics (knowledge, goals, prerequisites, cognitive style, learning style, maturity, general ability, confidence, motivation, experience, preferences, etc.);
- User modeling technique (Artificial Intelligence methodologies, heuristics, etc.);
- Tasks being performed (nature, priority, etc.);
- Information characteristics (nature, purpose, etc.);
- Etc.

These characteristics are gathered in several models, such as *task model, user model, dialogue model, application model*, etc. Additionally, depending on the requirements of the particular application, other adaptivity determinants may be found:

- The goals and characteristics of the information producer (e.g., affect perceiver's knowledge, opinion, emotional state), and the receiver of information (e.g., knowledge, interest, opinions) [Are 1993];
- Dialogue acts, such as:

- o Informative subject: **enable** - communicate actions to achieve a task subgoal, **result** - give information about the outcome of a task subgoal, **cause** – give information concerning the causality of a task subgoal, and **inform** - display information as is;
- o Subject-organizing: **sequence** - specify a succession of linked steps, **summary** – provide overview of task subgoals, and **condition** - a particular subgoal is a precondition;
- o Presentational: **locate** - draw attention to an information type, **foreground** - give further detail of an information type, **background** - give content information, and **emphasize** - make an information type prominent [Sut 1994].

- Expressiveness (i.e., ability to present all the information using specified techniques) and effectiveness criteria (i.e., amount of redundancy) [Mac 1986], [Gar 1988];
- Information about generally shared world knowledge applicable across different task domains [Nea 1991], e.g., common sense about the business world, office work, human communication [Tho 1987];
- Graphics design aspects, e.g., empirical studies on graphic tool usage, theoretical distinctions between tools [Cha 1993];
- Teaching strategies (particularly in Intelligent Tutoring Systems) [Fer 1989], [Dan 1992], [Gut 1994], [Per 1995].

Even when researchers agree on the set of adaptivity determinant characteristics, the concept of significativity may differ substantially. For example, information content is characterized or classified as:

- Linguistic or non-linguistic, analogue or non-analogue, arbitrary or non-arbitrary, static or dynamic, etc. [Ber 1993];
- By the data types, properties of relational structure, arity, user information seeking goal, etc. [Rot 1993];
- Descriptive, spatial, operational-action or operational-procedural, temporal, etc. [Sut 1994].

Adaptivity Goals

The goals that the adaptivity process attempts to fulfill vary substantially in current systems, according to the requirements of the application and user group. Dieterich in [Die 1993] provides the following list of adaptivity goals:

- Easy, efficient, effective use
- Make complex systems usable
- Present what the user wants to see
- Speed up use
- User Interface that fits heterogeneous user groups
- User Interface that dynamically considers increasing experience

In each application domain, there is a major goal that the system has to reach. For example, in the case of an air-traffic control system, the overall goal is the effective and error-free use; for a computer game, the overall objective might be the user's satisfaction. In several other cases, however, more than one (sometimes conflicting) goal is significant. For a public interface, for example, efficiency and effectiveness might both be desired.

Adaptivity Rules

The rules that guide the adaptivity vary in current implemented systems. For example:

- MacIDA [Pet 1990], uses a set of selection rules of the form:
- *"A window is selected for each entity, a simple edit box is selected for each attribute of an entity, a table is selected for each repetitive aggregate of attributes, and a push button is designated for each function."*
- [Ste 1993] addresses the adaptivity for people with special needs, using rules of the form:

    "If user task = X

    ($X \in \{selection, position, quantification, command input\}$),

    and,

    user load = Y

    (where user load refers to cognitive, perceptual and motor load,

    and,

    $Y \in \{low, medium, high\}$), and ...,

then use Z

(where Z ∈ {direct screen selection, direct selection on a tactile surface, ...})".

- Many other adaptivity rules may be found in the literature concerning the assignment of adaptivity constituents to adaptivity determinants, such as:
  - o *"**If** what has to be displayed is a structural analysis of a complex abstract domain, **then** use network charts"* [Ber 1992];
  - o *"**If** the task sub-goal requires spatial information - prefer visual media resource"* [Sut 1994];
  - o *"**If** information is urgent, **then** choose a medium with low default detectability and a channel with no temporal variance"* [Are 1993];
  - o *"**If** the data type is alphanumeric or numeric, and discrete, and the range of values is greater than 6, **then** use a list box"* [Jan 1993];
  - o *"**If** a Basic Unit of Learning exists, **then** select the Basic Unit of Learning in process"* [Fer 1989].

Global architecture for adaptive systems

Benyon in [Ben 1993] has proposed a global architecture for adaptive systems. According to him, adaptive systems must have three essential parts: a *user model*, a *domain model* and an *interaction model* (see Figure 5). However, the complexity of the system and the requeriments of the application have an impact on the detail contained in each component. The advantage of this architecture development is that it enables researchers to talk in the same language, to compare different systems and to develop appropriate representation techniques. This particular architecture has been adapted for information systems, electronic mail filtering systems, multimodal systems and other similar systems.

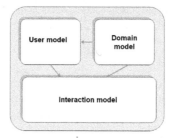

Figure 5.   Global architecture of an adaptive system

An adaptive system has a model of the system with which it is interacting. Very often that other system is a human being, and its representation is the *user model* part of the above architecture. An adaptive system also includes some representation of the application which is to have the adaptive capability. This is the *domain model*. The interaction of user and system is described in the *interaction model*. In the following, these three models are desscribed in detail.

The user model

The user model is required in an adaptive system because it can alter aspects of the system in response to certain given, or inferred, user characteristics. These characteristics represent the knowledge and preferences that the system "believes" that a user (which may be an individual, a group of people or a non-human agent) possesses. The model can be separated by the system from the rest of its knowledge and contains explicit assumptions about the user.

This model is used to provide adaptivity either by intervention or by co-operative agreement with a user. Providing adaptive functionality requires that a user model controls an inference engine. It may infer perceived goals and courses of actions and it acts upon such decisions, altering features of the interaction to meet the task and personal needs of individuals.

User models may be highly practical in the sense that they only represent what is required in order to facilitate adaptation. User models may contain the types of knowledge that the system has about the user. Firstly, the user model may hold data about what the system believes the user believes about the domain. It is **domain dependent data**. Because of the similarity of this data to that held by Intelligent Tutoring Systems, this portion of the user model is refered as the *student model* in Benyon's architecture (see Figure 6). The *Student model* component is created directly from the *domain model*, and data may be kept at the following levels:

- The *intentional* or *task level* that describes the user goals in the domain;
- The *logical level* that describes the user knowledge of the domain; and
- The *physical* level that records the user (inferred) knowledge.

At each of the above levels the user model should record the user knowledge and the user erroneous beliefs.

Domain independent data may be considered either as fundamental psychological data or as profile data. Psychological data is concerned with essential cognitive and affective traits of users and is held in the *psychological model* component of the *user model*. There is increasing experimental evidence that confirms that users differ in cognitive skills and personality traits, which significantly affect the quality of certain interaction styles and user requirements [Ega 1988], [Van 1990], [Jen 1992]. These characteristics of users are particularly resistant to change by the user and hence they are particularly important for adaptive systems. If users find difficult, or impossible, to change aspects of their make-up, these are exactly the characteristics that the system should adapt [Van 1990], [Ben 1993b]. For instance, spatial ability is a peculiarly relevant characteristic to Human-Computer Interaction (HCI) ([Vic 1987], [Ega 1988], [Vic 1988]) particularly where users have to navigate through the conceptual space of file structures or system modes.

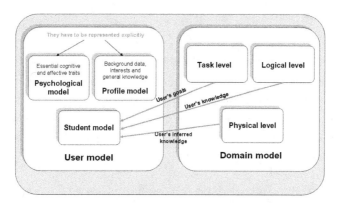

Figure 6.   Elements to build a user model

Data concerning the background, interests and general knowledge of users is maintained in a *profile model* component of the user model. This data is not psychological in nature, but may interact with cognitive characteristics in a number of ways. For example, users with poor spatial ability may be able to deal effectively with an interface style if they have a certain level of experience using that style [Jen 1992]. Knowledge of generic applications is stored in the user profile like much of the *stereotype-inherited data* such as being a business traveller [Mor 1989] or a feminist [Ric 1983].

Both the *psychological* and *profile* components have to be represented explicitly, preferably using some user modeling software. All aspects of the user model will require considerable prototyping, evaluation and refinement before they capture appropriate and relevant aspects of users with sufficient accuracy for a given domain.

Summarizing, a user model contains explicitly modeled assumptions that represent the characteristics of the user which are pertinent to the system. The system can consult the user model to adapt the performance of the system to the user characteristics. User modeling allows the system to personalize the interaction between the user and the contents. To achieve effective learning this personalization should put the content in a context which the user can understand and relate to. There are several techniques for modeling the user and tuning this model.

Type of user models

User modeling comes in two varieties, *knowledge-based* and *behavioral* [Kob 1993]. *Knowledge-based* user modeling is typically the result of questionnaires and studies of users, hand-crafted into a set of heuristics. *Behavioral models* are generally the result of monitoring the user during his/her activity. *Stereotypes* as stated by Rich [Ric 1983] [Ric 1989] can be applied to both cases, classifying the users into groups (or stereotypes), with the aim of applying generalizations to people in those groups.

Behavioral user models can also be classified in *overlay* and *perturbation* models.

Overlay models are widely used in adaptive hypermedia systems for education. A model of the student knowledge is built on a concept-by-concept basis and updated as the user progresses through the system. This allows for a flexible model of the student knowledge for each topic [Bru 1996b]. For this model the domain knowledge must be modularized into specific topics or concepts. The complexity of the model depends on the granularity of the structure of this domain knowledge and the granularity of the estimation of the student knowledge. This estimation is build up by examining the sections the student has read and the test he/she has performed. Uses of this model can be observed in systems like HANDLEBAR [Cla 1979], SCHOLAR [Sha 1987], INTZA [Gut 1994], MetaDoc [Boy 1994], HYPERTUTOR [Per 1995], CAMELEON [Lar 2001] and WebPVT [Vir 2001].

Perturbation models [Kas 1989] can be used to represent beliefs which are outside the expert's view of the domain. 'Buggy' models [Bur 1982] and 'mal-rules' [Sle 1981] may be used to represent common misconceptions which users may have about the domain.

Stereotypes represent a structured collection of traits or characteristics, stored as facets, to which a value and, optionally, a confidence-level and a rationale are attached. *Stereotypes* model users in a variety of dimensions and represent characteristics of users in a hierarchy. Creating fixed stereotypes is one of the simplest ways of carrying out user modeling. New students (if the system is for education) are categorized and the system will customize its performance based on the category which has been set for each student. A common example would be the notion of *novice, intermediate* and *expert* users.

The *stereotype* and *overlay* techniques of student modeling are often combined in adaptive hypermedia systems for education. The student may be categorized by stereotype initially and then this model is gradually modified as the overlay model is built from the information acquired from the student interaction with the system.

Other user models are also used for modeling the learners' knowledge and faculties. This is the case of the Fuzzy models that use Fuzzy Logics to allow a more realistic evaluation of the student performance [Kav 2001].

The domain model

The domain model is required in order to define the aspects of the application which can be adapted or which are otherwise required for the operation of the adaptive system. Other terms which have been used for this concept include *application model, system model, device model* and *task model*. The domain model serves a number of purposes. Firstly, it forms the basis of all the inferences and predictions which can be made from the user-system interaction. It is important, therefore, that the model is at an appropriate level of abstraction to allow the required inferences to be made. There may be mechanisms which, as a result of some observed behavior or stated characteristics, predict a problem that would occur or infer a user attempt to achieve a specific goal. In order to make these inferences the system must have an appropriate representation of the domain.

In TRACK [Car 1989] the domain model includes sequences of actions (plans) which are required to achieve a particular goal. This model is used to infer the user's goal from their observed actions. In addition to inferences, the domain model forms the basis for all the adaptations which the system may make. The system can only change aspects of the application which are described by the domain model. For example, in HAM-ANS [Mor 1989], the domain model contains a representation of hotels which includes 'quietness' as an attribute. The system exploits this representation in making a recommendation of a hotel to a particular user by emphasizing that a particular hotel is quiet. This adaptation is only posible because the domain model contains this attribute. In TAILOR [Par 1989] the domain model represents two levels of description of components of complex devices, such as telephones, so that it can provide appropriate explanations for different users.

Any system which is capable of evaluating its own actions also requires a domain model. The domain model contains the characteristics of the application which are measurable, so that they may be evaluated for the required criteria effectiveness.

The final use of the domain model is to form the basis of the student model component of the user model (mentioned before in Figure 6). The system needs to record what it believes the user believes about certain aspects of the application. The domain model must describe the system so that it can store data about the user's understanding of the various concepts and functions in the application.

In most adaptive systems the domain model is implicit. The representations are embedded in the system code or are only available after a significant amount of processing. For example, in GRUNDY [Ric 1983] the classification of suitable books for particular types of people may only be obtained from the *stereotype* user model. There is no explicit representation of the domain.

The benefits to be gained from having an explicit and well-defined domain model are considerable and have long been recognized in Artificial Intelligence [Dav 1977]. A separate domain model provides improved domain independence, which means that refining the domain model is much easier. This is most important as it is unlikely that any adaptive system design will generate a perfect representation of the domain on the first attempt. A separate and explicit domain model is used more easily for multiple purposes such as providing explanations of the system behavior.

The domain model might be seen as a description of the application which contains facts about the domain, i.e., the objects, their attributes and the relationships between objects. The domain model is the designer definition of the aspects of the application relevant to the needs of the adaptive system. A central question in designing a domain model is deciding what level of description should be represented. Since the domain model forms the basis of the student model component of the user model, it is important that the domain model be to a great extent *cognitively valid*. That is, it should capture a view of the domain which is appropriate to human information processing.

The knowledge representation and articulation in educational systems implementation will determine the content of the tutorial interaction and the structure that will govern an adaptive instruction [Car 1970].

For the instruction process, in adaptive systems is necessary to know, for example, the order in which the concepts will be presented, the existing relationships among them and the way in which those relationships help in the process, in the learning difficulties, in their prerequisites, in representing points of view or in explaining concepts, etc. Therefore, a great quantity of didactic information exists which is associated to each concept or group of concepts that one should know when teaching and that should be collected in the domain description.

Fink in [Fin 1991] states that in the area of Artificial Intelligence, domain knowledge refers to the subject matter material, and that there are various ways of representing it depending on the nature of the knowledge itself. Furthermore, she states that these methods do not necessarily need to have a psychological foundation, since the goal is to find an internally useful representation to be implemented. Based on her research, she summarizes the domain representation in adaptive educational systems as follows:

- The knowledge representation could be of two types: *declarative* and *procedural*. In most of the developed tutors these two types of knowledge have been represented by means of different profiles as *production rules*, *frames*, *semantic networks*, *scripts* or different combinations of the same. Currently these techniques are used in most of the existing ITS (i.e., TUTOR [Fer 1989] and INTZA [Gut 1994]).
- Representation of the knowledge from multiple points of view. Depending on the type of task the tutor wanted to assign, it is important to include different types of knowledge representation.

- Representation of models. These models are used to substitute real physical systems and to simulate their behaviors.

The interaction model

This component represents the actual and designed interaction between the user and the application. An interaction is the action of the user to work with the system at a level which can be monitored. Data gathered from monitoring may be used to make inferences about the user beliefs, plans or goals, or about long-term characteristics, such as cognitive traits or profile data. The system may tailor its behavior to the needs of a particular interaction or, given suitably 'reflective' mechanisms, the system may evaluate its inferences and adaptations and adjust aspects of its own organization or behavior (i.e., it must decide the appropriate moment to provide some indications based on user interaction). The next figure shows in detail the interaction model architecture as proposed by Benyon [Ben 1993].

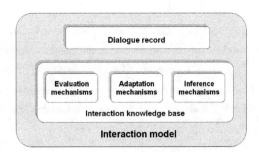

Figure 7.   The interaction model architecture in adaptive systems

Summary of aspects concerning adaptive systems

The following schema summarizes the main aspects concerning the development of adaptive systems:

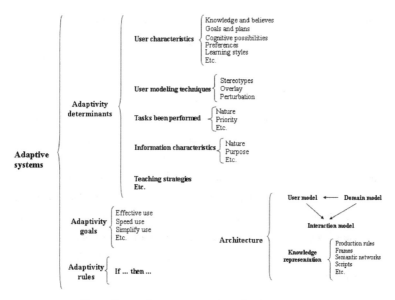

Figure 8.   Aspects concerning adaptive systems

2.6.4   Web-based Adaptive Educational Systems

Introduction

A distance education system must support, to the extent possible, the problems caused by the physical distances between teacher, student, and classmates. The classic approach of education with regard to knowledge transmission has been changing into a model of practical experimentation and interaction that promotes changes in concepts and student's strategies, until he/she reaches proficiency. In this context, teachers perform the role of significative assistant instead of information provider. This requires more efficient mechanisms of adaptivity and assistance in problem-solving processes. The system must perform the teacher's role as much as possible, building a robust student model for each user that would enable: adapting the curriculum to each user; helping him/her to navigate through the course activities; giving support in task accomplishment and in exercise and problem solving; and providing help resources anytime they are needed.

Some traditional static Web-based application systems, as well as other complex hypermedia systems with a large variety of users, suffer from an inability to satisfy heterogeneous needs. A Web course presents the same static explanation of a concept to students with widely differing knowledge of the subject. A Web bookstore offers the same selection of bestsellers to customers with different reading preferences. A Web museum offers the same "guided tour" and the same narration to visitors with very different goals and interests. A remedy for the negative effects of the traditional "one-size-fits-all" approach is to enhance the system's ability to adapt its own behavior to the goals, tasks, interests, and other features of individual users. Starting in the 1990s, many research teams began to investigate ways of modeling features of the users of hypermedia systems. This has led to several interesting adaptation techniques and adaptive hypermedia systems. The application areas for these systems range from educational hypermedia to information retrieval systems with a hypertext interface. Various research groups have developed different original techniques to adapt hypermedia systems to individual characteristics of the user.

A comprehensive review of adaptive hypermedia techniques and systems can be found in [Bru 1996] where Brusilovsky states that a hyperdocument (hypermedia document) could basically be adapted in two ways:

- The information content on a page may be modified to better suit the needs of the user. Short prerequisite explanations may be added, as may comparisons to subjects described on other pages the user has seen before, additional details for advanced users, etc. Changes in the presentation "style" are also possible, selecting different media (text, images, audio, video) or changing the length of the presentation.
- The link structure and/or presentation may be modified so as to make suggestions to the user about where to go next. Links or link destinations may be added, changed, removed, sorted or annotated.

Most of the focus in adaptive hypermedia for educational courseware has attempted to alleviate the difficulties of content comprehension (cognitive overload) and orientation (getting lost in hyperspace).

Adaptive presentation techniques which effect changes to both the selection of different media depending on user preferences and individual adaptation of the content are beginning to be successful.

The use of adaptive navigation which effects changes to the link structure between elements of the hypermedia courseware based on an individual user's (mental) model has proven effective since learners using such systems have demonstrated faster learning, more goal-oriented attitudes and fewer steps to complete a course.

To achieve the maximum effectiveness when using non-adaptive educational hypermedia there are some learner features that are particularly significant. These include pre-knowledge, cognitive style, maturity, general ability, confidence and motivation. These features influence the ability of students to effectively accept the additional mental load caused by the need to monitor and self-evaluate as well as learn [Spe 1998].

Many developers of educational systems consider Intelligent Tutoring Systems (ITS) and learning environments as different and even contradictory ways of using computers in education. Some well-known Intelligent Learning Environments (ILE) such as Sherlock [Laj 1989] and Smithtown [Shu 1990] showed that these ways are not contradictory, but rather complimentary. ITS are able to control learning adaptively at various levels, but they generally do not provide tools to support free exploration. Learning environments and microworlds support exploratory learning, but they lack the control of an intelligent tutor. Without such control the student often works inefficiently and may never discover important features of the subject.

The same situation exists now with ITS and educational hypermedia systems. They are often considered as two different approaches to using computers in education, but these approaches are in fact complimentary. Research has demonstrated that hypermedia can provide the basis for an exploratory learning system but that, by itself, such a system is insufficient, and needs to be supplemented by more directed guidance [Ham 1989]. That guidance can be provided by an intelligent tutoring component. By comparison, hypermedia can add new dimensions to traditional ITS/ILE by providing a tool for student-driven acquisition of domain knowledge.

In this section, the state of the art of web-based adaptive hypermedia systems development for education is presented.

Adaptation issues in web-based educational systems

According to Brusilovsky's studies, currently adaptation technologies applied in Web-based adaptive educational systems are adopted from either the *ITS* area [Bru 1995] such as: Curriculum sequencing, Intelligent analysis of student solutions, Interactive problem solving support, Example-based problem solving support, and Collaboration support; or the adaptive hypermedia area [Bru 1996] such as: **Adaptive presentation,** and **Adaptive navigation** support.

A detailed explanation of these topics is presented next.

- Adaptation technologies adopted from the ITS area
  - o *Curriculum sequencing*

    The goal of *curriculum sequencing* technology (or *instructional planning* technology) is to provide the student with the most suitable individually planned sequence of knowledge units to learn and to sequence learning tasks (examples, questions, problems, etc.). In other words, it helps the student to find an "optimal path" through the learning material (see [Ste 1998], [Bru 2000] and [Hen 2001]). In this context, two kinds of curriculum sequencing techniques are distinguished: *knowledge sequencing,* which determines the next concept or topic to be taught, and *task sequencing,* which determines the next learning task (problem, example, test) within the current topic [Bru 1992a].

    In the context of Web-based education, curriculum sequencing technology becomes very important to guide the student through the hyperspace of available information. Actually, this is the oldest and the most popular technology for Web-based adaptive educational systems. Curriculum sequencing was implemented in different ways in the following adaptive educational systems: ELM-ART [Bru 1996b], InterBook [Bru 1997], MANIC [Ster 1997)], DCG [Vas 1997], TANGOW [Car 1999b], KBS Hyperbook [Hen 2000], [Hen 2002] and WLog [Bal 2001], [Bal 2002].

o *Intelligent analysis of student solutions*

This deals with students' final answers to educational problems (which can range from a simple question to a complex programming problem), no matter how these answers were obtained. Unlike non-intelligent checkers which may say (not more than) whether the solution is correct, intelligent analyzers may say exactly where the mistake is or what the incompletion consists of. Intelligent analyzers may provide extensive error feedback and may update the student model. The classic example from the domain of teaching programming is PROUST [Joh 1986]; other examples are CAMUS-II [Van, 1994] and ELM-PE [Web 1995].

The intelligent analysis of solutions is a suitable technology in the context of slow networks. Only one interaction between browser and server is needed for a complete solution. It can provide intelligent feedback and perform student modeling when more interactive techniques are hardly useful. Currently, there are some adaptive educational systems on the Web which implement intelligent analysis of student solutions (i.e., students with different student models may get different feedback): ELM-ART, an ITS for programming in LISP [Bru 1996b]; WITS, an ITS for Differential Calculations [Oka 1997]; VCPROLOG, an ITS for teaching PROLOG [Pey 2000]; and WebPVT, a computer-assisted language learning system [Vir 2001].

o *Interactive problem solving support*

The goal of *interactive problem solving support* is to provide intelligent help at each step of problem solving - from giving a hint to executing the next step for the student. The systems which implement this technology may monitor the actions of the student, understand them and use this understanding to provide help and to update the student model. The classic example from the domain of teaching programming is the LISP-TUTOR [And 1985]; other examples are the ACT Programming Tutor [Cor 1992] and

GRACE [McK 1992]. However, such direct observation of single problem solving steps cannot be performed as easily in WWW-based tutoring systems because the delay caused by the correspondence with the server would be excessive. The current tendency of research is to try to solve this problem by creating intelligent on-site agents based on JAVA applets. A well-known development is PAT-Online [Bru 1997b] which uses a server-based approach (i.e., a form-based CGI interface) and lets the student submit several problem solving steps for checking in the same transaction (It is a combination of interactive problem solving support and intelligent analysis of student solutions).

o **Example-based problem solving**

In an *example-based problem solving* context, students solve new problems using previously experienced examples. In this context, ITS helps students by suggesting to them the most relevant *cases* (examples explained to them or problems solved by them earlier). An example from the domain of teaching programming is ELM-PE [Web 1995]. Example-based problem solving does not require extensive client-server interaction and can be naturally used in adaptive educational systems on the Web. A working system which uses this technology on the WWW is ELM-ART [Bru 1996b]. A similar approach can be also observed in the Adaptive Educational System Object Model (AESOM) [Fun 2001].

o **Adaptive collaboration support**

Adaptive collaboration support is a new ITS technology which has been developed within the last 5 years along with the evolution of networked educational systems. The goal of adaptive collaboration support is to use the system's knowledge about different users (stored in user models) to form a matching collaborating group. Existing examples include forming a group for collaborative problem solving at a proper moment of time [Hop 1995], [Ike 1997] or finding the most competent peer to answer a question about a topic (i.e., finding a person with a model showing good knowledge of this topic) [Bis 1997], [McC 1997]. Currently, the AESOM system [Fun 2001] proposes the use of this technique.

- Adaptation technologies adopted from the adaptive hypermedia area

  o *Adaptive presentation*

    Brusilovsky [Bru 1996] uses this term to indicate the adaptation of what is shown on a single screen or page. In a system with adaptive presentation, pages are not static, but adaptively generated or assembled from pieces for each user. For example, with several adaptive presentation techniques, expert users receive more detailed and comprehensive information, whilst novices receive additional explanations.

    Basically, there are two different aspects of adaptive presentation:

    - *The same information may be presented in different ways.*

      An Adaptive Hypermedia System (AHS) may offer different alternative presentations and allow the user to choose one (or more). From repetitions in this choice the system can deduce the user preference automatically. An example would be a system where the user can click on a button to get the page read out to him/her. After a number of subsequent page accesses where the user systematically asks to get the audio fragment, the system may decide to play the audio automatically. (Another alternative is to let the system offer an explicit choice through an initial questionnaire or a configuration form. This would result in the definition introduced for an *adaptable* system). Examples of this kind of *adaptive presentation* are:

      o **Media selection**: the same information can be presented as text, audio (spoken text) or video. The AHS learns the user preference and presents information in that format by default.

o **Level of difficulty**: essentially the same information can be conveyed using different wording. Technical terms which the user might not understand should be avoided. Non-essential details can be left out, etc. It is, of course, difficult to decide the level of difference which should be considered in the presented information.

o **Verbosity or style**: the same information may be provided using long or short sentences, with few or many details, using a different user perspective (for instance using "we", "you" or "one"), etc.

- *The same page may also offer different information to different users*: The AHS may offer *additional explanations* to advanced users, or users with a specific background or knowledge. The difference between additional explanations and just a more detailed or reworded version of the same page is, of course, not very clear.

  o The AHS may offer *prerequisite explanations* to compensate for missing pre-cognition. If some information about a concept used on a page is needed in order to understand the rest of the page, a short (prerequisite) explanation of that concept may be added. Such a prerequisite explanation is not a substitute for a whole page (or even a set of pages) about that concept, but it is just enough to enable the user to understand, the current page.

  o The AHS may offer *comparative explanations* to users who have read about two related concepts. After reading the first concept no comparison can be made with the other concept. But once the second concept is studied, it becomes available for comparison. Such a comparison is added to whichever page is read last.

In current AHS the adaptation is always dynamic. Prerequisite explanations disappear when they are no longer needed. Comparative explanations appear not only on the page about the second concept but also on the first one, etc.

In order to achieve adaptive presentation, several **techniques** can be used. The two most common ones are:

o *Page variants*: different versions of the "same" page exist. Based on the user model the AHS decides which variant to use for a specific user (at a specific moment). Page variants are most useful to implement media selection or the choice between long and short versions of pages.

o *Conditional inclusion of fragments*: a page is constructed from small content fragments which are conditionally included (or omitted). From the user model the AHS deduces which prerequisite, additional or comparative explanations to include in the page or not.

An example from the domain of teaching programming is the "conditional text" technique applied in Lisp-critic [Fis 1990] and ITEM/IP [Bru 1992b].

Adaptive presentation is very important in the WWW context where the same "page" has to suit very different students. Only two Web-based adaptive educational systems implement full-fledged adaptive presentation: C-Book [Kay 1994] and De Bra's adaptive course on Hypertext [Cal 1997]. Both systems apply the conditional text technique. Some other systems use adaptive presentation in special contexts. Medtec [Eli 1997] is able to generate adaptive summaries of book chapters. ELM-ART [Bru

1996b], AST [Spe 1997] and InterBook [Bru 1997] use adaptive presentation to provide adaptive insertable warnings about the educational status of a page. For example, if a page is not ready to be learned, ELM-ART and AST insert a textual warning at the end of it and the InterBook inserts a warning image as a red bar. The page variant technique is used in Anatom-Tutor [Bea 1994], C_Book [Kay 1994] and ORIMUHS [Enc 1995].

o *Adaptive navigation support:*

The goal of the *adaptive navigation support technology* is to support the student in hyperspace orientation and navigation, by changing the appearance of visible links. Adaptive Navigation Support (ANS) can be considered as an extension of curriculum sequencing technology into a hypermedia context. It shares the same goal - to help students to find an "optimal path" through the learning material. At the same time, adaptive navigation support is less directed than traditional sequencing: it guides students implicitly and leaves the choice of the next knowledge item to be learned and the next problem to be solved to the user.

The management of links that are presented within nodes (pages) is typically done in one or more of the following ways:

- *Direct guidance*: A "next" or "continue" (link) button is shown. The destination of this link is the node which the AHS determines to be most appropriate.

- *Sorting of links*: A list of links is sorted and presented from most relevant to least relevant. This technique is useful in information retrieval systems and in goal-oriented educational systems.

- *Link annotation*: Link anchors are presented differently depending on the relevance of the destination.

- *Link hiding*: Links leading to inappropriate or non-relevant information are hidden. This can also be done by presenting the link as "normal text".

- *Link disabling*: Inappropriate links are disabled. Whether the link anchor is visible depends on the combination of this technique with link annotation or link hiding.

- *Link removal*: Inappropriate links (and anchors) are simply removed. This works well in lists, but removing the anchor text does not work for anchors that appear in running text.

Two examples of ANS-based standalone systems from the domain of teaching programming are ISIS-Tutor [Bru 1994], which uses adaptive hiding and adaptive annotation, and Hypadapter [Hoh 1996], which uses adaptive hiding and adaptive sorting. In a WWW context where hypermedia is a basic organizational paradigm, adaptive navigation support can be used very naturally and efficiently. The most popular form of ANS on the Web is annotation. It is implemented in ELM-ART, InterBook, WEST-KBNS [Bru 1997c], and AST. InterBook also applies adaptive navigation support by sorting. Link disabling was implemented in De Bra's adaptive course about Hypertext [Cal 1997] (Links are made completely non-functional then nothing happens when the user clicks on it).

Summary of adaptation issues in web-based educational systems

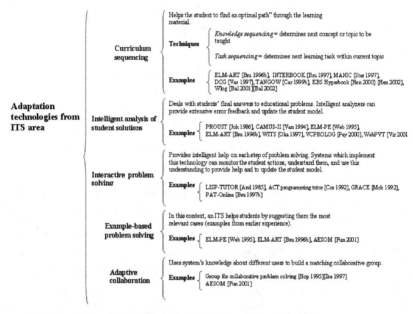

Figure 9.   Summary of adaptation technologies from ITS area

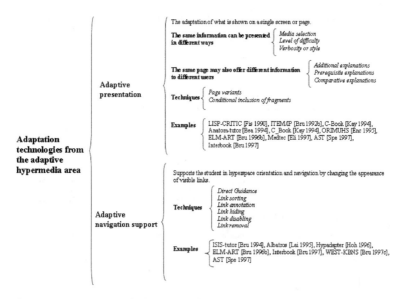

Figure 10. Summary of adaptation technologies from the adaptive hypermedia area

Adaptive presentation and adaptive navigation considering cognitive and learning styles

With the application of individual characteristics in hypermedia, such as the *cognitive* and *learning style,* a few adaptive hypermedia systems have been developed. Some of these systems are:

- **RAPITS** [Woo 1995], is an adaptive teaching system that compares student model to domain knowledge and automatically changes the presentation style. The lessons are set up in a hypertext structure but the system controls the tutoring strategy. The student can proceed through the lessons sequentially and adaptively, and exit, choose another topic or switch to a non-linear hypertext mode through the courseware. Student knowledge is assessed at the end of each topic and teaching strategies are adapted at this point for the subsequent topics.

- In **CS388** [Car 1999], a range of learning style tools are available to students. The learning styles are assessed using the Felder-Silverman Learning Style Model (FSLSM.). Students are allowed to traverse the courseware according to their own learning style. In this approach the key was to determine what type of media was applicable and appropriate to different learning styles (such as graphs, movies, text, slideshows, etc.).

- **Arthur** [Gil 1999], a web-based system that provides adaptive instruction based on learning styles. Basically, an adaptive presentation is achieved using different teaching strategies. Student learning style is detected and tuned by means of case-based reasoning (CBR) techniques. Adaptive navigation is not considered.
- In **INSPIRE** [Gri 2001], the authors adopted Kolb's theory of experiential learning (activists, pragmatists, reflectors and theorist learning styles). The user model consists of two parts: general information about user (age, sex) and current knowledge of the level unit. As users progress through the system, they are monitored. Lessons are divided into layers which are dynamically generated. There is also a presentation module responsible for modifying the appearance of knowledge modules. A*daptive presentation* techniques are used for different orders of knowledge modules. Learning style elements can also appear inside a lesson, and *adaptive navigation* techniques such as *link annotation* in the 'navigational' area of the system are used.
- **CAMELEON** [Lar 2001] is a system running across the Internet / Intranet that helps a learner studying the course (presentation of the course material, assessments, etc.) via an adaptive interface. The domain model is composed of elementary bricks or fragments. Adaptive presentation is based on the user's knowledge level and learning style (using the Felder-Silverman Learning Style model). Adaptive navigation is achieved by applying hypermedia metrics to create adaptive links to concepts.
- The **AEC-ES** [Tri 2002] system is based on field dependent/independent cognitive styles. It uses *navigational support tools* (concept map, graphic path, advance organiser) and *adaptive presentation* techniques. Students are provided with instructional strategies that suit their preferred cognitive style with an option to switch to a non-preferred version.
- **iWeaver** [Wol 2002] aims to create an individualized learning environment that accommodates specific learning styles. The system is built on the Dunn & Dunn learning style model. The key of this approach is determining which media representation is allocated to each learning style and the underlying rationale for such allocation. A crucial concept of iWeaver is that this media-style allocation is flexible. It may change dynamically according to learner behavior. This learner-centered approach makes an effort to increase motivation, retention of knowledge and understanding for learners. *iWeaver* supports *adaptive presentation*: it varies different media representations and uses conditional text with regard to the user learning style. Adaptive navigation is not considered.

Benefits and Drawbacks of Adaptive Hypermedia Techniques

Adaptive hypermedia techniques have many potential benefits and drawbacks [DeB 1999b]:

- Information *should* be presented in the right media, at the right level of difficulty, and with the right writing style for each user. However, different versions of fragments or pages must all be authored, and often an author will also need to define the Adaptive Hypermedia System (AHS) so as to decide which version to show to which user. An adaptive system "must" support authors offering a way to describe dependencies between concepts and the relationship between such concepts and their contents.

- Users may be guided towards information relevant for them at that moment, and for which they are "ready" (i.e., hey have the necessary previous knowledge and the information is not redundant). This guidance is again based on an application *domain model* designed by the author. If prerequisite relationships are omitted, or are just wrong, the user may be guided towards pages that are not relevant or that the user cannot understand (yet). Bad guidance is worse than no guidance.

- When a hyperdocument is adapted to an evolving user model, each time a user revisits a certain page, this page may look different. Fragments may be added or deleted and links may be shown, hidden or annotated differently. Such an "unstable" appearance of pages may cause confusion among users. A possible solution would be to keep track of how each page was shown to a user initially, and to minimize the later variations.

2.7   Conclusions

In this chapter, the hypertext and hypermedia technologies have been reviewed according to the research interest of this book applied to educational systems throughout the web. It paid special attention to the state of the art in the generation of architectures for web-based adaptive educational hypermedia systems and their methods and techniques to achieve an adaptation based on parameters such as user characteristics (focused in cognitive and learning styles), user modeling techniques, tasks being performed, information characteristics, etc.

The Web offers the technological base for implementing most of the adaptive technology that has been implemented on other platforms. Most of the web-based systems are being used in educational environments as has been shown in the presented literature.

Adaptive technologies have contributed to several directions of research and development of Web-based educational systems. According to the cited research experiences, adaptive presentation can improve the usability of course material presentation and adaptive navigation support, and adaptive sequencing may be used for overall course control and to help the student select the most relevant tests and assignments. Problem solving support and intelligent solution analysis can significantly improve the work with assignments providing both interactivity and intelligent feedback. Adaptive collaboration support opens new possibilities for communication and collaboration.

Chapter 3.   Intelligent Agents in Education

3.1   Introduction

One of the major problems of traditional computer-based learning systems is how
to provide adaptive teaching which is suitable to each student. Most recent
advances in the field of Interactive Learning Environments (ILE) have proposed
the use of Artificial Intelligence (AI) techniques such as Multi Agents or Agent
Society-based architectures. The principles of Multi-Agent systems have shown
adequate potential in the development of teaching systems. This is due to the fact
that a cooperative way facilitates the solution of many teaching-learning
problems. In this scenario, intelligent agents introduce a new paradigm for
instruction. It is focused on the concept of shared abilities and cooperative
learning between humans and computers [Kea 1993]. Altogether, user interfaces
may enable the system to dynamically personalize applications and services to
meet user preferences, goals and desires [Cag 1997]. In AI methodologies, the
intelligence may be applied through user models to make assumptions about the
user's state of knowledge, which may in turn help determine the user's learning
needs [Woo 1996].

By using intelligent agents to simulate instructors, agent-based learning
environments can serve as a powerful research tool to investigate teaching and
learning. The agent metaphor provides a way to operate and simulate the "human"
aspect of instruction in a more natural and valid way than other controlled
computer-based methods. Additionally, from an architectural perspective, since
agents are independent objects in the learning environment, they allow for more
flexibility in research design.

This work is focused on the use of agent technology to accomplish adaptive
intelligent learning environments; hence the most relevant aspects of intelligent
software agent technology applied to web-based education are described in this
chapter.

3.2   Agent Terminology

Software agents have their roots in the work conducted in the fields of Software Engineering, Human Interface research and Artificial Intelligence (see Figure 11). Their concepts can be traced back to the late seventies when their predecessors, the so-called 'actors' were introduced. These actors were self-contained objects, with their own encapsulated internal state and some interactive and concurrent communication capabilities. Software agents developed up to now have been classified as Multiple Agent Systems (MAS), one of the three branches of distributed AI research. The others are Distributed Problem Solving (DPS) and Parallel Artificial Intelligence (PAI) [Nwa 1997].

Technically, Software Agents exhibit many of the properties and benefits of distributed AI systems. These may include:

- *Modularity*. Add/remove elements without affecting others (specialized agents can be added as needed). A modular programming approach reduces the complexity of developing software systems.
- *Speed*. The concurrent execution of co-operating programs (parallelism) increases the execution speed of the overall system.
- *Reliability*. Built-in redundancy increases the fault tolerance of an application, thus enhancing its reliability.
- *Operation at the knowledge level*. Utilization of AI techniques allows high-level messaging.
- *Others*. For instance: maintainability, reusability and platform independence.

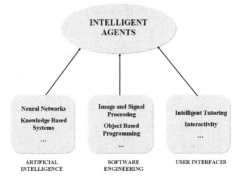

Figure 11.   Roots of intelligent agents

Many agent definitions can be considered, taking into account different points of view to understand important aspects of their world and application. According to the dictionary presented in [MER 1993], an agent is:

- Something that takes place or is able to produce an effect.
- Something that acts for or instead of another by means of an authorization.
- A means or instrument by which a result is achieved through a given intelligence.

In the Computer Science community or more specifically among the Artificial Intelligence researchers, intelligent agents have a wider meaning. Some of these definitions are:

- An intelligent agent is considered as a computing system that substitutes a person or process to carry out an activity or to fulfill a requirement. The substitute entity offers capacities to take similar decisions to those described by the human intentions. An intelligent agent can operate between the boundaries of a general necessity or accurately represented among the limits of a given information space [Kin 1995].
- Russell and Norvig in [Rus 1997] define the intelligent agents in three ways (considering *behavior*, *rationality* and *autonomy* properties) ordered by their sophistication degree or intelligence:

    o In a generic sense and considering *behavior*, an agent is something that one can see perceiving its environment through sensors and acting on the same through effectors (see Figure 12).

o With respect to *rationality*, for each possible sequence of perceptions, an ideal rational agent can do something to maximize its measuring efficiency on the base of the evidence offered by the sequence of perceptions and any integrated knowledge it may have.

o A rational agent is *autonomous* to the extent that its actions and preferences depend on its own experience instead of the knowledge immersed in the environment built by the designer.

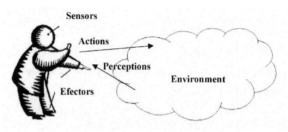

Figure 12.   Agent behavior

• Wooldridge in [Woo 2000] states that *autonomy* is the main characteristic that identifies intelligent agents and therefore differentiates them from any expert system. He defines an agent as a computer program which is able to carry out, in some environments, flexible and autonomous actions. In such a case, flexibility is considered to be possessing *reactivity*, *pro-activity* and *sociability* characteristics:

o A *reactive* system is maintains a continuous relationship with its environment and responds to the changes that happen in it.

o A *proactive* system directs its behavior to achieve some particular goals. Therefore, it is not only managed by events but rather it can also take the initiative.

o *Sociability* is an important aspect in agent communities. The real world is considered as a Multi-Agent environment where some objectives cannot be reached without considering others. Some goals can only be achieved with the cooperation of others.

• Depending on the agent application area, Wooldridge also states that agents may exhibit the following properties:

- o *Mobility*: the ability of moving through the net.
- o *Truthfulness*: an agent will not communicate any information that it considers false.
- o *Benevolence*: agents do not have conflicting goals and therefore they should always try to do what the designer has commanded.
- o *Learning/Adaptation*: agents increase their efficiency through time.

- Atkinson in [Atk 1995] defines agents using the *agency* and *intelligence* terms:

  - o *Agency* is considered to be the degree of autonomy and authority given to the agent and can be measured, at least qualitatively, by the nature of the interaction between the agent and other entities of the system. The agency degree increases if an agent somehow represents the user. A more advanced agent can interact with other entities such as data, applications and services, and can collaborate and negotiate with other agents.
  - o *Intelligence* is the reasoning degree and learning capacity or the agent's ability to accept the instructions of the user and to carry out the delegated task. Initially, some preference instructions should exist, normally in the form of rules with an inference motor or some other mechanism that can act on these preferences. High intelligence levels include users' models or some other way to understand and to reason about what the user wants to do.

Intelligent agents then, are software entities that carry out a group of operations on a user's behavior (or on another program) with a degree of independence or autonomy. Therefore, they use knowledge or representation of goals, objectives or the user's desires.

- Finally, Hendler in [Hen 1996] states that there are three main characteristics which identify software agents:
  - o The minimum characteristic is *behavior*: a program is an agent if it exhibits agent behavior or it assumes agent responsibilities (such as carrying out high level tasks for its owner).

o The second characteristic is *communication*: a program is an agent if it carries out all the communications with its pairs in an expressive agents' communication language.

o The third characteristic is *implementation*: a program is an agent if it maintains and reasons about the explicit representation of its goals, beliefs and capacities.

3.3 Artificial Intelligence Methodologies for Customization and Personalization

One of the greatest impacts of Internet information processing is the distribution of information management responsibilities to give end-users greater power to shape their computing environments and manage their personal information needs. Designers can program services to enable users to traverse their own path through the networked information. Software agents have been proposed as a mechanism to help users with work and information overload [Mae 1995]. In that way, intelligent agents introduce a new paradigm for instruction including the concept of shared abilities and cooperative learning between humans and computers [Kea 1993]. Programming AI into user interfaces may enable the system to dynamically personalize applications and services to reach user preferences, goals and desires [Cag 1997].

Blankenhorn, in [Bla 1997], identifies some of the AI methodologies which may be applied to customization. They are:

- *Rule-based* techniques that can generate user profiles or patterns, which are transformed into rules to predict user behaviors.
- *Case-based* techniques that may use questions which are based on previous cases and examples, to continually narrow options.
- *Collaborative filtering* systems that seek user profiles in utilization patterns. These profiles are then matched with other users to produce intelligent/likely recommendations.

The rapid commercial acceptance of AI, agent and mobile object technologies and their programmable and dynamic intelligence have resulted in new opportunities for media designers. They can align Internet experiences with the cognitive styles and preferences of users applied to learning environments. This methodology may include the application of agents for collecting patterns from the experiences of users. The selection of branching options (navigation paths), and interactive options in simulations, are the most suitable measurement data. The result is a database of learning options, based on the experiences of users. Expert libraries can be built to guide future experiences.

To adapt the presentation to perceived user needs, AI may also help [Woo 1996]. Rather than isolating users, the Internet and agent technology may provide socialization and continuity through online experiences by grouping those of like interest and allowing multiparticipant interaction, collective experiences, and intimate knowledge-sharing within personalized and customized virtual environments. Thus, at the cognitive level, intelligent agents may help to make the online experience more enjoyable by making users feel more comfortable. The intelligence can help the system reason about the user's idiosyncratic actions, and determining the problems/issues to be solved [Woo 1996].

3.4   Agent Classification and Applications

3.4.1   Introduction

The various definitions presented in section 3.2 involve a host of properties of an agent. Franklin and Graesser, in [Fra 1996] as shown in Table 4, summarize properties that help further classification of agents in a useful way.

Table 4. Summary of agent properties

Property	Other Names	Meaning that an agent
Reactive	(sensing and acting)	responds in a timely fashion to changes in the environment
Autonomous		exercises control over its own actions
Goal-oriented	proactive purposeful	does not simply act in response to the environment, it also directs its behavior to achieve some goals
Temporally continuous		is a continuously running process
Communicative	socially able	communicates with other agents, perhaps including people
Learning	adaptive	changes its behavior based on its previous experience
Mobile		is able to transport itself from one machine to another
Flexible		actions are not scripted
Character		is a believable "personality" and emotional state

Three major views of agency can be distinguished in the literature. First, computer scientists and software engineers have used agents as an abstraction to conceptualize, design and implement complex systems. This class of agents is referred to as programmed agents. Second, agents may be viewed as autonomously migrating entities that act on behalf of network nodes in a distributed environment. This class is referred to as network agents. Finally, agents have been proposed as an abstraction for end users to interact with computer systems. This view defines the class referred to as user agents.

Agents involved in this work belong to the user agents' class (considering all the properties summarized in Table 4 but removing the mobility). The next section, then, describes a detailed agent classification.

3.4.2   User Agents

End users have attributed autonomy and other aspects of agency to computer systems. For example, in an experiment conducted by Friedman in [Fri 1997], eighty three percent of the participating users attributed autonomous decision making capabilities or intentions to computer programs. Such an attributed autonomy may be increased by a natural next step in the development of human-computer interfaces, which is to make the agent abstraction explicitly available to the end users.

Since user agents directly affect the way that human-computer interfaces are perceived, the term interface agents has frequently been associated with this view of agency (for example, see [Lau 1990], [Koz 1993], [Woo 1995a] and [San 1993]). However, *interface agents* is a more precise way to refer such agents; after all, "interfaces" also exist between software modules and communicating computers (or within any independent system).

Interface agents characteristics

Maes in [Mae 1994] describes the interface agents as follows:

"Instead of user-initiated interaction via commands and/or direct manipulation, the user is engaged in a co-operative process in which human and computer agents both initiate communication, monitor events and perform tasks. The metaphor used is that of a personal assistant who is collaborating with the user in the same working environment."

The motivating concept behind Maes' interface agents allows the user to delegate mundane and tedious tasks to an assistant agent. Her own agents follow this direction; scheduling and rescheduling meetings, filtering emails, filtering news and selecting good books. Her goal is to reduce the workload of users by creating personalized agents to which personal work can be delegated.

There are many interface agent systems and prototypes inspired by Maes's work, allocated within a variety of domains. A common point in these systems is that there are three aspects that must be addressed before successful user collaboration with an agent can occur: knowing the user, interacting with the user and competence in helping the user.

Knowing the user

This involves learning user preferences and work habits. If an assistant is ready to offer help at the right time, and of the right kind, then it must learn how the user prefers to work. On the other hand, an eager assistant, always interrupting with irrelevant information, would just annoy the user and increase the overall workload.

The following are challenges for systems which are trying to learn about users:

- Extracting the user goals and intentions from observations and feedback
- Getting sufficient context to set the user goals
- Adapting to the user's changing objectives
- Reducing the initial training time

At any given time, an interface agent should know in advance what the user is trying to achieve in order to offer effective assistance. In addition to knowing what the user intentions are, there must be sufficient contextual information about the user's current situation to avoid irrelevant agent help. Another problem is that regular users typically have numerous concurrent tasks to perform. If an agent is helpful with more than one task, it must be able to discover when the user has stopped working on one job, and is progressing towards another.

Users are generally unwilling to invest much time and effort to learning software systems. They want results early, before committing too much to a tool. This means that interface agents must limit the initial period during which the agent learns enough about the user to offer useful help.

In learning environments, lessons have been learned from direct manipulation interfaces. In consequence, users need to feel in control, expectations should not be unduly inflated and user mistakes should not be penalized [Nor 1994].

Interacting with the user

This approach presents the following challenges:

- *Deciding how much control to delegate to the agent:*

  It is known from direct manipulation of interfaces, that users want to feel in control of what their tools are doing. By the nature of an autonomous interface agent, some control has been delegated to it. Shneiderman and Maes in [Shn 1997] argue for a combination of direct manipulation and indirect Human Computer Interaction (HCI), promoting user understanding of agents and the ability for users to control agent behavior directly.

- *Building trust in the agent:*

Trust provides a new method for filtering information. It is one of the most important social concepts that helps human agents to cope with their social environment and is present in all human interaction [Gam 1990] [Mon 2002].

- *Choosing a metaphor for agent interaction:*

Interface metaphors, such as the desktop metaphor, guide users in the formation of useful conceptual models of a system. New metaphors will be required for indirect HCI, presenting agents in a helpful way to new users.

- *Making simple systems that novices can use:*

Ideally, interface agents should be so simple to use, that delegating tasks becomes a natural way of working, amenable to the novice user.

Competence in helping the user

Once the agent knows what the user is doing and has a good interaction style, it must still formulate a plan of action that helps (not hinders) the user. The challenges are:

- Knowing when (and whether) to interrupt the user
- Performing tasks autonomously in the preferred way of the user
- Finding strategies for partial automation of tasks

There is little current research on how users can be helped in the best way. Work from other disciplines, such as Computer Supported Co-operative Working (CSCW) can help, but real user trials are needed to demonstrate and evaluate effectiveness and usefulness of the personalized services performed by interface agents [Nwa 1996]. If an agent does not reduce the workload of a real user in a real working environment, its utilization is worthless.

Summarizing, interface agents provide for personalized user interfaces, for sharing information learned from peer-observation and for alleviating the tasks of application developers. Interface agents adapt to user preferences by imitating the user, by following immediate instructions of the user or through the Pavlov effect (learning from positive and negative responses of users). It should be noticed that interface agents can only be effective if the tasks that they perform are inherently repetitive and if the behavior is potentially different for different users. If the tasks are not repetitive, the agents will not be able to learn, and if the user behavior is similar to other users, it may use a knowledge base.

Interface Agents Classification

Interface agents can be classified according to the role that they perform, the technology they use or the domain they inhabit. Interface agents are moving from research to commercial exploitation, increasing significantly the roles and domains of agents as "businessmen" finding new ways to exploit new markets. The fundamental technology behind the agents, however, is undergoing less radical change, and thus provides a more stable basis on which to build a useful taxonomy.

From an application perspective, Sanchez in [San 1997] proposed an agent interface classification. This one, complemented with Middleton appreciations in [Mid 2001] is disaggregated as *Information, Task and Synthetic agents*, and listed next.

- Information agents
  - o Social agents
    - Recommender systems
  - o Agents with user models
    - Behavioral model
    - Knowledge-based model
    - Stereotypes

- Task agents
    - Agents that learn about the user
        - Monitor user behavior
        - Receive user feedback
            - Explicit feedback
            - Initial training set
        - Programmed by user
- Synthetic agents
    - Character-based agents

Information agents

An *information* agent is considered as a software entity that accesses multiple heterogeneous and distributed sources of information and proactively obtains, serves as a broker and maintains relevant information on users' representations or on other agents. They are classified as collaborative or non collaborative depending on the collaborative work they carry out during the execution of their tasks. They can be rational if they decide 'rationally' on when and how to execute tasks. They can be adaptive if they are able to adapt themselves to changes of the environment (users, networks, information). Additionally, they can be mobile if they can travel in an autonomous way through the Internet to execute their tasks in different servers [Klu 2000].

Information agents help users in dealing with information domains that are typically unorganized and highly dynamic. In this context, intelligent agents are not just used to search and filtrate information but also to categorize and to give priority and selective dissemination of this information.

In the field of collaborative work, information agents' infrastructures have been created to share resources in robust and scalable ways, taking advantage of the network resources. This is the case of social agents that talk to other agents (typically other interface agents) in order to share information. This technique is often used to train new, inexperienced interface agents using the experience of older interface agents (attached to other users).

Recommender systems

Recommender systems are a specific type of *social agent*. They are also referred to as collaborative filters [Mon 2003]. They find relevant items based on the recommendations of others. Typically, the user's own ratings are used to find similar users, with the aim of sharing recommendations on common areas of interest.

Technologies for Information agent's generation

Specific interface agents will often implement different types of technology, and appear then, in a multiplicity of cases. A common example is an agent that learns about the user and also supports a user model. The presented taxonomy ought to be robust enough to deal with the increase in new systems, since the fundamental technologies of machine learning and user modeling are unlikely to change as quickly.

The World Wide Web (WWW) looks very attractive for testing various implementations of information agents as it is seen in: LETIZIA [Lie 1996], AMALTHAEA [Mou 1997], and MARGIN NOTES [Rho 2000] among others. LETIZIA conducts a breadth-first traversal search for pages that are related to the current document or to the user's inferred interests; heuristics infer user preferences and interesting pages are briefly displayed in suggestion windows. AMALTHAEA observes user browsing behavior and assists the user in finding interesting WWW information. The browser history, bookmarks and other agent profiles initialize the system. Relevant feedback is recorded. MARGIN NOTES add a suggestion list to the side of the web browser. The user provides an initial list of interesting documents. The current web page provides the context for suggestions, with the top suggestion being displayed (summary and a link).

Task Agents

Task agents help users perform computer-supported tasks. These agents run concurrently with user applications, watch user activity, learn from them and offer to automate certain actions.

Agents, employing a learning technology are classified according to the type of information required by the learning technique and the way the user model is represented. Algorithms requiring an explicit training set employ supervised learning, while those without a training set use unsupervised learning techniques [Mit 1997]. There are three general ways to learn about the user: monitoring the user behavior, asking the user for feedback or allowing explicit programming by the user.

Monitoring the user's behavior produces unlabelled data which is suitable for unsupervised learning techniques. This is generally the hardest way to learn, but it is also the least intrusive. If the monitored behavior is assumed to be desirable of what the user wants, a positive example can be inferred.

Asking the user for feedback can be on a case-by-case basis or based on an initial training set which produces labeled training data. The disadvantage of it is that a feedback must be provided, requiring an investment of effort (often significant) in the agent by the user.

User programming involves the user changing the agent explicitly. Programming can be performed in a variety of ways, from complex programming languages to the specification of simple cause/effect graphs. Explicit programming requires significant effort by the user.

Two kinds of task agents can be distinguished: personal agents that assist individual users; and group agents who participate in computer-mediated collaborative tasks.

Some examples of personal task agents include intelligent tutors such as COACH [Sel 1994], a NOTE-TAKING APPRENTICE developed by Schlimmer and Hermens' [Sch 1993], MAXIMS [Mae 1994], an e-mail filter, and GALOIS [Sag 1997], an intelligent adviser. COACH provides personalized advice to students using a computer to learn about specific domains, such as the Lisp programming language or the Unix operating system.

NOTE-TAKING APPRENTICE continuously predicts likely completions for notes taken on a pen-based computer; the user can select the agent' predictions in order to produce faster and more accurate notes.

MAXIMS filters email by learning the repetitive actions performed by the user. It monitors user actions to discover patterns using memory-based reasoning. Agents can share expertise with other agents, and user programming is allowed.

GALOIS monitors the use of an application and offers expert advice when users are lost or being inefficient. An initial knowledge-based user profile is constructed from personal information, and then a behavioral model is built by observing user actions. Stereotypes are used to classify users, thus allowing customized help.

In contrast, DAVE [Lak 1994] is an agent that provides assistance to groups of users working cooperatively. It has access to all objects in a large, shared display and becomes another actor during a performance by intervening from time to time when certain patterns in a special-purpose visual language are recognized. Kautz et al. [Kau 1995] have designed an environment in which user agents communicate with each other to locate subject expert users, a common problem in collaborative work settings.

Synthetic Agents

Synthetic or character-based agents create engaging environments for users by introducing advanced "character"-based interfaces, representing real world characters (such as a pet dog or a human assistant [Mae 1995]). They promote a *suspension of disbelief* [San 1997] from the user and provide the illusion of autonomous, animistic entities. Such agents draw on existing real-world protocols already known to even novice users, to facilitate more natural interaction. There are also applications in the entertainment domain, creating state of the art virtual worlds populated by believable agents. Examples of these applications are:

- JULIA [Mau 1994], an agent that participates as an independent player in TINYMUD, a *multi-user dimension* (MUD) [Cur 1992]. JULIA may converse with other players, explore the MUD's "rooms" and objects, assist users in navigating the environment, and answer questions about *herself*, other players, rooms and objects.
- WOGGLES [Bat 1994] are real-time, interactive, self-animating creatures immersed in a simulated world. These agents are designed to have individual personalities, display emotions, engage in social behaviors and react to their environment, which includes a fourth Woggle controlled by a human interactor.

- ALIVE [Maes 1995] is an environment in which users can immerse themselves and interact with animated three-dimensional creatures with different behaviors. Gesture recognition, and competing goal architecture is employed.

As a result of developments in *believable* intelligent agents [Bat 1994], the intelligent tutoring system community is currently presented with opportunities for exploring new technologies for *pedagogical agents* and the roles they can play in communication. Up to now, pedagogical agents have not been developed very much, but significant progress is being made on two fronts. First, research has begun on pedagogical agents that can facilitate the construction of component-based tutoring system architectures and communication between modules as stated in [Rit 1997] and [Wan 1997], provide multiple context-sensitive pedagogical strategies [Fra 1997], reason about multiple agents in learning environments [Eli 1996a], and act as co-learners [Dil 1997]. Secondly, projects have begun to investigate techniques by which animated pedagogical agents can behave in a lifelike manner to communicate effectively with learners both visually and verbally [And 1996] and [Ric 1997]. This second category is considered to include lifelike animated pedagogical agents.

Lifelike pedagogical agents are very promising, because they could play a central communicative role in learning environments. Through an engaging "fiction character", a lifelike pedagogical agent could simultaneously provide students with contextualized problem-solving advice and create learning experiences that offer high visual appeal. Perhaps as a result of the inherent psychosocial nature of learner-agent interactions and of the human tendency to anthropomorphize software, recent evidence suggests that an ITS with a lifelike character can be pedagogically effective [Les 1997b] while at the same time can have either a strong motivating effect on learners [Les 1997] or can cause learners to feel that on-line educational material is less difficult [And 1998]. But more importantly, animated pedagogical agents make it possible to model more accurately the kinds of dialogs and interactions that occur during apprenticeship and one-on-one tutoring. Factors such as gazing, eye contact, body language and emotional expression can be modeled and exploited for instructional purposes [Joh 1998a].

Pedagogical agents bring a fresh perspective to the problem of facilitating on-line learning, and address issues that previous intelligent tutoring work has largely ignored [Wen 1987]. Because pedagogical agents are autonomous agents, they inherit many of the concerns that autonomous agents should address.

Johnson and Hayes-Roth in [Joh 1998] argue that practical autonomous agents must manage complexity. They must exhibit robust behavior in rich, unpredictable environments; they must coordinate their behavior with that of other agents, and they must manage their own behavior in a coherent fashion, arbitrating between alternative actions and responding to a multitude of environmental stimuli. In the case of pedagogical agents, their environment includes both the students and the learning environment in which the agents are situated. Student behavior is by nature unpredictable, since students may exhibit a variety of aptitudes, levels of proficiency, and learning styles.

Developments in the pedagogical agents' area are varied. Those mentioned below are some of the interesting developments that have influenced in one or another way this work:

- ADELE (Agent for Distance Learning Environments) [Ell 1997], a pedagogical agent that runs on each student's computer, and interacts with each student as they work through the Web-based course materials. ADELE is responsible for monitoring the student, recording student actions, adapting courseware presentation as needed and reporting student performance to the central server at the end of the session.
- PPP *Persona* (Personalized Plan-based Presenter *Persona*) [And 1998], an animated pedagogical agent for interactive WWW presentations. The *persona* appears in many forms (cartoon figures and 3D models). The *persona* guides the learner through Web-based material using presentation acts (e.g., pointing) to draw attention to elements of the Web pages, and provide commentary via synthesized speech.

  The PPP system generates multimedia presentation plans for the *Persona* to deliver. *PPP persona* executes this plan adaptively, modifying it in real-time based on user actions such as repositioning the agent on the screen or asking questions.

- COSMO [Tow 1999], a lifelike pedagogical agent with real-time full body emotive expression. COSMO inhabits the *Internet Advisor* environment for the domain of Internet packet routing. An impish, antenna-bearing creature that hovers about a virtual world of routers and networks provides advice to learners as they decide how to ship packets through the networks to specified destinations.

  COSMO has been used to investigate how to combine various agent behaviors in order to enhance the ability to refer to objects in their environment through judicious combinations of speech, locomotion and gesture, in a manner similar to humans. Emotive behaviors of agents can help to engage and motivate the learner. They could also relieve student's frustrations by appearing to commiserate with them. COSMO possesses a large emotive behavior space. Behaviors such as applause are used with congratulatory speech acts. COSMO also uses behaviors such as head scratching, and shrugging when posing rhetorical questions.

- CU ANIMATE [Jiy 2002] consists of a set of software tools to enable conversations with animated characters. The animated agents have been incorporated into interactive book-multimedia learning environments to help children learn to read and acquire knowledge through reading.

3.5   Multiagent Systems

3.5.1   Introduction

Much of the current research in intelligent agents has focused on the capabilities and structure of individual agents. However, in order to solve more complex problems, these agents must work cooperatively with other agents in a heterogeneous environment. This is the domain of *Multi-Agent Systems* (MAS) and the area of interest for developing the idea proposed in this book.

3.5.2   Definition and Characteristics

Demazeau in [Dem 2000] defines a Multi-Agent system as a group of possible organized agents that interact in a common environment and have the following four (**A-E-I-O**) fundamental elements:

- **A** (Agents): internal architecture of the processing entities.

- **E** (Environment): domain dependent elements to build external interactions among entities.
- **I** (Interactions): elements to build internal interactions among entities.
- **O** (Organizations): elements to structure groups of entities according to their functions in the Multi-Agent system.

The concept of Multiagent systems arose under the influence of the work done by Marvin Minsky entitled "The society of mind" [Min 1986], where a complex system could be understood as a group of simple agents specialized in a concrete domain (the philosophy currently applied to intelligent agents that live in Internet).

Developing Minsky's idea even further, Rodney Brooks in [Bro 1991] proposed a completely different design concerning intelligent behavior. Brooks stated that intelligent behavior consists of the establishment of complex behavior by means of the interrelation of simple behaviors. Agents were considered to be those whose activation is the responsibility of control architecture. This assumption was later adopted by the IA community, combining the predominant knowledge-based systems with the behavior-based systems proposed by Brooks.

Therefore, research in MAS is concerned with the study, behavior and construction of a collection of possible preexisting autonomous agents that interact each other and with their environments. The study of such systems goes beyond the study of individual intelligence to consider, in addition, problem solving that has social components. In this scenario, a *MAS* can be defined as a loosely coupled network of problem solvers that interact to solve problems that are beyond the individual capabilities or knowledge of each problem solver [Dur 1989]. These problem solvers, or *agents*, are autonomous and can be heterogeneous in nature.

In order to reach its goals, a MAS should exhibit some basic characteristics as Sycara states in [Syc 1998]. Those characteristics are summarized in the following figure.

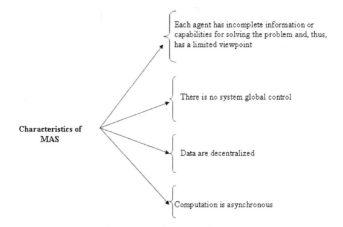

Figure 13.   Characteristics of a MAS

The increasing interest in MAS research has been motivated by their ability to carry out the following actions (extracted and organized considering Sycara work in [Syc 1998]):

1. To solve problems that are too large for a centralized agent to solve because of resource limitations

2. To allow for the interconnection and interoperation of multiple legacy systems

3. To provide solutions to problems that can naturally be regarded as a society of autonomous interacting components-agents

4. To provide solutions that efficiently use information sources that are spatially distributed

5. To provide solutions in situations where expertise is distributed

6. TO ENHANCE PERFORMANCE ALONG THE FOLLOWING DIMENSIONS:

Computational efficiency — Because concurrency of computation is exploited

Reliability — Graceful recovery of component failures

Extensibility — Because the number and the capabilities of agents working on a problem can be altered

Robustness — The system's ability to tolerate uncertainty, because suitable information is exchanged among agents

Maintainability — Because a system composed of multiple components-agents is easier to maintain because of its modularity

Responsiveness — Because modularity can handle anomalies locally, not propagate them to the whole system

Flexibility — Because agents with different abilities can adaptively organize to solve the current problem

Reuse — Because functionally specific agents can be reused in different agent teams to solve different problems

Figure 14.   MAS actions that increase research interest

3.5.3   MAS technologies

To allow agents to interoperate, some communication mechanisms (which can be used independently or together) have been proposed from the research field (see Table 5).

Table 5.   Components of an Agent Communication Language (ACL)

ACL component	Description	Related with
KIF [Gen 1994] Knowledge Interchange Format	First order logic set theory. An interlingua for encoded declarative knowledge. Common language for reusable knowledge.	ACL Syntax
Ontology [Gru 1993] Explicit specification of a conceptualization	A common vocabulary and agreed upon meanings to describe a subject domain. *Ontolingua* is a language for building, publishing, and sharing ontologies.	ACL Semantics
KQML [Fin 1994] A high level interaction language	High level, message-oriented, communication language and protocol for information exchange independent of content syntax and ontology.	Pragmatics

However, many efforts tend to maximize this interoperability across agent-based applications, services and equipment. In such a direction, the Foundation for Intelligent Physical Agents (FIPA) has developed specifications for interaction protocols, communicative acts, and content messages for agent communication (see [FIPA]).

The most relevant aspects of FIPA specifications are:

- They provide the normative framework within which FIPA agents exist and operate. They establish the logical reference model for the creation, registration, location, communication, migration and retirement of agents. The entities contained in the reference model are logical capability sets (that is, services) and do not imply any physical configuration. Additionally, the implementation details of individual Agent Platforms (APs) and agents are the design choices of the individual agent system developers.

- The agent management reference model consists of the following logical components, each representing a capability set (which can be combined in physical implementations of APs):

    o An **agent** that is a computational process that implements the autonomous, communicating functionality of an application. Agents communicate using an Agent Communication Language and must support at least one notion of identity. This notion of identity is the Agent Identifier (AID) that labels an agent so that it may be distinguished unambiguously within the Agent Universe.

    o A **Directory Facilitator (DF)** that is an optional component of the platform. It provides yellow page services to other agents. Agents may register their services with the DF or query the DF to find out what services are offered by other agents.

    o An **Agent Management System (AMS)** that is a mandatory component of the platform. The AMS exerts supervisory control over the access to and use of the platform. Only one AMS will exist in a single AP. The AMS maintains a directory of Agent Identifiers which contain transport addresses for agents registered in the AP. The AMS offers white page services to other agents. Each agent must register with an AMS in order to get a valid AID.

    o A **Message Transport Service (MTS)** that is the default communication method between agents on different Agent Platforms (Aps).

    o An **Agent Platform (AP)** that provides the physical infrastructure in which agents can be deployed. The AP consists of the machine, the operating system, the agent support software, the FIPA agent management components (DF, AMS and MTS) and agents. The internal design of an AP is still an open issue for agent system developers, but it is not a subject of standardization within FIPA. AP's and the AP agents may use any proprietary method of inter-communication. FIPA is concerned only with the way communication between agents occurs. Agents are free to exchange messages directly by any mechanism that they can support.

o Software that describes all non-agent, executable collections of instructions accessible through an agent. Agents may access software, for example, to add new services, acquire new communication protocols, acquire new security protocols/algorithms, acquire new negotiation protocols, access tools which support migration, etc.

The FIPA message

The basic element in a FIPA ACL communication is the *message*. Next figure shows its structure:

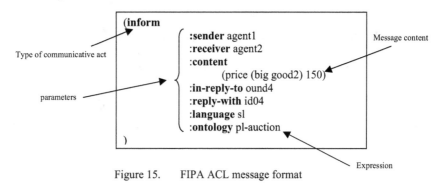

Figure 15.   FIPA ACL message format

The message parameters may be divided in five categories according to their mission. These categories are:

1. Definition of the message type

In this category, only one parameter exists and it is named *:performative.* It indicates the communication type that is wanted to carry out by means of the message. For example: to transmit a data, to ask a question, to request a service, etc.

This field appears immediately after the parenthesis that indicates the beginning of the message. This is the only field that includes its contents directly (i.e.

:performative contents).   It may take twenty-two possible values. The most commonly used values are:

- Inform: to transmit data to the receiver
- Query-ref: to ask a question to the receiver
- Query-if: to ask a question to the receiver using a Boolean answer
- Request: to request the receiver to carry out an action
- Accept-proposal: to accept a request for carrying out an action
- Failure: to indicate a request failure
- Not-understand: to indicate that the message is not understandable.

2. Identification of the agents that participate in a communication:

This category defines: who sends the message (**:sender** field), who receives the message (**:receiver** field) and optionally, the third agent that might be answered (receive the information if it is different from the receiver) (**:reply to** field). Each one of these three fields should have as value an agent identifier.

3. The message contents

In the **:content** field, the properly content of the message is placed. This contents should be understandable by the receiver agent. The message contents have three fields that are described next.

4. The message contents description

A message contents have three fields that allow the receiver to understand the message. These fields are:

- **:language,** that defines the language used to write the message contents (i.e. FIPA-SL, Java, Prolog, Lisp, etc.). FIPA-SL allows the specification of logical expression predicates.
- **:encoding,** that shows if the message is encoded.

- **:ontology**, that defines the ontology used to transmit the message. It allows a formal description of the concepts. It includes the agent knowledge domain, its properties and its attributes. The objects that are part of this knowledge domain are modeled as classes and the attributes are considered as properties of these classes.

5. The dialogue control

It allows grouping a set of messages in a dialogue. To carry out this action the following fields are used:

- **:protocol**, that identifies the protocol used in the dialogue. Different protocols allow agents' interaction in different ways. Some of them are:

    - FIPA request, to request the agent to carry out an action.
    - FIPA query, to request data from another agent.
    - FIPA Contract Net, to make a consensus for carrying out an action.
    - FIPA brokering. In this case, a broker agent that knows the services offered from a group of agents should exists. This protocol requests the broker agent, to carry out an action. This broker agent in turn, requests this action to the agent group. A specialized agent from this group that knows how to develop the involved task will carry out the action.

- **:conversation-id**, that identifies the dialogue in which the agent is immersed.
- **:reply-with,** that allows knowing the point of the dialogue in which the participants are (the step in the protocol).
- **:in-reply-to,** that indicates the point of the dialogue to which the agent should response, i.e., when an agent has received a message that includes the **:reply-with** field with

an X value, it should response to it using the **:in-reply-to** field with the same X value.

- **:reply-by**, that specifies the limit date and time to answer the message.

AGENTUML: the language to design agents

Research in agents' oriented software is a relatively new field, since as all new technology; it needs a time to be accepted by the enterprises that develop software due to the extra dimension of risk that this technology may carry out. To reduce that risk, some techniques have been proposed to represent this new technology as an incremental extension of well-known and accepted methods, offering tools to support the analysis and a methodical development. These techniques applied to the agents' area involve the following processes [Bau 2000]:

- Introduce agent technology as an extension of object technology including particularities that represent the autonomy feature:

  o An agent is an object that may decide in a semi-autonomous way, when to carry out an action.

  o An agent is an object that may decide to carry out an action with variations or not to carry out it at all, according to the request or to its state.

- Promotes the use of standardized tools to support the analysis, specification and design of the agent software.

To achieve this goal, FIPA and OMG [OMG] groups have been working together to create a new standard denominated agentUML [AUML] to adapt the UML language (Unified Modeling Language, that is gaining wide acceptance for the representation of engineering artifacts in object-oriented software) to the requirements of the agent technology. Table 6 describes the UML based modeling approaches that contribute in the agent modeling.

Table 6. The UML based modeling approaches vs. the agent modeling

MODEL	DESCRIPTION	PROBLEMS AND SOLUTIONS TO MODEL AGENTS
Use cases	The specification of actions that a system or class can perform by interacting with outside actors.	Since agents are active (may take the initiative), a problem in the specification of use cases and static models appears.
	They are commonly used to describe how a customer communicates with a software product.	The use cases diagrams and the static models should be adapted to extend the actor concept and to allow the agent's autonomy representation based on the
Static models	The conceptual description (static semantics) of data and messages (i.e. class diagrams).	state of the agent's environment where the agent acts.
Dynamic models	Include interaction diagrams (i.e., sequence and collaboration diagrams), state charts, and activity diagrams.	
	Interaction diagrams (sequence and collaboration): Are used to define the behavior of groups of objects. One of these diagrams picks up the behavior of one use case. These diagrams are mainly used to define basic interactions between objects at the level of method invocation.	The interaction diagrams are not well-suited for describing the types of complex social interaction as they occur in multiagent systems.
	State charts : Are used to model the behavior of the complete system. They define all possible states an object can reach and how an object's state changes depending on messages sent to the object.	The state charts are not appropriate to describe the behavior of a group of cooperating objects. Since *interaction protocols*, (i.e. the definition of cooperation between software agents) define the exact behavior of a group of cooperating agents, in AgentUML the sequence diagrams with the notation of state diagrams for the specification of interaction protocols, are combined.
	Activity diagrams: Are used to define courses of events / actions for several objects and use cases.	According to the literature, the activity diagrams can be used to model agents without any modification

Next section shows the relevant characteristics of the *AgentUML* language.

The protocol diagrams in AgentUML

A protocol diagram is the result of the combination of the sequence diagrams and the state diagrams to specify the interaction protocols between agents (AIP – Agent Interaction Protocols – using FIPA notation). As an example, the representation of the FIPA-query protocol (Figure 16) by means of a protocol diagram is shown in Figure 17.

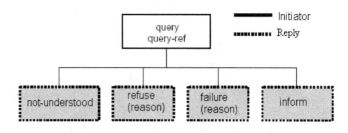

Figure 16.   The FIPA query protocol

In the FIPA-query protocol, the agent *initiator* requests some information to the agent *Reply*. The following messages may be sent to respond to this request:

- *Not-understood*, if the agent does not understand the request
- *Refuse*, if the agent does not want to respond
- *Failure*, if an error occurred when the agent is going to respond
- *Inform*, if the agent is able to respond (the message content is taken from the agent ontology)

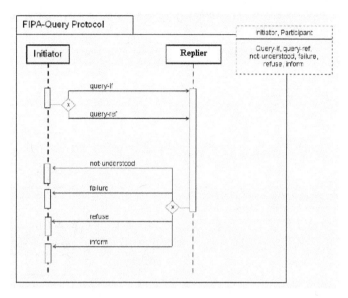

Figure 17.   The protocol diagram of the FIPA-query protocol

The description of the protocol diagram elements considering: the role of the involved agents, the agents' lifelines and threads of interactions, the nested and interleaved protocols and the communication protocols are shown in Tables 7 and 8.

Table 7. *Protocol diagram elements to represent agent roles, agent lifelines and agent threads of interaction*

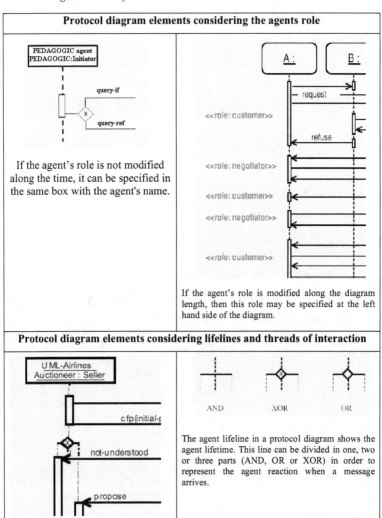

Protocol diagram elements considering the agents role

If the agent's role is not modified along the time, it can be specified in the same box with the agent's name.

If the agent's role is modified along the diagram length, then this role may be specified at the left hand side of the diagram.

Protocol diagram elements considering lifelines and threads of interaction

AND   XOR   OR

The agent lifeline in a protocol diagram shows the agent lifetime. This line can be divided in one, two or three parts (AND, OR or XOR) in order to represent the agent reaction when a message arrives.

Table 8. Protocol diagram elements to represent nested and interleaved, and communication protocols

Protocol diagram elements to represent nested and interleaved protocols	
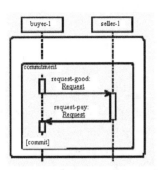 This is the representation of a protocol within another protocol (nested).	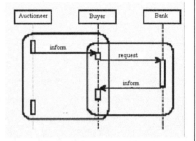 This is the representation of an interleaved protocol. In the example, an agent interacts with two more agents using two interleaved protocols.

Protocol diagram elements to represent communication protocols	
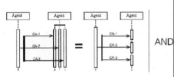 AND This representation is used when an agent has to send more than one message.	This representation is used when an agent has to send some messages chosen from a given set. OR

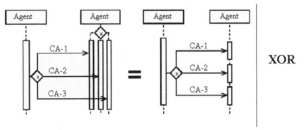 XOR

This representation is used when an agent has to send just one message chosen from a set of possible
.

3.6   Conclusions

The bibliography reviewed for this chapter allows one to define *Intelligent Agent* as an independent 'object' that behaves more flexibly by simulating human aspects, exhibiting all or some of the following properties: reactive, autonomous, goal-oriented, temporarily continuous, communicative, able to learn, mobile, flexible and with character.

Additionally, it shows several applications to the educative environment. Intelligent agents have introduced a new paradigm for learning. First, they allow the concept of shared abilities and cooperative learning of humans and computers. Second, Intelligent Agents in ITS assess the state of learner knowledge and tailor the overall context of courses, curriculum sequencing and tutorial objectives to the individual's needs. The Intelligent Agents may have specific images (representations of themselves through the user interface) that make the user more comfortable when working with an ITS. They may adapt to the user's needs and feelings.

Finally, it appears upon observing the literature that having multiagent architectures such as those provided by FIPA is a necessity since they facilitate and standardize the development of ITS with agent technology.

This work impels further development to integrate the stated concepts within adaptive web-based courses. The next chapter presents this proposal.

Chapter 4.   Intelligent Agents to Improve Adaptivity in a Web-based Learning Environment

4.1   Introduction

Generally, an e-learning (web-based) environment should replace those activities typically found in a face-to-face classroom. These may include: presentation of information, interaction among students, interaction between students and instructors or interaction among students, instructors and contents in an educational setting [LaR 2000]. However, Coppola, Hiltz and Rotter [Cop 2002] stated that instructors in this context must simultaneously play the following three crucial roles: *cognitive*, *affective* and *managerial*.

- The cognitive role refers to mental processes of learning, information storage and thinking, and shifts to a process of deeper cognitive complexity.
- The affective role relates to influencing the relationships between the students, the instructor and the classroom atmosphere. It is necessary for the faculty to find new tools to express emotion to make students feel more confident. This role involves personal motivation and satisfaction of the learner [Dan 2002].
- The managerial role deals with class and course management, and requires greater attention to detail, more structure and additional student monitoring.

The Internet provides an infrastructure that supports unprecedented communication capabilities and opportunities for collaboration. In the field of education, the Internet allows collaboration between various domain experts and teachers when designing novel approaches to teaching and co-operation. It offers a vast store of information that can be accessed in a structured manner or explored in an unstructured manner, providing opportunities for designing tutoring systems with diverse pedagogic strategies.

One, however, has to be aware of the possibility of wasting time, effort and resources, if the designer of the tutoring system does not take into account that the freedom and flexibility offered by the Internet may involve immense educational processes and many educational technologies.

Although web technology has allowed the use of multimedia in the presentation of teaching materials, most web-based learning environments are nothing more than a set of static, impersonalized electronic pages. The creation of interactive on-line courses and tutorials must use a combination of hypertext and multimedia (hypermedia) and consider a number of issues before the true potential of e-learning environments can be exploited [Nik 1999]. These issues are adaptivity, a broader range of educational material and the existing slow access to course material.

This work focuses on the use of intelligent agents in on-line learning environments in which educational organizations can equip students with lifelong learning skills for today's society. In this scenario, and for this case, a web agent can be thought of as a software package with the potential to improve the guidance provided to the user through personalized contents considering learning styles and cognitive states.

The current infrastructure of the USD platform (Teaching Support Units) [Fab 2000a] has been used as a base for this proposal. The proposed agents will provide the students with personal assistants than can help them to carry out learning activities according to their learning styles and knowledge level. The student's progress is tracked and his/her motivation during learning is also taken into consideration. The agent's environment is built by means of a multiagent architecture called MASPLANG [Peñ 2002a], designed to support adaptivity (adaptive presentation and adaptive navigation) in a hypermedia education system used for distance learning on the web.

A distinguished feature of the proposed approach is the ability to build a hybrid student model beginning with a student stereotype model which considers the student's learning style and is gradually modified as the overlay model is built from information acquired from the student's interaction (subjective likes) within the learning environment.

Within the context of this work, learning is defined as the internal change process that, under factors of change, results in the acquisition of an internal representation of a notion (knowledge) or an attitude. This internal process cannot be measured directly, but can be measured through the external observable demonstrations that constitute the behavior related to the object of the knowledge. Finally, this change is a result of the experience or training on the web and has durability which depends on factors such as motivation and compromise [Hui 1999].

4.2   General Features of the USD E-learning Environment

4.2.1   Modular Architecture

At the University of Girona (Spain) an interdisciplinary group of researchers from the Informatics and Applications Institute and the Pedagogy Department developed the USD e-learning platform (a Course Management System where teachers could perform only the managerial role). In this framework, teachers could create and publish dynamic and interactive didactic materials which make comprehensive use of the new possibilities opened up by the Information and Communication Technologies and more specifically by the Internet. There, students could access materials in a decentralized manner using the WWW as an interface in a closed and controlled environment [Peñ 2000a]. The platform also offered tools for communication between students and teachers at various levels (see the USD conceptual architecture in the next figure).

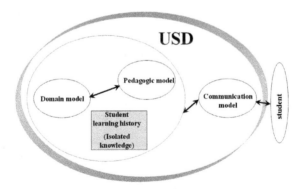

Figure 18.   USD conceptual architecture

A username and a password customized access to the platform; hence a user's activity could be tracked and recorded. In order to perform the managerial role in this system, teachers used the following tools:

- the Interactive Exercise Generator
- the Document Organizer
- the Glossary Editor
- and the Teaching Units Editor.

Figure 19 shows the modular architecture of this environment. While the teacher could access all modules, the student only had access to the Navigation Module.

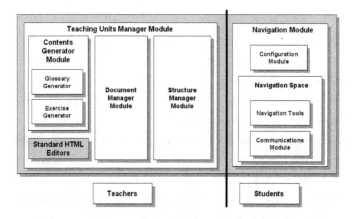

Figure 19.   USD Modular Architecture

Modules were independent of each other, but they worked with the same database. Therefore, by knowing the database design and the defined access methods, the system could grow as desired and new modules could be developed and then divided and sorted by different users.

The USD system allowed teachers to create and manage *teaching units* for established sequential or free navigation. A teaching unit consisted of a set of HTML pages that encompassed the didactic material and a navigation structure (see Figure 20). The navigation structure is provided by a directed graph prepared by the teacher following his/her criteria about the course curriculum. Students could customize the learning environment by selecting the working language; the icon's shapes and the icon's position (characteristics of an adaptable learning system). The navigation environment also offered tools that allowed the following activities to be carried out:

- navigating the learning contents in a guided or free way (using punctual navigation tools such as forward or backward buttons or positional navigation tools such as content maps);
- searching terms in predefined glossaries;
- making interactive self-assessment exercises;
- communicating with the student and teacher community (e-mail, chat, forum);
- printing the learning contents; and
- making a follow-up of the students' learning activities.

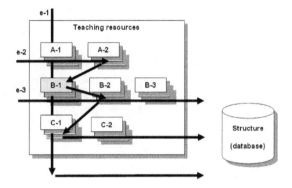

Figure 20.   Navigation structures (e-1, e-2, e-3) and learning contents (A-1, A-2, B-1, B-2, etc.) representation in a USD teaching unit

The centralization of the information in just one database allowed a permanent updating of data and access to the correct information module. The possibility of storing students' activities (navigation undertaken, exercise results, communications, etc.) allowed students' behavior to be studied and improved their academic performance.

4.2.2   General Performance

Teachers could write the didactic material to build teaching units, using standard tools (to create HTML files, images and any other additional object) or the tools included in the USD Contents Generator Module, such as the Glossary Editor and the Interactive Exercises Generator.

The glossaries and the exercises created by the Contents Generator Module were stored directly in the system. The Document Manager Module had to be used to store the materials made with other tools. The Structure Manager Module allowed the establishment of the navigation structure to be followed according to the contents, which had been previously organized.

Students could access teaching units through the Navigation Module, with prior identification and authentication. The next figure shows the different steps in this USD performance.

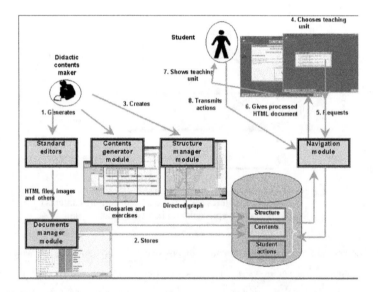

Figure 21.   USD general performance

4.2.3   Advantages and Drawbacks

Experience using this platform has allowed us to identify its advantages and drawbacks from the teacher's point of view when preparing and presenting a course and from the students' point of view when going through it.

Advantages:

- It is an educational platform designed with web technology that allows, through a web browser, easy access from any place and student learning at any pace.

- It offers a configurable learning environment in some aspects of the working desk presentation (colors, icon shapes and language).
- It offers teachers ergonomic and easy tools for creating and managing didactic materials.
- It offers students navigation tools to follow up a course (direct guidance, glossaries, concept trees, etc.).
- It offers teachers and students tools to follow up the learning activities undertaken (pages visited and time of the visit, actions more commonly carried out, exercises completed, global evaluation of the exercises, etc.).

Drawbacks:

- The navigation structure is fixed and there is only one, defined by the teacher according to his/her approach, to follow the curriculum.
- The pages of contents are static (the same format and the same instructional strategy for all the students).
- The navigation tools are general for all the students.
- Because of the first three of these disadvantages, personalized instruction does not exist. This is also a consequence of the absence of a student's model in the conceptual architecture (see Figure 18).
- A clear idea to motivate the student to learn or to fulfill the objectives does not exist.
- Feedback mechanisms for student learning do not exist.
- In spite of existing tools for communication between professors and students and among students, the students demonstrate a feeling of isolation during their learning process.

4.3 A Solution to Eliminate Drawbacks in the USD E-learning Environment

4.3.1 Introduction

Considering the drawbacks in the USD mentioned in the previous section, the MASPLANG multiagent architecture is proposed to introduce adaptive characteristics (adaptive hypermedia, motivation and affective behavior) based on students' learning styles (following the directions of the FSLSM learning style model, adopted for this study) and students' cognitive states (see Figure 22). To achieve this goal, we began modifying the USD conceptual architecture according to the adaptive systems approach proposed by Benyon in [Ben 1993] and revised in Chapter 2 of this document. Figure 23 shows this architecture.

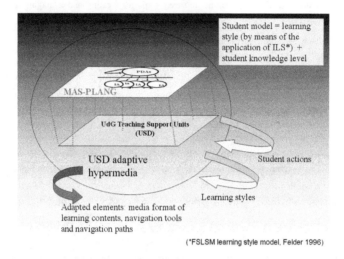

(*FSLSM learning style model, Felder 1996)

Figure 22.   MASPLANG basic infrastructure

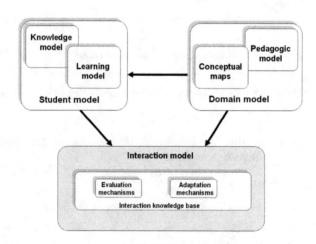

Figure 23.   MASPLANG conceptual architecture

The conceptual architecture shown in Figure 23 has three main models: the domain model, the student model and the interaction model. The *domain model* contains the information the student will receive and a set of rules that decides how to transmit that information (*pedagogic model*). The **student model** registers information about the knowledge and abilities acquired by the student (*knowledge model* and *learning profile*). The **interaction model** supervises the student interactions and offers adaptive mechanisms to give the student suitable information (with assistantship) according to the established adaptive determinants.

Adaptive hypermedia for educational courseware is normally focused on the alleviation of the difficulties of content comprehension (cognitive overload) and orientation. Adaptive presentation techniques which effect changes to both the selection of different media depending on the user's preferences and adaptation of the contents based on an individual's user model have proven effective as stated by Eklund in [Ekl 1998], among others. In addition, the use of adaptive navigation which changes the link structure between elements of the hypermedia courseware based on an individual user's (mental) model has confirmed that learners using such systems achieve faster learning, have a more goal-oriented attitude and take fewer steps to complete a course [Car 1999].

MASPLANG, by carrying out the following assignments, has implemented processes to convert the USD into an adaptive hypermedia system:

- Directing, controlling and coordinating the user's interactivity with the system and its contents. For instance, allowing the automation of certain tasks according to the user's preferences, making suggestions on ways of executing tasks in special situations, tracking the user's actions, showing the navigational paths allowed, adapting exercises to student knowledge level, etc.
- Creating and maintaining a student's model.
- Carrying out the filtering database information according to established patterns.
- Evaluating the student's knowledge based on his/her student model.

4.3.2   Multiagent Architecture

Figure 24 shows the proposed two-level MASPLANG architecture made up by Intermediary agents, called IA (*Information* agents), at the lower level and *Interface* Agents, called PDA (Assistant agents), at the upper level.

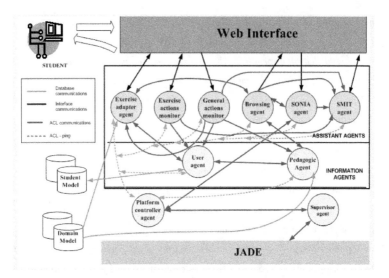

Figure 24.   MASPLANG two level agent architecture

The Assistant agents attend the students when working with the didactic material arranged for the course. Such assistance consists of collecting student actions and motivating the students with attractive interfaces. Collecting the students' actions allows particular behaviors that fine-tune the student model to be identified, and students are motivated by using animated life-like characters and adapting exercises to the students' knowledge level or preferences.

The Information agents are in charge of the student and pedagogic model maintenance. They are very close to the system databases (students' learning activities dossier and domain model).

4.3.3   Agent Activities

SONIA (Student Oriented Network Interface Agent) is a programmable agent that tries to automate learning tasks, either allowing the student to program the activities based on examples, or imitating the student's behavior and adapting the learning tasks to it. This is a simple reflective agent that operates using data for the desired tasks and certain events occurring in the learning environment.

SONIA can be programmed to do the following:

- To inform the student when a specific classmate comes on-line.
- To suggest the revision of bibliographical references in some sections of the lesson.
- To suggest doing the interactive exercises proposed when the student gets to particular sections of the lesson.
- To alert the student if he/she has gone beyond a specific time of study.
- To remind the student with personalized messages at a determined time.
- In the special case of a professor's message, to get the attention of some students currently connected to the system so that they could revise specific sections of the lesson, solve a particular problem or enter the chat room to carry out an on-line discussion.

SMIT (Synthetic Multimedia Interactive Tutor) is a synthetic agent. It is introduced in the environment using an animated interface (anthropomorphous). Its goal is to present the student the messages (warnings, motivation, feedback, etc.) coming from the other agents of the environment (for example, to interrupt the student with a warning message coming from *SONIA*). Representing each message requires the selection of certain animations and corporal movements to define the SMIT behavior in a particular situation. The aim of using this agent is to "humanize' the learning environment and to make it more friendly and closer to the student. Next figure shows the generic aspect of this agent.

Figure 25.   Generic aspect of the agent SMIT

The *MONITOR* agents' purpose (two agents, one saves the mouse-click actions and the other saves the exercise solutions) is to supervise the students' activity in the learning environment. The information collected by these agents allows student behavior to be interpreted (to verify his/her learning profile or to fine-tune it by means of CBR techniques) and the student knowledge state to be evaluated.

The *EXERCISE ADAPTER* agent is in charge of building the exercises for the student in an adaptive way (considering the student knowledge state or the student preferences). The agent may choose a suitable level of difficulty for the questions according to the student's progress.

The *BROWSING* agent shows, builds and refreshes the navigation tree of the course following the link adaptation techniques (*link hidden and link annotation*). This agent also chooses and sets up the suitable navigation tools for each particular student.

The *USER* agent, by evaluating the student actions' and the student knowledge state, creates and maintains the student model (to enable data personalization and collaborative filtering) using Rule-based methodologies and CBR techniques.

The *PEDAGOGIC* agent builds and maintains the pedagogic model of the course. It evaluates the pedagogic decision rules established by the teachers when building the conceptual graph and, as a result, introduces suitable actions to adapt the course presentation and to define the course navigation patterns.

The *SUPERVISOR* and the *CONTROLLER* agents carry out tasks for controlling the operation of the MASPLANG platform.

4.3.4   MASPLANG Features Concerning Adaptive Parameters and Learning Environment Tools Offered to Students

As a base for the student modeling, the student's learning style and level of knowledge demonstrated as he/she worked through the concepts to be learned were considered. To obtain the learning style, the ILS questionnaire [ILS] of the FSLSM model [Fel 2002] was applied (see the questionnaire contents in annex 1). However, the categories concerning the format for the reception of the information (visual, verbal or neutral) and the style of processing the information (active, reflexive or neutral) were the most representative for this study.

The student's level of knowledge is obtained from the completed exercises and from the visits carried out to the hyper-documents that explain the concepts. According to the approach revealed by the student's actions (picked up by the *Monitoring Agents*), the system offers different ways of motivating the student (generally using the assistant agents) so that he/she advances and improves his/her learning level.

The adaptive presentation depends on the appropriate selection of contents according to the student learning style, considering Felder's category for information reception. For adaptive navigation, *link hidden* and *annotation* techniques [Bru 1996] are implemented using the evaluation of the pedagogic decision rules carried out by the *Pedagogic Agent* during the student interaction with materials. During the process of completing exercises, there exists the possibility of exercise adaptation (by means of the *Exercise Adapter Agent*) according to student progress and applying the repetition principle of Gagne's cognitive theory [Gag 1992] if necessary.

All of the students (independent of their learning profile) have in their working environment general tools to:

- consult the user's manual
- review the project information
- change personal data
- personalize the environment language
- personalize the working desk colors
- change a password
- see statistical data of accesses and learning activities carried out
- access the available communication tools such as chat, forum and e-mail
- program some assistant tasks (by means of the *SONIA* agent)

The MASPLANG knowledge domain is declarative and built considering static and progressive tendencies. All didactic material is organized into several Learning Objects and stored in a Course Material File System (a teaching unit structured in a pedagogic domain using pedagogic decision rules according to the teacher's criteria). In this case, a learning object is a logical container that represents anatomic web-deliverable resources such as a lesson (an HTML page), a Simulation (a Java Applet), or a Test (an HTML page with an evaluation form).

When a student is visiting a teaching unit, he/she will have a new bar with personalized navigation tools allowing him/her to move comfortably through the proposed didactic material (structural and punctual tools). Those tools are: *backward* and *forward* arrows to go back or advance through learning pages, a button to access the bibliography of the course, a button to access the *Exercise adapter* agent to request a configured or an adapted exercise, a button to access the *SMIT* agent for reviewing the message history that it has displayed, a button to consult the glossary of terms if it exists, a button to review the help information and a button to print the contents of the current page if the teacher allows it.

In addition, students with an active learning style (according to Felder's classification) will not have the *backward* and *forward* arrows but instead a new tool to freely search the knowledge in the materials proposed by the teacher or in the information found on the Internet.

4.4   Conclusions

The objective of this chapter was to describe in global terms an approach (using agent technology) to bring adaptive characteristics to the USD e-learning environment (a Course Management System).

The USD basic infrastructure was examined and its advantages and drawbacks were identified. A MASPLANG intelligent agent system was proposed to eliminate the USD drawbacks (following directions to create adaptive hypermedia considering learning styles) and to reinforce motivation and affective behavior.

In summary, this chapter showed **what** the MASPLANG system will carry out to accomplish the USD adaptive goals. The next part will show, in three more chapters, **how** this proposal was developed.

Conclusions Part 1

The first part of the book was directed to review the theoretical foundation and the state of the art of educational systems through the web, considering their cognitive implications (cognitive domain, cognitive/learning styles), and the technologies used for their implementation.

Through some of the ITS systems explored in Chapter 1, it was observed that they suffer from an inability to satisfy heterogeneous needs of many students. As it was stated by authors in this research area, this handicap had its roots during the process of learning environment design. The developers did not consider learning styles despite their importance to adapt the course behavior to the goals, tasks, interests, and other features of students (individual or groups). Some empirical testing of learning styles and contents design using hypermedia technologies have demonstrated that style may influence the students' motivation in following a course successfully.

Learning styles are considered basic parameters to build the adaptive e-learning environment proposed in this job. In consequence, various learning style models were studied allowing to adopt Felder-Silverman FSLSM model because of its use and great testing in the domain of Engineering Education. Felder model originally had five dimensions to learning styles (involving reception of information and information processing), however a recent update deletes one of them and leaves the following four dimensions: information processing (active/reflective), information perception (sensitive/intuitive), information input (visual/verbal) and information understanding (sequential/global).

Furthermore, in Chapter 2 there were examined features of different adaptive hypermedia systems, guided to solve the learners' problem of being lost in the hyperspace. It was observed that the common design elements for these systems require a mechanism to gather data about the student (current knowledge state and learning preferences) and then incorporate it into a module that builds a student model. This model, then directs the adaptive issues for that particular person.

Analyzing the above appreciation and in order to re-design the USD behavior (the behavior of the e-learning environment taken as base for this study) to obtain the USD adaptive performance, the following three models that make up the conceptual model for adaptive systems were studied:

- The student model (considering the construction of the student knowledge level and the identification and tuning of the learning profile).
- The domain model (considering the structure of the domain by means of conceptual maps and its integration with the pedagogic domain represented by pedagogic decision rules).
- The communication model (set in the adaptation engine and that allows students to interact with the system and to receive feedback to enhance learning motivation).

To turn on the development of the proposed idea, different methods and techniques from the following five disciplines were explored:

- From the Artificial Intelligence (AI), the modeling and the representation of the domain model and the student model, the ways for knowledge acquirement and the multiagent and agent society based architectures.
- From the Human Computer Interaction (HCI), the interaction with the training tasks, the sociability of the interface, the contents and link adaptation between concepts, and the student assistance during learning.
- From the Cognitive Psychology, the ergonomics of the interfaces (ways for information presentation) and the student modeling (referred to models to identify the knowledge state).
- From the Cognitive Sciences, the definition of the global educational approaches to propose styles of training corresponding to the fixed objectives and to the different types of learners.
- From the Adaptive Hypermedia, the methods and techniques to obtain adaptive presentation and adaptive navigation.

In Chapter 4, using agent technology, the Multi-Agent architecture MASPLANG was proposed as an environment that allows the objective accomplishment of this work: to improve USD feature adaptivity. The principles of Multi-Agent systems have showed an adequate potential in the development of teaching systems, this is due to the fact that a cooperative way facilitates the solution of many teaching-learning procedures. In this scenario, intelligent agents introduce a new paradigm for instruction. It is focused on the concept of shared abilities and cooperative learning between humans and computers as affirmed by authors in the literature.

By using intelligent agents to simulate instructors, agent-based learning environments may serve as powerful research tools to investigate teaching and learning. As stated by some authors the agent metaphor provides a way to operate and simulate the "human" aspect of instruction in a more natural valid way than other controlled computer-based methods. This research tries to prove this theory.

Part 2

MASPLANG E-Learning Environment

Adaptive Presentation, Adaptive Navigation and Affective
Behavior in an E-Learning Hypermedia System with
Intelligent Agents

Introduction Part 2

This part shows the logical and technological solutions proposed for the development of MASPLANG. The conceptual architecture for the adaptive hypermedia system is presented in Chapter 5. In Chapter 6, we describe in detail the interaction model of the architecture enhancing the collaborative work carried out by all the agents in order to achieve the main goal: adaptive presentation and adaptive navigation in an e-learning environment. In Chapter 7, we present the results of experimentation on the test bench accomplished with a MASPLANG prototype.

Chapter 5.   MASPLANG Conceptual Model

5.1   Introduction

As explained in Chapter 4, the conceptual model of the USD adaptive hypermedia system based on the MASPLANG agent approach, is composed basically of three models: the *domain model*, which determines the concepts to be taught and their interrelationships in order to provide a global structure of the domain concerned (knowledge domain); the *student model*, which allows the different features of the student (such as expertise, knowledge, preferences, objectives, etc.) to be considered in the learning process; and the *interaction model*, which encapsulates the adaptive engine that provides adaptive presentation and adaptive navigation by means of supervising the student interaction.

The next formulation represents an abstract model of the MASPLANG performance, taking into account the conceptual model described above:

$$\text{IS:} \quad S \leftarrow LP_{ls} \tag{1}$$

$$D_{ls}: \quad C * O \rightarrow \sum_{i=1}^{n} HTML \tag{2}$$

$$\text{ES:} \quad SM_S \leftarrow LP_{ls} * K_S(D_{ls}) \tag{3}$$

Where:

IS means that at the beginning of the session, a *learning profile* based on *learning styles* (*LP_{ls}*) is assigned to the student *S*. The first value of this learning profile is obtained by evaluating the ILS questionnaire (the learning style diagnostic instrument of the FSLSM model adopted for this study - this questionnaire can be found in Annex 1 in English, Spanish and Catalan) given to students. Later on, after collecting a representative number of student actions, this profile is fine-tuned through a case-based reasoning process carried out by the agents of the HabitatPro[TM] tool (a tool for personalization and market prospecting developed by Agents Inspired Technologies Corporation [AIT]).

Dls defines the knowledge domain model based on learning styles. It consists of a set of concepts (*C*) with an organization structure (*O*). In the end, what the student receives from this domain model is a set of HMTL pages.

Finally, **ES** means that at the end of the learning session, the student model (SM_S) is updated with the student learning profile (LP_{ls}) and the student knowledge state (K_S) taken into consideration.

In this chapter, we describe the characteristics of the domain model and the student model of the MASPLANG conceptual architecture (most of the ITS theory applied in this study was taken from the work of Ana Arruarte [Arr 1998]).

Aspects of the *interaction model* are described in detail in Chapter 6 (the agent model of MASPLANG).

5.2   Domain Model

5.2.1   Description

The domain model (D_{ls}), as part of an adaptive hypermedia system for education, represents both the knowledge about a particular domain that will be transmitted to the student and the way of presenting that information (rules defined in a pedagogic model). The domain model knowledge and its structure determine the contents of the tutorial interaction, together with the structure that governs the adaptive instruction.

The domain model of the MASPLANG is *declarative* and its knowledge is represented by means of a conceptual map (see Figure 26) whose structure takes into account the *static (*the **what**) and *evolutionary (*the **how**) focus.

From the **static** point of view, the teaching concepts are represented by means of a conceptual network structured using different taxonomies. Each node corresponds to a domain concept and it is disaggregated in other nodes using *class-subclass* relationships (i.e. tree like structure). The resultant conceptual network is a static representation of the knowledge in the teaching domain (i.e., **what** will be taught).

From the **evolutionary** point of view, the conceptual network is structured using relationships to describe the pedagogic rules needed to select the contents and/or determine their sequencing. In this study, conceptual (i.e. *property* relationships, such as "X is part of Y") and *procedural* relationships are considered. The procedural relationships are used to determine the *order* in which the concept nodes should be learned or the *decisions* that should be evaluated to reach any instructional objective (i.e. if condition A is true then the student may study nodes 1.1 and 1.2 of the *Concept* 1). This structure corresponds to the didactic organization of the domain (i.e., *how* the concepts will be taught).

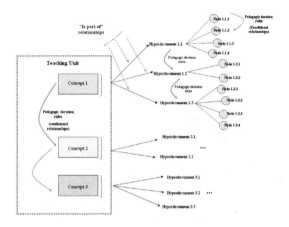

Figure 26.   Example of the MASPLANG domain model organization

5.2.2   Content Types that consider Learning Styles

Supporting quality teaching and learning has been one of the critical issues in distance education. In distance learning scenarios, one of the key things to consider is how the student feels about the educational material. This raises several critical issues concerning learning styles and dynamic pedagogic material adapted to particular student preferences.

Selecting the learning style model is crucial to the development of an effective adaptive hypermedia course that addresses different learning style preferences. For this study, the FSLSM learning style model [Fel 2002] was adopted since it has been well tested in web-delivered courseware for Engineering and Computer Science education (our field of interest). The experiences of Carver [Car 1999] using this model, have demonstrated that students are empowered to learn using their own unique learning style instead of being forced to learn according to the instructor's point of view.

The FSLSM model, described briefly in Chapter 1, offers four dichotomous dimensions that identify eight learning styles that may be associated to moderate or strong tendencies, as described below:

- The *Processing* dimension involves *active/reflective* learning styles.
    - *Active learners* tend to acquire knowledge by doing something. They like to try out things, and bounce other people's ideas around. In addition, they feel comfortable with group work.
    - *Reflective learners* process the information introspectively, and normally they think things through before trying them out. Generally they prefer to work alone or in pairs.
- The *Perception* dimension involves *sensitive/intuitive* learning styles.
    - *Sensitive learners* learn better when the information presented includes facts and procedures.
    - *Intuitive learners* tend to be imaginative, prefer interpretations and concepts, like variety in their work, do not mind complexity and get bored soon with too much detail and repetition.
- The *Input* dimension involves *visual/verbal* learning styles.
    - *Visual learners* get more information from visual sources, such as pictures, videos, diagrams, graphs, schematics and demonstrations.
    - *Verbal learners* are comfortable with written and spoken communications.
- The *Progress* dimension involves *sequential/global* learning styles.
    - *Sequential learners* prefer to approach knowledge in small steps of connected chunks (blocks of information).
    - *Global Learners* like to approach information in apparently unconnected chunks and achieve understanding in large holistic leaps, connecting all the chunks intuitively.

Following the experimental work applied by Carver in [Car 1999] and using a similar approach that takes advantage of the versatility offered by the teaching tools of the MASPLANG environment, the teaching contents and the navigation tools to match learning styles have been adapted. Adapting some traditional instructional strategies and building the learning objects by means of HTML pages (since MASPLANG teachers have worked well developing contents in this format) which have subjects embedded in different media format, Table 9 offers a useful distribution of criteria for selecting the right instructional strategies, instructional complementary materials, interactive and assessment elements and navigation tools for adaptive presentation and adaptive navigation.

As can be seen in Table 9c, the navigation tools proposed could cater for almost all learning styles. In any case, the main idea of identifying the components previously is to be able to offer the learning content and the learning environment that best fits the learning profile obtained by evaluating the ILS questionnaire.

Table 9. Hypermedia course components for MASPLANG considering Felder learning styles

a. Instructional Strategy

	Lesson Objectives	Case studies	Lectures	Knowledge nucleus	Conceptual maps	Synthesis
Active				√		
Reflective	√	√	√		√	
Sensing		√			√	
Intuitive	√				√	
Visual		√			√	√
Verbal	√		√		√	
Sequential					√	
Global	√					√

b. Media format

	Slideshow		Media clips			Lineal Texts
	Text	Multimedia	Graphics	Digital movies	Audio	
Active						√
Reflective	√					√
Sensing		√	√	√	√	√
Intuitive	√	√	√	√	√	√
Visual		√	√	√		
Verbal	√				√	√
Sequential	√	√		√	√	√
Global			√	√		

c. Navigation tools

	Punctuals			Structurals		Collaborative work		
	Arrows (back & forward)	Printings	On-line help	General vision maps	Filters	Chat	Forum	e-mail
Active	√	√		√	√	√	√	√
Reflective	√	√	√	√	√			√
Sensing	√	√	√	√	√	√	√	√
Intuitive	√	√	√	√	√	√	√	√
Visual	√	√	√	√	√	√	√	√
Verbal	√	√	√	√	√	√	√	√
Sequential	√	√	√			√	√	√
Global				√	√	√	√	√

5.2.3   Domain Model Representation

The MASPLANG domain model is represented by a semantic graph based on a set of concepts to teach. Each concept is considered as a *basic learning unit* with its own properties (i.e. associated learning style, required level of knowledge, requisites, etc.). As was shown in Figure 26, a concept in the semantic graph is disaggregated in hyperdocuments and these in turn are disaggregated in nodes. For this work, the node contents were prepared by teachers using HTML pages while ensuring that they matched learning styles. The relationships between concepts and hyperdocuments and between hyperdocuments and nodes are represented by links in the graph.

The graph may have different types of nodes and links as shown in Figure 27.

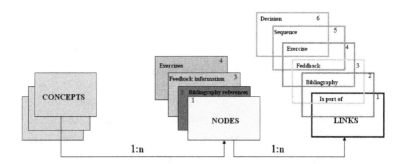

Figure 27.   Nodes and links types in the semantic graph

The main nodes should contain:

Basic information (corresponding to theoretical explanations – node 1 in Figure 27) or information for *enforcing student assessment* (nodes that correspond to exercises – node 4 in Figure 27).

Additionally, there are two optional types of nodes that may be associated to each main node of theoretical explanations (these nodes will be available when the main nodes are being studied). These are:

- The *bibliography* nodes (node 2 in Figure 27) that provide a review of the bibliography, and
- The exercise nodes (node 4 in Figure 27) that provide *exercises for student self assessment* (notice that exercise nodes may be of the *main* or *optional* types depending on how they are linked in the graph).

There are six types of links as follows:

The *is-part-of* link - link 1 in Figure 27 - which connects the nodes that are part of a hyperdocument used to explain a concept or part of a concept.

The *bibliography* link - link 2 in Figure 27 - which points to an optional bibliography node (node 2 in the set of nodes). This link may be enabled from any of the main nodes of the graph.

The *feedback* link - link 3 in Figure 27 - which points to a feedback information node (node 3 in the set of nodes). This link may only be enabled in a *decision* link.

The *exercise* link - link 4 in Figure 27 - which points to an optional exercise node (node 4 in the set of nodes). This link may be enabled from any of the main nodes of the graph.

The *sequence* link - link 5 in Figure 27 - which points to the next node to be visited, thus establishing a mandatory sequence.

The *decision* link - link 6 in Figure 27 -which allows the user to visit the next node once a particular condition is satisfied.

The information concerning exercises is the only one that is not prepared directly by teachers using HTML pages. Instead, before making the graph, teachers should build (and save in the database) a global exercise skeleton with questions and answers (using the Exercise editor – a MASPLANG teaching tool) organized according to the hierarchy shown in Figure 28.

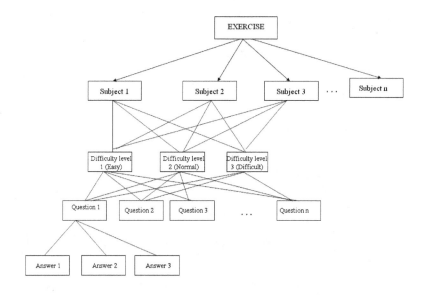

Figure 28.   Exercise hierarchy organization

The exercise nodes referred in the semantic graph are built during the student learning session by the *Exercise adapter* agent, in HTML format, using instances from the global exercise skeleton. At this point, the agent (which appears as an icon in the navigation tool bar) allows the student to decide if he/she wants to configure an instance of the exercise or to leave the agent to adapt the exercise according to the student knowledge state (applying principles of the Gagné theory [Gag 1992]). The following rules show aspects of this mechanism for exercise adaptation [Per 1995]:

- *If* the student has failed the last exercise (i.e. achieved less than 5) *then* propose an exercise with the same level of difficulty (based on the *repetition principle*; repetition of the same schema under different appearance improves learning).
- *If* the student has passed the last exercise with a score above 7, *then* propose another one with a higher level of difficulty (based on the *logic order principle*).

Figure 29 shows the data model structure of the domain model organization.

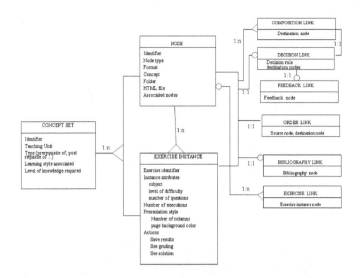

Figure 29.   Domain model data structure

In order to build this domain model, the MASPLANG offers teachers the *Teaching Units Editor* which allows the semantic graph to be represented graphically. This way of working (i.e. physically drawing the graph) with the facilities afforded by the editor (ergonomic and easy-to-use environment) was found to be highly acceptable by the MASPLANG teachers.

Figure 30 shows an example of the semantic graph built for the course "*Study of the TCP/IP protocol*s" used as a prototype in the MASPLANG experimentation and evaluation.

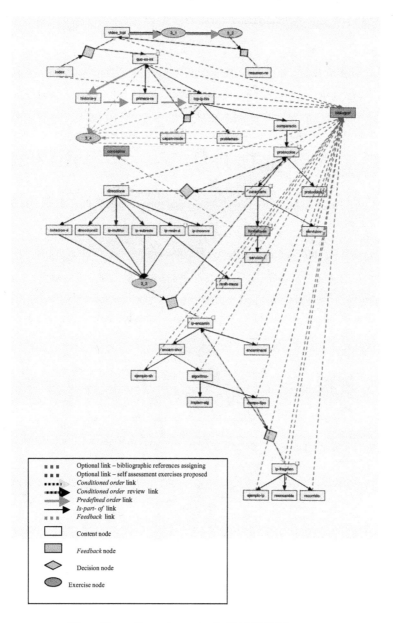

Figure 30.   Semantic graph of a MASPLANG course

5.3 Student model

5.3.1 Description

A student model defines a knowledge base that establishes: the learning characteristics of a student; the knowledge that he/she has about the domain; the didactic material that he/she has used to learn; the history of the learning sessions that he/she has carried out; etc. This information is used by other components of the system to achieve a more efficient process of instruction which is better adapted to the student.

In this section, we describe how the student is modeled in MASPLANG by means of the *User* agent within the multiagent architecture.

5.3.2 Student Modeling in MASPLANG

Two elements are taken into account when modeling the student in MASPLANG: the *student model* knowledge base and the *User* agent (i.e., the student manager – an agent based on knowledge). Figure 31 shows these two elements in the context of the multiagent architecture.

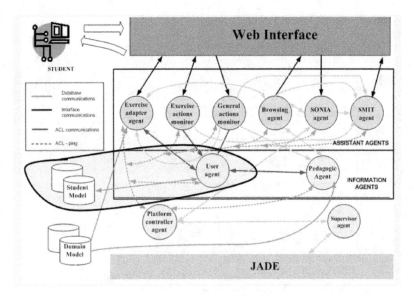

Figure 31.   Student modeling elements in MASPLANG

The student learning characteristics are established in the knowledge base. MASPLANG uses a *hybrid* model, a combination of an *overlay* model [Car 1977] and an *inferred* model, to represent the student knowledge about the domain. This model is in turn divided into two more conceptual models: one is *permanent* and the other is *temporal*.

The **permanent model** contains information concerned with data about the student's personal characteristics and his/her learning profile (based on Felder-Silverman learning styles); the knowledge that he/she has about the domain; the didactic material that he/she has used to learn and the history of the learning sessions carried out (common actions, history of exercises, etc.). This model is available during the whole instruction process and is updated session by session.

The first data acquired for the *learning profile* comes from the ILS questionnaire (a task carried out by the *general monitor agent* of the multiagent architecture). Later, it is fine-tuned by analyzing the student's interactions with the system, using a procedure described in the next section.

The *knowledge about the domain* is the knowledge that the student has acquired through the learning process and how this knowledge was acquired. The particular structure of the domain is modified to include new attributes to control the acquisition characteristics (the navigation through the graph is adapted to the student knowledge state). These attributes are: the acquired-level to indicate the level of knowledge that the student has about a concept and the concepts that the student has learnt.

The *didactic material that the student has used to learn* (basic contents and exercises) identifies the material used by the system to present the learning content or to assess it. This information is used by the *pedagogic* agent of the MASPLANG multiagent architecture to make a suitable choice of the content that the student should learn at any particular time. The *exercise adapter* agent uses the information concerned with the exercises already solved by the student to adapt exercises to the student knowledge state.

In the student model, the information about the development of the instruction process is also considered. Data about the last session summarizes the learning session events that took place in the last session. This information is important for setting up certain elements to be represented in the next session.

The *history of the whole instructional process* is represented by a set of actions commonly carried out, which nodes were visited along with the time spent on each visit and information about the student development when solving exercises (a list of the exercises that the student has made and the way they were solved). This information is available through the learning statistics button in the general tool bar of the learning environment.

The ***temporal model*** makes sense only for the current session. Its data is managed for the *User* agent who at the end of the session updates the ***permanent model*** with relevant information that should alter the student knowledge state.

The *User* agent is the student manager. Its job is mainly to identify the student's objectives, updating the student model and fine-tuning the learning profile.

5.3.3 Tuning the Student Learning Profile

Introduction

An interactive system, in order to adapt its behavior to the needs of the user, must be capable of dynamically building a representation of the user's interests and characteristics. The MASPLANG *user* agent models the student according to the student learning profile (with the learning style first assigned by evaluating the ILS questionnaire) and the student knowledge state. The learning profile is then fine-tuned by analyzing the student interaction in the environment using the Case Based Reasoning (CBR) approach implemented in the HabitatPro™ tool.

The main idea of CBR is to solve a new problem by retrieving a previous similar situation and by reusing information and knowledge of that situation. Finding a similar past case and reusing its solution can solve a new problem in a new situation. In CBR terminology, a *case* usually denotes a *problem situation*. A previously experienced situation, which has been captured and learned in a way that can be reused for solving future problems, is referred to as a past case, a previous case, a store case or a retained case. Correspondingly, a new case or unsolved case is the description of a new problem to be solved. Case-Based

Reasoning is – in effect – a cyclic and integrated process of solving a problem, learning from this experience, solving a new problem and so on. If two problems resemble each other, their solutions are similar and therefore it is possible to apply an adaptation of the former solution to the current problem [Aam 1994].

In the MASPLANG, the information of the student model allows the adaptation of the learning environment to the needs of the individual students. Adaptive presentation (concerning the media format of the contents and the best subject for a particular situation) and adaptive navigation (concerning the appropriate navigation techniques and suitable navigation tools for comfortable navigation through the subjects) are the adaptive hypermedia aspects applied in this approach.

System performance for student profiling

Subjectivity comprehension: images and counter images

In order to get an agent to act correctly in the best interests of the individual that it represents, it is indispensable that it incorporates knowledge, in some way, of his/her likes, preferences and personality. This knowledge is, in general, extremely diffuse and contradictory (subjective) and therefore difficult to represent and manage. The MASPLANG User agent obtains this subjective knowledge by means of images and counter images of the student it is representing.

Characterization of the subjective particularities of the educational units by means of attribute-value pairs.

The agent's personalization techniques involved in the student profiling by the HabitatPro use the concept of ***attribute-value*** pairs, which are used widely in Artificial Intelligence to represent knowledge. The attribute applicable to a teaching unit or to a student is equivalent to a property or a characteristic.

For the didactic contents, some of the following possible attributes are considered:

- The media format for content presentation (i.e. graphic, text, hypertext, audio, etc).
- The type of interactivity that the content offers (i.e. sensitive maps, simulations, and exercises)
- The instructional strategy used to explain the situations (i.e. objectives, summaries, examples, synthesis, and lectures).

Each attribute may have one value among a group of possible values. If a group of products is defined, the products to which certain sets of attributes are applicable can be identified. In the MASPLANG, three groups of products are considered:

- the didactic contents,
- the navigation techniques and
- the navigation tools.

The following structure represents the attribute-value pair for each of these three groups:

Table 10. Attribute-value pair for MASPLANG groups of products

GROUP	ATTRIBUTE	VALUE
Didactic contents	Media format	graphic, audio, slide shows, hypertext, text and video
	Interactivity element	sensitive maps, simulations, exercises
	Type of contents	objectives, summaries, examples, interactive graphics, lectures, nucleus of knowledge, synthesis, conceptual maps, pictures
	Presentation style	menus, hypertexts, glossaries, slide shows, digital libraries, videos, lineal texts.
Navigation strategies	Navigation techniques	Direct guidance, link annotation and hidden links.
Navigation tools	Single click	Backward and forward arrows, print and help
	Structural	General vision maps, local maps, filters and indexes
	Historical	Historical follow-up (logs), tracks and marks
	Collaborative work	Chat, forum and e-mail

The values that the attributes can take are generally of a subjective nature, because the meaning of each one depends on the person that uses or defines it (one student may learn a teaching unit better in a graphic format than one in a text format) and therefore sophisticated techniques are needed for their manipulation. In this case, adding more values of this type does not make sense. The algorithms used to deal with these values in the system are based on AI techniques, such as Case-Based Reasoning and fuzzy logic.

The image of a product is defined as a set of pair attribute-values that characterize the product. For instance, the image of the *Introduction to Computers* teaching unit for an *active* student (as defined by the FSLSM model) may contain the following attribute-value pairs:

> *Media format:* hypertext
>
> *Interactivity elements:* simulations
>
> *Type of Contents: conceptual* maps
>
> *Presentation style:* hypertext

While for a *sensitive* student it might be:

> *Media format:* video
>
> *Interactivity elements:* simulations
>
> *Type of Contents: examples*
>
> *Presentation style:* video-clips

Using the concept of product images, it is possible to define the new concept of **distance** between products using Fuzzy logic techniques. This distance allows us to obtain, from the images of two products, a numerical value that represents the degree of similarity existing between the products. This distance is a function:

$$d_p : P \ x \ P \rightarrow R$$

Where P is the set of product images and R is the set of real numbers.

Characterization of the subjective particularities of the students by means of the triple elements attribute-value-weight

A set of *attribute-value* pairs related to a student can reflect his/her preferences with respect to the teaching units and the learning environment. For instance, an *active* student (categorized by Felder) could be characterized for a specific teaching unit with the following set of pairs:

{*Media format*/hypertext,
Interactivity element/simulations,
Type of Content/conceptual maps,
Presentation style/hypertext's links,
Navigation techniques/direct guidance,
Navigation tools/arrows,
Collaborative work/forum}

Representing student preferences by means of an *attribute-value* pair is not efficient because it does not take into account the intensity of the preferences or the importance that the student gives to each of the attributes. To solve this problem, a weighting is associated to each attribute and to each student. Each student will give to each attribute his/her own weighting, which will indicate the importance the attribute has for him/her when assigning a degree of preference to a product.

The set of weights that can be associated to the attributes is configurable. In this system the following weights are used:

W= {Indifferent, Less Important, Medium Important, Important, Very Important and Necessary}

The variable values for these are {0, 1, 2, 4, 8 and 1000}. At this point it can be observed that *W* will always contain two special constants: *Indifferent* with value zero and *Necessary* with a very big value.

From this point, the image of the student in a group is defined as a set of three elements: ***attribute/value/weight*** which encodes the student's preferences and the importance given to the values of the attributes for the products of the group.

By introducing the weight parameter, the following examples show the characteristics of the Teaching Units preferred by a student with an *active* learning style and by a student with a *reflexive* learning style:

Teaching Unit for an active student:

{Media format/hypertext/very important
Interactivity elements/simulations/important
Type of contents/conceptual maps/very important
Presentation style/hypertext links/important
Navigation techniques/direct guidance/important
Navigation tools/backward and forward arrows/necessary
Collaborative work/forum/important}

An *active* learner tries to acquire the knowledge by doing; he/she likes to work in groups and is comfortable navigating the contents by means of the direct guidance navigation technique, whereby the backward and forward navigation arrows are necessary.

Teaching Unit for a reflexive student

{Media format/graphic/very important
Interactivity elements/simulations/very important
Type of contents/conceptual maps/indifferent
Presentation style/hypertext links/very important
Navigation techniques/direct guidance/indifferent

Navigation tools/backward and forward arrows/indifferent
Collaborative work/forum/less important}

A *reflexive* learner processes the information introspectively, acquires the knowledge better by means of graphical contents, thinks a lot before acting and prefers to work alone or in pairs.

By extending the concept of ***distance*** between products introduced above, and generalizing it to include the ***weights*** of the attributes, two new concepts are included:

1. The distance between a student and a Teaching Unit, which is defined by:

$$d: P \times C \rightarrow R$$

Where **P** is the set of teaching Unit images and **C** is the set of student images.

Given an image, **c,** of a student and an image, **p,** of a Teaching Unit, we get the function:

$$d (p, c) \quad (1)$$

This function considers, simultaneously, all the attributes used in the two images, along with their values and weights in order to return a numerical value representing the distance between the student and the product. Therefore function **d** takes the subjective information representing the student and the teaching unit images to obtain a concrete numerical measure of the affinity between them.

2. The distance between two students, which is defined by:

$$d_c : C \times C \rightarrow R$$

- where **C** is the student image set.

Given two student images, **c** and **d**, we get the function:

$$d (c, d) \quad (2)$$

This function considers, simultaneously, all the attributes used in the two images along with their values and their weights, in order to return a numerical value that represents the distance between the two students.

In a similar way to the function **d (p, c)**, the d_c function uses the subjective information representing two student images to obtain a concrete numerical measure of the affinity between them.

The applications of these two functions (1 and 2 above) are immediate. With them, it will be possible to tell a student about the didactic materials that will work best for him/her, to put students into groups according to related preferences or to use the information studied by a student in a teaching unit to promote the same didactic materials for other students of similar learning styles (collaborative filtering). Another type of application of great importance for these functions is the analysis and the prospecting of new teaching units.

Upgrading student images

As was mentioned previously, an essential characteristic of intelligent agents consists of being capable of learning from its interactions with other agents and with the environment. In this case, where the agents are incorporating knowledge on student preferences and personality, the learning process will consist of continuously fine-tuning the student images so that, gradually, they reflect a more faithful likeness.

To this end, each time the student carries out a Teaching Unit, his/her image will be updated and adjusted to the new situation. Not only will the system maintain something like an average value for each one of the attributes, but it will also automatically upgrade the weightings, so that the attributes for which the student always chooses the same values (or nearly the same) will have higher weightings, while the attributes for which the student has no marked preference for a particular value or range of values will have a lower weightings.

The magnitude of the image upgrade will be controlled according to different factors:

a) *The demonstrated student interest:* If a student more or less carries out all of the learning activities proposed in a teaching unit that has certain attributes, the system will assume that he/she likes this unit and therefore the magnitude of his/her image upgrade for that specific unit, should be bigger than for another teaching unit that presents the same learning contents with different attributes but which the student has never gone into or, if he/she has gone into it, has only carried out a minimum of the learning activities proposed there.

b) *The quality of the student interaction:* the magnitude of the student image upgrade will be related to the quality or quantity of interactions that he/she has had within the learning environment.

c) *The type of teaching unit:* the system can more faithfully upgrade the image of a student if the teaching unit is rich in content with diverse learning activities.

d) *The time:* it has to be remembered that people's preferences change with time. Therefore the upgrade of the student image will be more representative **if a moderate time has passed** since the last upgrade.

e) *The student's preferences:* the system should be sufficiently open to allow the student to change his/her image according to his/her own preferences.

Images and counter-images

Previously it was seen how the images of the students might be upgraded to reflect the fact that they show interest in a specific type of teaching unit, carrying out a high percentage of the proposed learning activities there, either visiting a certain number of pages, carrying out exercises with X or Y degrees of difficulty, participating in the programmed chats or contributing and analyzing information through the discussion forums, or using certain navigation tools. All of these types of actions have something in common: they provide *positive information*, that is to say, information on what the student likes. It has already been observed how the system can take advantage of this type of information, using student preferences to upgrade their image. But, just as important as knowing what they *do* like in order to provide them with suitable teaching materials, we need to know **what they dislike**, i.e. what they find boring or uninteresting or unsuitable, didactically. There are different ways to get this kind of information:

- Identifying the types of teaching units that fail to arouse interest despite being repeatedly offered to the student.
- Asking the students directly

At this point, the problem arises of how to use the negative information provided by the student. This negative information is always of the same type: the student rejects a teaching unit presented in a particular style with more or less intensity. One way to manage this type of information consists of some kind of negative adjustment of the student image, defining, for example his/her *counter-image*. The counter-images are also groups of three elements, *attribute/value/weight*, associated to each student. Therefore, the counter-image of a student **c** is the image of an imaginary student **c'** with preferences that are totally opposed to those of **c**.

The way to manage the negative information is now clear: every time that a student rejects a teaching unit with a type of specific learning content, the student's counter-image will be upgraded, just as if he/she had shown interest in it. The magnitude of the upgrade of the counter-image will be proportional to the magnitude of the rejection. In this way, positive information will upgrade the image and negative information will upgrade the counter-image. Consequently, using the function of distances between students and teaching units, not only can the teaching units be ranked from the one that is most adjusted to the student's learning style and which the student feels comfortable working with, to the one that is least adjusted to the student's learning style (using the image), but also from the one that the student least dislikes to the one that he/she dislikes the most (using the counter-image).

5.4 Conclusions

In this chapter the conception of the domain model and the student model of the MASPLANG were described.

The domain model in this context is represented by a semantic graph that encloses the concepts to be taught and the way they would be taught. Concepts are "explained" by sets of descriptive contents (taking learning styles into account) or exercises linked together in a particular way. It is shown that the structure of the links in the graph determines the order to follow. A decision link encloses a selection rule that establishes one of two things: the next content or the next instructional objective that will be presented to, or achieved by, the student. The optional links allow additional contents to be presented to the student when a main node is being studied.

The information stored in the domain model is used by the *pedagogic* agent in the multiagent architecture, to carry out adaptive presentation and adaptive navigation.

The student modeling in MASPLANG involves two elements: the student model, which allows the different features of the students (i.e. expertise, knowledge, preferences, objectives, etc.) to be considered in the learning process and the *User* agent, which is the student manager that identifies the student objectives, updates the student model and fine-tunes the learning profile using the recommendation offered by the agents of the HabitatPro tool.

The features of the interaction model are described in Chapter 6.

Chapter 6.   MASPLANG Agent Design and Implementation Issues

6.1   Introduction

The proposed MASPLANG multiagent system designed to provide USD adaptivity and student assistance is built using a two-level agent architecture (*Information* and *Assistant* agents), as shown in next figure.

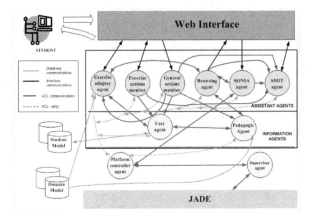

Figure 32.   MASPLANG two level agent architecture

The *assistant* agents are designed to assist students as they work with the didactic material arranged for the course. Such assistance consists of registering the student actions (by means of the *Monitor* agents) to identify patterns that can be used for personalizing the presentation of the learning content and the navigation tools the students use to move through the contents (by means of the *Browsing* agent) and to adapt exercises (by means of the *Exercise Adapter* agent) for self-assessment to the student's knowledge level or preferences. To make the student feel comfortable when he/she carries out the learning activities, an animated, life-like character (the *SMIT* agent) has been designed to display the reinforcement information and the programmed alert messages (by means of the *SONIA* agent).

There are two *Information* agents. The first is the *User* agent designed to maintain the student model and the second is the *Pedagogic* agent which evaluates the pedagogic decision rules that are embedded in the pedagogic model of the course. The *Information* agents are very close to the system databases (students' learning activities dossier and domain model).

Table 11 summarizes the services that MASPLANG agents offer to the USD learning environment.

Table 11. The MASPLANG agents' service

MASPLANG agent:	Services
SMIT	• Shows messages to the user via a life-like animated character • Interacts with the student when he/she wants to recall the message history that it has shown.
SONIA	• Receives instructions from the user regarding the personalized tasks to be carried out (reminders, connected users search, alerts for the existence of bibliography or exercises in the lesson, etc.) • Asks the *Controller agent* to execute programmed tasks concerning the system's events • Asks the *Browsing agent* to execute programmed tasks concerning particular aspects of the learning materials (links to bibliographical references or exercises)
CONTROLLER	• Supervises the lifecycle of all the MASPLANG agents (using testing by means of ACL ping messages) • Carries out tasks concerned with system events (especially those tasks programmed by means of the *SONIA* agent, such as alarm clocks, users connections, etc.)
GENERAL ACTIONS MONITOR	• Monitors the general user's actions • Requests the *Exercise adapter agent* to build an adapted exercise for the student if the student clicks on the *Exercise adapter agent* button of the interface • Updates the knowledge base of the *user agent*
EXERCISES' MONITOR	• Monitors the user's actions during exercises (collecting the student's answers) • Updates the knowledge base of the *user agent* • Sends feedback information to *SMIT* agent
EXERCISE ADAPTER	Builds an adapted exercise for the student, based on his/her exercise history at the *User agent's* request or based on the default parameters at the *Pedagogic agent's* request
SUPERVISOR	• Maintains a list of the users connected to the platform (extension of the JADE DF agent) • Sends a message to the *Controller agent* when a particular user is connected to the platform
USER	• Models the student during session (maintains a temporary student model) • Updates the permanent student model • Responds to *Pedagogic agent* and *Exercise adapter agent* petitions
BROWSING	• Receives the adapted learning information from the *Pedagogic* agent • Adapts navigation paths in the student interface • Adapts navigation tools in the student interface • Manages the motivation information
PEDAGOGIC	• Evaluates the pedagogic decision rules of the pedagogic domain • Asks the *User agent* for relevant information about the user included in rules • Adapts contents presentation

In this context, the MASPLANG agents are designed with the following properties taken into account:

- *Reactivity*: agents need to maintain a continuous relationship with their environment and respond to the changes that happen in it.
- *Interactivity*: agents need to interact with each other in order to achieve the goals.
- *Autonomy*: agents need to know when and how to carry out the tasks assigned to them.
- *Proactivity*: agents have goals or explicit objectives (i.e. to find didactic contents in graphic media, to select structural navigation tools, etc.) and need to act accordingly and in an autonomous manner to achieve them.
- *Learning*: the User agent learns from student interactions in order to adapt the learning environment to the student model (learning profile and student knowledge state).

The agency and personalization model of this system follows the behavior shown in Figure 33. Students (rectangles) interact with an environment (USD platform) through agents (circles) that represent them. The agents have a double function: ***interacting*** with each other and with the habitat on behalf of the student and ***filtering*** the information (type and style of didactic contents, navigation tools and navigation techniques) that the students receive from other agents and the habitat. The agents are individuals (each student has his/her own agent) and they all have knowledge about the objectives and learning styles of the students they represent; they are also capable of learning from interactions with the environment.

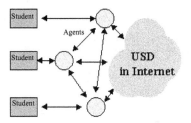

Figure 33.   MASPLANG model of agency and personalization

6.2   Client-Server Architecture

The MASPLANG is built on the FIPA compliant multiagent system (see [JADE]), using Java, JavaScript, Flash, PhP, JSP, HTML and XML languages at different stages of the agents' programming. Figure 34 shows the reference model of this architecture.

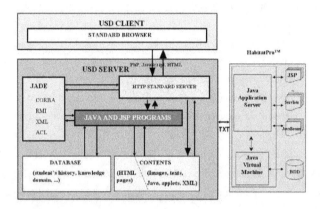

Figure 34.   MASPLANG client-server architecture

The USD teaching and learning working space (the virtual desktop) was programmed using HTML, CSS Style Sheets, JavaScript and ActionScript (Macromedia Flash) languages. Its interface was divided into the following four frames to facilitate the working area definition for each assistant agent (see Figure 35):

- The frame on the right (number 4 in Figure 35) displays all the working windows of the environment (tool interfaces, learning contents, exercises, etc.).
- The frame on the bottom (number 3 in Figure 35) displays the general tool bar of the environment.
- All assistant agents are invisible in frame 1, where a JADE container (a Java applet) is loaded. The *Exercise adapter* and the *SMIT* agents have a visible representation in the navigation tool bar (at the top of the screen in frame 1).
- The *SONIA* agent has a visible representation in frame 2. In the background, the monitor agents' register student actions in all frames (except the *exercise action* monitor which goes into action only during events happening inside an exercise opened in the right-hand frame).

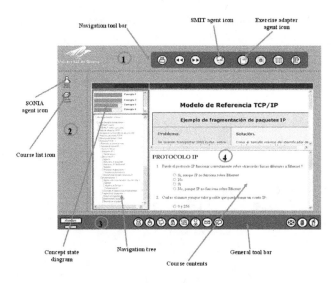

Figure 35.   Aspect of the USD working space

6.3   Working scenario

The working scenario of the MASPLANG multiagent system is defined by the type of users and the type of the content offered. If the working environment is an adaptive hypermedia system for education, the users are classified as *professors*, who prepare and set up the teaching content for adaptive learning and *students* who carry out the learning activities in a personalized way.

In order to create the initial student learning profile, the system asks the student to answer the ILS questionnaire. This questionnaire consists of a set of questions of a psychological nature whose goal is to determine the student's wants, habits and reactions that will act as a guide, in part, for personalizing the content and the learning environment. The student model is built by taking into account this learning profile and the student knowledge state obtained by analyzing the student actions.

The teachers' interaction with the system may be summarized as follows:

Teachers build the teaching content based on a set of HTML pages that comprise the theoretical definitions (declarative knowledge – **what** should be taught) using different instructional designs and media formats (to match the Felder learning styles for the information processing and reception dimensions). Subsequently, using the teacher's tools available in the environment, they proceed to define **how** these contents should be taught (domain model building), in which case they build the concept structure and the relationships between the concept elements. Finally, this knowledge is stored in the system database. The following figure shows this working scenario.

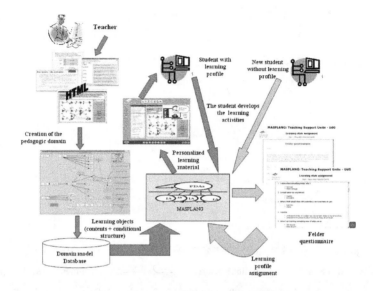

Figure 36.   MASPLANG working scenario

The student carries out the learning activities in a pleasant and assisted environment through the personalized user interface.

6.4   Analysis and Design of the *Monitor* Agent

6.4.1   Introduction

The aim of the *Monitor* agent is to register student activity from the student learning environment as the learning tasks are carried out. These monitoring tasks consist of registering the student mouse-clicks on relevant buttons of the entire working desk during a learning session - when he/she studies a lesson, completes exercises or enters the system for the first time. Therefore, the student model is updated by the *User* agent performance which processes the collected information. The *SMIT* agent improves its operation by offering some information to help motivate the learning experience or to reinforce the knowledge the student has acquired.

The collected activity also allows the fine-tuning of the student learning profile by the agents from the HabitatPro™ environment [AIT].

Figure 37 shows the agent communication flow (blue arrows) in which the monitor agent is involved. Table 12 summarizes the relevant data considered for each area of monitoring.

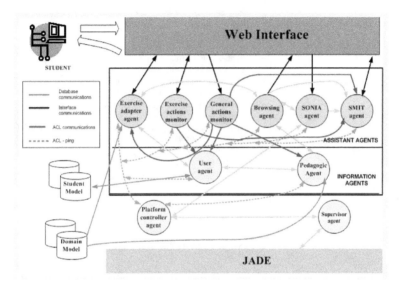

Figure 37.   Agent communication flow for the *Monitor* agent

Table 12. Student activity data, collected by the Monitor agent

MONITORING AREA	STUDENT ACTIVITY DATA
Initial access to the system	Answers to the ILS questionnaire
The entire learning session	• Session beginning and ending: date and time • Number of mouse-clicks on the chat button • Number of mouse-clicks on the e-mail button • Number of mouse-clicks on the forum button • Number of mouse-clicks on the agent *SONIA* button
The current learning lesson	• Number of mouse-clicks on the navigation tree links • Number of mouse-clicks on the navigation arrows (backward and forward arrows) • Number of mouse-clicks on the glossary button • Number of mouse-clicks on the bibliography button • Number of mouse-clicks on the search button • Number of mouse-clicks on the *SMIT* agent button • Number of configurable exercises (on student preferences) for self assessment carried out • Number of exercises (adapted to the state of student knowledge) for self assessment carried out • Names of visited nodes • Number of visits per node • Time spent in visiting a node
The exercises carried out	• Number of *Easy* questions carried out • Number of *Normal* questions carried out • Number of *Difficult* questions carried out • Answers to questions • Time spent in completing exercises • Exercise qualification

The first time students access the system, this action allows the *General Action Monitor* agent to ask the student to answer the ILS (Index of Learning Styles) questionnaire. The result of the evaluation of this questionnaire allows the initial student learning profile to be assigned.

6.4.2 Requirements: Use Case Diagram

Figure 38 shows the *use case diagram* of the monitor agent. Tables 13 and 14, summarize the description of its elements.

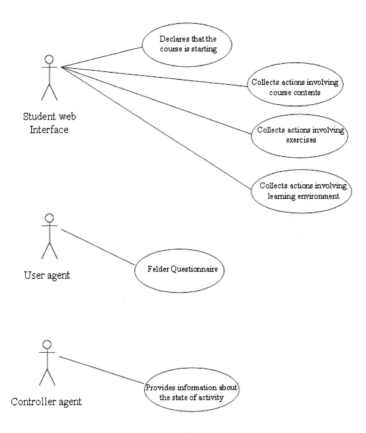

Figure 38.   Use case diagram of the *Monitor* agent

Table 13. Characteristics of the Monitor agent use case diagram elements (1)

USE CASE	FUNCTIONALITY	ROLE CONCERNING STUDENT ACTIVITY	ACTORS	PRECONDITION	POSTCONDITION
Declares that the course is starting.	Informs the Pedagogic and the User agents about the beginning of a lesson.	The information collected at this point is relevant to the functioning of the Pedagogic and User agents.	The student actions are collected from the virtual working desktop of the student Web interface.	The student should begin to study a new lesson.	Data collected concerning the beginning of a new lesson should be coded using the corresponding agent ontology and should be sent to the Pedagogic and User agents.
Collects actions involving course contents.	Collects data concerning the lesson learned in the current session.	The student carries out activities, such as navigating the page contents, reviewing the recommended bibliography, completing self-assessment exercises, etc.	The student actions are collected from the virtual working desktop of the student Web interface.	The student should begin to study a lesson.	Data collected from the learned lesson should be coded using the agent ontology and should be sent to the User agent. In this case, the User agent updates the temporary student model that it has in the memory. Mouse-clicks on the SMIT agent button will wake the SMIT agent to allow the student to check the history of the displayed messages.
Collects actions involving exercises.	Collects data concerning the exercises completed by the student.	The time spent when completing the exercise as well as the level of difficulty of the exercise and the answers given to the questions are relevant parameters for updating the student model by means of the User agent.	The student actions are collected from the virtual working desktop of the student Web interface.	The student should have completed a proposed exercise.	Data collected concerning the activities carried out when completing exercises should be coded using the corresponding agent ontology and should be sent to the User agent. Feedback information is sent to the SMIT agent if necessary.
Collects actions involving learning environment.	Collects data concerning the general actions carried out by the student during the entire learning session.	The mouse-clicks on available relevant buttons of the virtual desktop may represent particular student behavior tendencies that are important to detect. This collected data may be used to update the student model by means of the User agent.	The student actions are collected from the virtual working desktop of the student Web interface.	The student should have closed the current learning session.	Data collected concerning the general student actions in the learning environment should be coded using the corresponding agent ontology and should be sent to the User agent. The student is disconnected from the system.

Table 14. Characteristics of the Monitor agent use case diagram elements (2)

USE CASE	FUNCTIONALITY	ROLE CONCERNING STUDENT ACTIVITY	ACTORS	PRECONDITION	POSTCONDITION
Felder questionnaire	Collects the answers to the Felder questionnaire.	Allows the initial assignment of the student learning profile.	The information is requested by the *User* agent	This is the first time that the student accesses the system.	Initialization of the student learning profile.
Provides information about the state of activity	Provides information about its activity state (test of survival).	There is no role concerning student activity. This case is just for the agent activity control	The information is requested by the *Controller* agent.	The monitor agent should have received a control test message.	The monitor agent response should be coded using the corresponding agent ontology and should be sent to the *Controller* agent.

(Please refer to Annex 3.1 for more information about the agent behavior)

6.5 Analysis and Design of the *Exercise Adapter* Agent

6.5.1 Introduction

The aim of the *Exercise Adapter* agent is the construction of suitable exercises for a student learning session. This process is carried out with the following two features taken into account:

- The student's preferences, in which case it is the student who configures the topics and the types of questions that he/she wants to answer (configured exercise).
- The student's knowledge level, in which case it is the agent who selects the topics and the types of the questions that the student should answer in a given moment (adapted exercise).

An exercise is in fact a group of multiple choice questions. Each one of these questions is associated with a topic and a level of difficulty according to the domain model structure. There are three levels of difficulty and they are described as 1-*easy*, 2-*normal* and 3-*difficult*.

There are two types of exercises in a lesson:

- *Mandatory* exercises. These are represented as prerequisite nodes in the navigation map. In this case, it is the teacher who determines the general characteristics of the exercise that the agent should create for the student, for example, the number of questions to complete, their level of difficulty, the number of possible attempts at the exercise that the student is allowed, the total time that the student may spend on the exercise, etc.
- *Optional* exercises or self-assessment exercises. In this case, the student may determine the general characteristics of the exercise to complete. The student may also request an adapted exercise from the *Exercise Adapter* agent according to his/her level of knowledge.

Figure 39 shows the agent communication flow (blue arrows) in which the *Exercise Adapter* agent is involved.

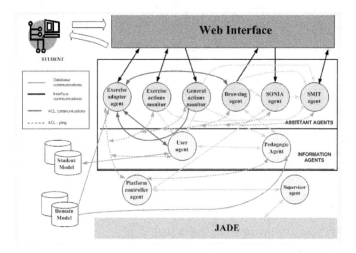

Figure 39.   Agent communication flow for the *Exercise Adapter* agent

The use case diagram of this agent is described next. Please refer to Annex 3.2 for complete information about the *Exercise adapter* agent behavior.

6.5.2   Requirements: use case diagram

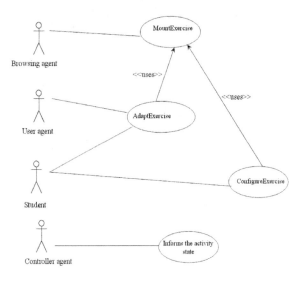

Figure 40.   Use case diagram of the *Exercise Adapter* agent

Table 15. Characteristics of the Exercise Adapter agent use case diagram elements (1)

USE CASE	FUNCTIONALITY	ROLE CONCERNING STUDENT ACTIVITY	ACTORS	PRECONDITION	POSTCONDITION
MountExercise.	Constructs an exercise and shows it to the student.	Enables evaluation of the student's knowledge (self assessment or from the teacher's point of view)	The basic characteristics of an exercise are handled by the *Pedagogic* agent from the pedagogic domain. For optional exercises, the student decides the exercise characteristics or allows the *Exercise Adapter* agent to configure an exercise. From the student interface, it is the *Browsing* agent that requests this task for the lesson that has been learnt by the student.	A request to make an exercise should exist.	The *Exercise Adapter* agent shows the exercise by means of the student interface and the student may begin to complete it.
AdaptExercise	Chooses the exercise characteristics according to the student progress, applying some of the learning principles proposed by Gagne [Gag 1985].	Allows the student to do exercises adapted to his/her level of knowledge.	The student requests this type of exercise. The *User* agent provides information with data about the student model.	A request to make an adapted exercise should be made by the student.	The *Exercise Adapter* agent presents the exercise via the student interface and the student may begin to complete it.
ConfigureExercise	Allows the student to configure an exercise according to his/her preferences.	Allows the student to do exercises adapted to his/her preferences.	The student requests this type of exercise	A request to make a configured exercise should be made by the student.	The *Exercise Adapter* agent shows the exercise by means of the student interface and the student may begin to complete it.
Informs about the activity state	Provides information on state of activity (test of survival).	There is no role concerning the student activity. This case is just for the agent activity control	The information is requested by the *Controller* agent.	The *Exercise Adapter* agent should have received a control test message.	The *Exercise Adapter* agent response should be coded using the corresponding agent ontology and should be sent to the *Controller* agent.

- Page 186 -

6.6 Analysis and Design of the *User* Agent

6.6.1 Introduction

The student model represents the computer system's belief about the learner's knowledge. In order to allow instruction to be individually tailored, it is first necessary to capture the student's understanding of the subject. With this information, the difficulty of the material and any necessary remediation can be controlled within the instructional system. Building a student model involves defining:

- The "*who*", or the degree of specialization in determining who is modeled and what the learner history is;
- The "*what*", or the goals, plans, attitudes, capabilities, knowledge and beliefs of the learner;
- "*how*" the model is to be acquired and maintained;
- And "*when*" to give assistance to the learner, to provide feedback to the learner, or to interpret learner behavior.

In maintaining the student model, the factors that need to be considered include the fact that students do not perform consistently, they forget information randomly and then exhibit large leaps in understanding. The student model, which is the essential component when offering individualized learning in e-learning systems, is the one that builds and maintains the system's understanding of the student.

In the context of the MASPLANG, it is the *User* agent that builds and maintains the student model - taking into consideration the domain model (domain and pedagogical knowledge) and the student performance. The *Monitor* agents collect all the information concerning the student performance for the *User* agent (see Table 16) and the *Pedagogic* and the *Exercise Adapter* agents consult the *User* agent for information about the student model in order to adapt the contents and the navigation paths for a particular student. Figure 41 shows the agent communication flow (blue arrows) in which the *user* agent is involved.

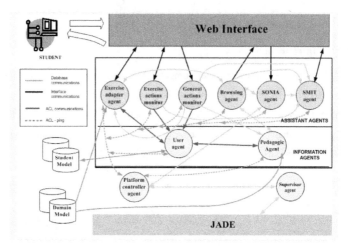

Figure 41.   Agent communication flow for the *User* agent

Table 16. Information that builds and maintains the system's understanding of the student

Type of information	Description
Student learning profile	This information is assigned at the beginning of the course by means of the ILS (Index of Learning Styles) questionnaire evaluation. This profile is later fine-tuned using CBR techniques.

Student knowledge state (student progress during the learning session or during the study of the complete lesson)	Student progress in a course is measured by the evaluation of certain variables that may determine how well a topic is "learned". Some of these variables are:
	• The *nodes visited* for the studied concepts: which nodes were visited, and how much time was spent on the visit.
	• The *exercises completed* (self-assessment or assessment):
	    o Number of exercises that were completed
	    o Levels of difficulty assessed
	    o Number of *Easy*- level questions that were answered correctly or incorrectly
	    o Number of *Normal*-level questions that were answered correctly or incorrectly
	    o Number of *Difficult*-level questions that were answered correctly or incorrectly
	    o Grading obtained for the best attempt at an exercise
	    o Time spent on doing the exercise
	    o Number of exercises that were configured by the student
	    o Number of exercises that were adapted by the *Exercise Adapter* agent.
	• Etc.

In this section, we will discuss various aspects of the *User* agent design.

6.6.2   Requirements: Use Case Diagram

Figure 42 shows the *use case diagram* of the *User* agent. A description of the elements in this diagram is given in Tables 17 and 18. (For more complete information about the *user agent* behavior, please refer to Annex 3.3)

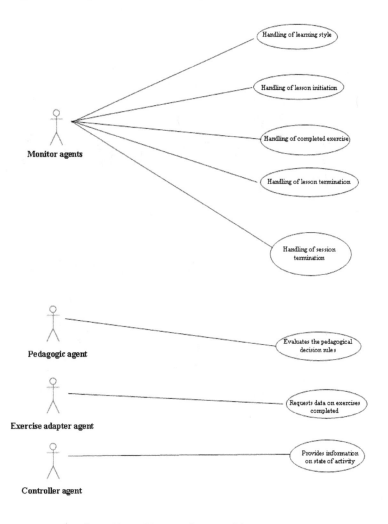

Figure 42.   Use case diagram of the *User* agent

Table 17. Characteristics of the User agent use case diagram elements (I)

USE CASE	FUNCTIONALITY	ROLE CONCERNING STUDENT ACTIVITY	ACTORS	PRECONDITION	POSTCONDITION
Handling of learning style	Requests the evaluation of the ILS questionnaire to assign the student learning profile.	If the student enters the system for the first time, he/she is assessed by the ILS questionnaire	The *Monitor* agent presents the *Monitor* agent requesting the information to initialize the student	The *User* agent should have sent a message to the temporary memory.	The *User* agent updates the temporary student model in the
		and collects the student answers.			
Handling of lesson initiation	Stores in the temporary student model base the information collected by the monitor agent with respect to the moment (date, time and entry number) in which the student begins studying a lesson in a learning session.	The student lesson access is captured by the *Monitor* agent because it represents relevant data for statistical analysis carried out by the *User* agent when building the student model.	The *Monitor* agent picks up this information	The *Monitor* agent should have sent a message regarding the beginning of a lesson (using the *newUnit* object of the ontology.	The *User* agent updates the temporary student model in the
Handling of completed exercise	Stores in the temporary student model base the information collected by the *Monitor* agent with respect to the student exercise performance.	The student performance when completing an exercise is captured by the *Monitor* agent because it represents relevant data for statistical analysis carried out by the *User* agent when building the student model.	The *Monitor* agent picks up this information.	The *Monitor* agent should have sent a message regarding the student performance (using the *Exercise* object of the ontology).	The *User* agent updates the temporary student model in the temporary student memory.
Handling of lesson termination	Stores in the permanent student model base (database) the information concerning the student performance during the lesson that was studied.	The information collected by the *Monitor* agent at the end of the lesson will indicate to the *User* agent that it can update the permanent student model in the database.	The *Monitor* agent picks up this information.	The *Monitor* agent should have sent a message regarding the termination of the studied lesson in a learning session (using the *Unit* object of the ontology.	The *User* agent updates the permanent student model in the database.

Table 18. Characteristics of the User agent use case diagram elements (2)

USE CASE	FUNCTIONALITY	ROLE CONCERNING STUDENT ACTIVITY	ACTORS	PRECONDITION	POSTCONDITION
Handling of session termination	Stores, in the permanent student model base (database), the information concerning the student performance when using the tools that help the development of the learning activities (e-mail, chat, forum, and the *SONIA* agent)	The student performance using the general tools that may help learning is captured by the *Monitor* agent because it represents relevant data for statistical analysis carried out by the *User* agent when building the student model (this information may reflect information about learning styles and may offer indicators to improve the tools for helping learning).	The *Monitor* agent picks up this information	The *Monitor* agent should have sent a message regarding the ending of the learning session (using the *Session* object of the ontology).	The *User* agent updates the permanent student model in the database.
Evaluates the pedagogical decision rules	Sends the necessary information that the *pedagogic* agent requires to evaluate a pedagogical decision rule concerning aspects of student behavior.	A pedagogical decision rule is evaluated when the student navigates through the learning contents. The result of this evaluation may lead to the discovery of new navigation paths for the student or may allow the reinforcement of what the student is currently learning.	The *pedagogic* agent makes the request.	The *pedagogic* agent should have sent a message asking for specific information about the student model that may evaluate a pedagogic decision rule	The *User* agent sends the requested information.
Requests data on exercises completed	The *Exercise Adapter* agent needs to know the student performance in the exercise, in order to evaluate the rules for adapting exercises according to the student knowledge level.	This procedure lets the *Exercise Adapter* agent know the development of the student's knowledge when completing exercises.	The *Exercise Adapter* agent requests this information.	The *Exercise Adapter* agent should have sent a message to the *User* agent requesting the information about the exercises that the student has completed.	The *User* agent responds to this request.
Provides information on state of activity	Provides information on state of activity (test of survival).	There is no role concerning student activity. This case is just for the agent activity control.	The information is requested by the *Controller* agent.	The *User* agent should have received a control test message.	The *User* agent response should be coded using the corresponding agent ontology and should be sent to the *Controller* agent.

6.7 Analysis and Design of the *Pedagogic* Agent

6.7.1 Introduction

In the context of the MASPLANG, it is the *Pedagogic* agent which defines the navigation paths and the content that a student may study progressively in a learning session according to the student model (learning profile and knowledge state) and the structure of the domain. To carry out these adaptive tasks, the *Pedagogic* agent evaluates the decision rules of the pedagogic domain, requesting suitable information about the student model from the *User* agent. The information that the student receives is presented by the *Browsing* agent through a personalized interface with ergonomic navigation tools.

Figure 43 shows the communication flow (blue arrows) in which the *Pedagogic* agent is involved.

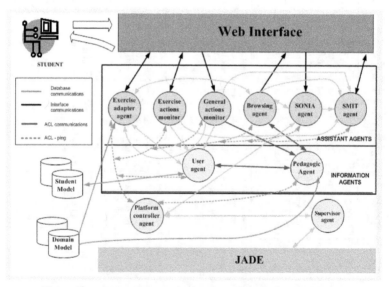

Figure 43.   Agent communication flow of the *Pedagogic* agent

6.7.2   Requirements: Use Case Diagram

Figure 44 shows the use case diagram of the *Pedagogic* agent. The description of its elements is shown in Table 19.

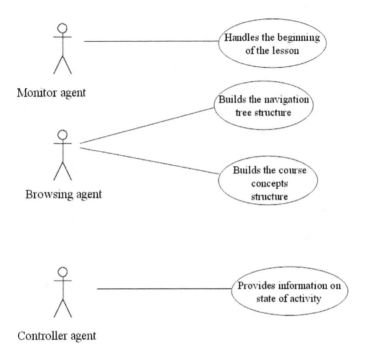

Figure 44.   Use case diagram of the *Pedagogic* agent

Table 19. Characteristics of the Pedagogic agent use case diagram elements

USE CASE	FUNCTIONALITY	ROLE CONCERNING STUDENT ACTIVITY	ACTORS	PRECONDITION	POSTCONDITION
Handles the beginning of the lesson	The course identifier that is sent by the *Monitor* agent will allow the *Pedagogic* agent to choose suitable learning material for the student	The student begins to study a new lesson.	The *Monitor* agent sends the information.	The student should have begun to study a lesson.	The *Monitor* agent informs the event of the course beginning to the *Pedagogic* agent.
Builds the tree navigation structure	By means of this request, the *Pedagogic* agent evaluates the pedagogic decision rules (using information from the student and domain models) to select suitable materials and the conditions that will allow the course navigation tree to be adapted for the student.	This procedure allows the student to navigate the course in an adaptive way.	The *Browsing* agent	The *Pedagogic* agent responds to the request with suitable information that will allow the navigation tree of the course for the particular student to be built.	
Builds the course concepts structure	By means of this request, the *Pedagogic* agent consults the *user* agent for information about the knowledge state of the student on the concepts that he/she has learnt.	The concepts structure allows the student to find out his/her knowledge state on the concepts that compose the course.	The *Browsing* agent	The *Pedagogic* agent should have received a message requesting the information.	The *Pedagogic* agent responds to the request with suitable information that will allow the concepts state diagram for the particular student to be built.
Provides information on state of activity	Provides information on state of student activity (test of survival).	There is no role concerning student activity. This case is just *Controller* agent activity control	The information is requested by the *Controller* agent.	The *Pedagogic* agent should have received a control test message.	The *Pedagogic* agent response should be coded using the corresponding agent ontology and should be sent to the *Controller* agent.

(Please refer to Annex 3.4 for more complete information about the *pedagogic* agent behavior)

The process of building the navigation tree or the concept diagram is carried out by means of a constructor (at the implementation level) which loads data from the domain model database and builds a tree data structure or a bar diagram respectively, after evaluating the pedagogic decision rules embedded in the pedagogic model using the information from the student model, which is managed by the *User* agent.

Figure 45 shows the diagram of this process. In the navigation tree structure (option a.) it is important to notice the construction of strong and light links which delimit the suitable path and nodes that the student may follow at that moment.

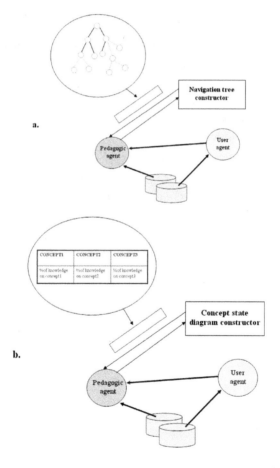

Figure 45.   Information flow and processes that allow the navigation tree and the concept state diagram to be built

6.8   Analysis and Design of the *Browsing* Agent

6.8.1   Introduction

The *Browsing* agent is an assistant agent which creates, in the student interface, the navigation structure of the learning content (HTML pages) adapted to the student learning profile and to the student level of knowledge. The adaptive navigation techniques, such as *hidden link*, *direct guidance* and *link annotation* as well as the selection of suitable navigation tools, are applied to assist the student in navigating the contents in a personalized way.

As it operates, the *Browsing* agent communicates with:

- the *Pedagogic* agent (which builds and maintains the navigation tree and the concept state diagram according to the student model) in order to refresh the information to be presented;
- the *SONIA* agent in order to indicate which nodes have particular information for review associated to them (i.e., bibliography or exercises), provided that the student has programmed it to provide such alerts.
- the *Exercise Adapter* agent if the lesson has exercises assigned or with the *SMIT* agent in order to send the information that should be represented to the student in a user-friendly interface (to motivate or to reinforce behaviors).

In short, the *Browsing* agent is used to adapt the features displayed in the interface to the needs of the learner. Figure 46 shows the agent communication flow between the agents involved with the *Browsing* agent operation.

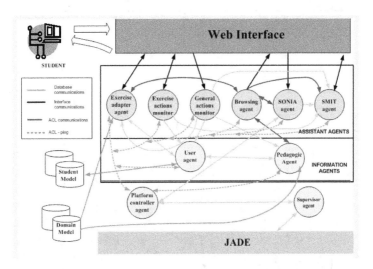

Figure 46. Agent communication flow for the *Browsing* agent

6.8.2 Requirements: Use Case Diagram

Figure 47 shows the use case diagram of the *Browsing* agent.

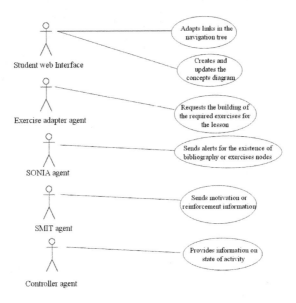

Figure 47. Use case diagram of the *Browsing* agent

The description of the elements of this diagram is presented in the next two tables.

Table 20. Characteristics of the Browsing agent use case diagram elements (1)

USE CASE	FUNCTIONALITY	ROLE CONCERNING STUDENT ACTIVITY	ACTORS	PRECONDITION	POST-CONDITION
Adapts links in the navigation tree	Builds and shows in the student interface the learning contents content via the navigation tree or by applying techniques for adaptive navigation.	The student is able to navigate the content via the navigation tree or by using the complementary navigation tools.	The student web studying a lesson in the learning environment	The student should be allows the student to navigate the content.	The Browsing agent allows the student to navigate the content.
Creates and updates the concepts diagram	According to the student knowledge state concerning the concepts of the course, it creates and updates, in the student interface, the concept state diagram. The information concerning the student knowledge state is updated by the Pedagogic agent.	The student is properly informed about his/her state of knowledge on the concepts of the course.	The student web interface.	The student should be studying a lesson in the learning environment	The Browsing agent allows the student to visualize his/her concepts of the course by the concept state diagram that it has built in the interface.
Requests the building of the required exercises for the lesson	Requests the exercise adapter agent to build the required exercises for the lesson.	The student may assess his/her knowledge by doing configurable or adapted exercises.	The Exercise Adapter agent	The learning material should have associated exercises.	The Browsing agent asks the Exercise Adapter agent to build the corresponding exercises for the lesson and to present them via the student interface.
Sends alerts about the existence of some nodes have bibliography or exercise nodes	Informs the SONIA agent if bibliographical references or to make exercises using the SONIA agent recommendation.	The student is able to review the bibliographical references or to make exercises using the SONIA agent recommendation.	The SONIA agent	The student should have programmed the SONIA agent for alerts on the bibliography or exercise nodes	The Browsing agent sends the alert to the SONIA agent if the nodes associated with bibliography or exercises that the student should revise, exist.

Table 21. Characteristics of the Browsing agent use case diagram elements (2)

USE CASE	FUNCTIONALITY	ROLE CONCERNING STUDENT ACTIVITY	ACTORS	PRECONDITION	POST-CONDITION
Sends motivation or reinforcement information	Sends the *SMIT* agent the motivation or the reinforcement information that should be presented by a user-friendly (affective) interface.	The student may correct certain behavior by analyzing this information. The student feels assisted during his/her learning process.	The *SMIT* agent	Some particular behavior of the student during the development of his/her learning activities should have motivated the presentation of this type of information.	The *Browsing* agent sends the corresponding information to the *SMIT* agent.
Provides information on state of activity	Provides information on state of activity (test of survival).	There is no role concerning student activity. This case is just for the agent activity control	The information is requested by the *Controller* agent.	The *Browsing* agent should have received a control test message.	The *Browsing* agent response should be coded using the corresponding agent ontology and should be sent to the *Controller* agent.

(Please refer to Annex 3.5 for complete information about the *browsing* agent behavior)

At the implementation level, the work developed by the Browsing agent consists of the dynamic construction of two HTML pages (by means of JSP programs) that enable the navigation tree and the concept state diagram (built by the *Pedagogic* agent) in the course interface. Figure 48, below, shows, a representation of this process in the USD environment.

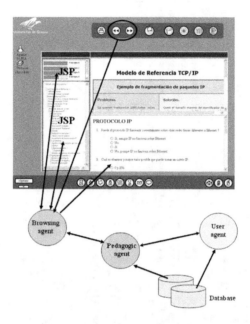

Figure 48.   Working space of the *Browsing* agent in the USD environment

6.9   Analysis and Design of the *SONIA* Agent

6.9.1   Introduction

SONIA (Student Oriented Network Interface Agent) is a very simple agent. It was designed to perform tasks that the users (teachers or students) may program. Some of these tasks are:

- To inform the student when a specific classmate comes on-line.
- To suggest looking at the bibliographical references in some sections of the lesson.
- To suggest doing the interactive exercises proposed when the student gets to particular sections of the lesson.

- To alert the student if he/she has gone beyond a specific time of study.
- To provide the student with personalized messages (reminders, scheduled events, etc.) at specified times.
- In the special case of a professor's message, to get the attention of students currently connected to the system so that they could revise some specific sections of the lesson, solve a particular problem or enter the chat room to carry out an on-line discussion.

To achieve these goals, *SONIA* agent works cooperatively with the *Controller*, *Browsing* and *SMIT* agents as follows:

- With the *Browsing* agent, by requesting alerts about the existence of bibliographical references to review or exercises to carry out.
- With the *Controller* agent, by requesting the information on certain system events (i.e. alarm clock, user's login, broadcast message, etc).
- With the *SMIT* agent, by reporting the messages that should be presented to the student if the tasks have been completed.

Figure 49 shows the communication flow (blue arrows) in which the *SONIA* agent is involved.

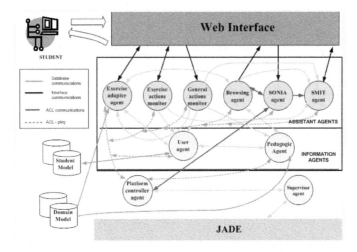

Figure 49.   Agent communication flow for the *SONIA* agent

6.9.2 Requirements: Use Case Diagram

The following figure shows the use case diagram of the *SONIA* agent. The characteristics of the elements of this diagram are shown in table 22.

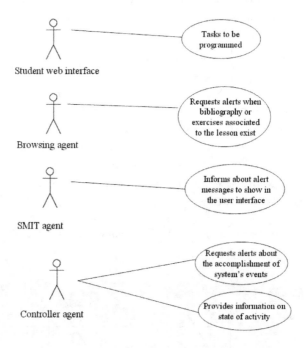

Figure 50.   Use case diagram of the *SONIA* agent

Table 22. Characteristics of the SONIA agent use case diagram elements

USE CASE	FUNCTIONALITY	ROLE CONCERNING STUDENT ACTIVITY	ACTORS	PRECONDITION	POSTCONDITION
Tasks to be programmed	Allows users (students or professors) to program the tasks that SONIA agent should carry out.	The student is able to program the actions for the agent using the SONIA agent interface in the learning environment.	The student web interface	The student should have used the SONIA interface to introduce the agent programming.	The SONIA agent processes the tasks.
Requests alerts when bibliography or exercises associated to the lesson exist	Requests the Browsing agent to search for this information.	There is no direct activity concerning the student in this phase.	The Browsing agent.	The student should have programmed these tasks.	The Browsing agent is continuously searching the learning contents for the requested information
Informs about alert messages to show in the user interface	Requests the SMIT agent to display the information concerning the accomplishment of the programmed task.	The student may receive the alert messages involving the accomplishment of tasks that he/she has programmed.	The SMIT agent	Agents that work together to perform tasks should have informed the SONIA agent about the accomplishment of these tasks.	The SMIT agent displays the messages on the user interface.
Requests alerts about the accomplishment of system events	Requests the Controller agent to monitor system events that allow the programmed task to be carried out.	There is no direct activity concerning the student in this phase.	The Controller agent	The student should have programmed these tasks.	The Controller agent is monitoring the system events that carry out the programmed tasks.
Provides information on state of activity	Provides information on state of activity (test of survival).	There is no role concerning the student activity. This case is just for the agent activity control	The information is requested by the Controller agent.	The SONIA agent should have received a control test message.	The SONIA agent response should be coded using the corresponding agent ontology and should be sent to the Controller agent.

(Please refer to Annex 3.6 for more complete information about the SONIA agent behavior)

6.10 Analysis and Design of the *SMIT* Agent

6.10.1 Introduction

SMIT (Synthetic Multimedia Interactive Tutor) is a synthetic agent. It is introduced in the environment using an animated interface (anthropomorphous). Its goal is to show the student the messages (i.e. warnings, motivation, feedback, etc.) coming from other agents in the environment. (e.g., to interrupt the student with a warning message from the *SONIA* agent). Each message representation demands the selection of certain animations and body movements to define the *SMIT* behavior in any particular situation. The aim of using this agent is to "humanize' the learning environment and to make it user-friendlier and closer to the student.

The messages that the *SMIT* agent may show come from the *Monitor*, *Browsing* and *SONIA* agents. Figure 51 shows the agent communication flow (blue arrows) in which *SMIT* agent is involved.

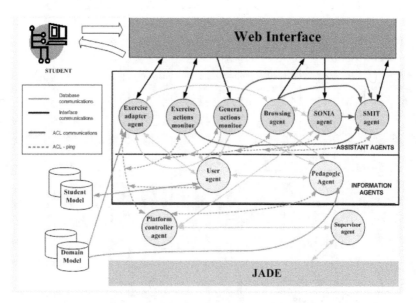

Figure 51. Agent communication flow for the *SMIT* agent

6.10.2   Requirements: Use Case Diagram

The following figure shows the use case diagram of the *SMIT* agent.

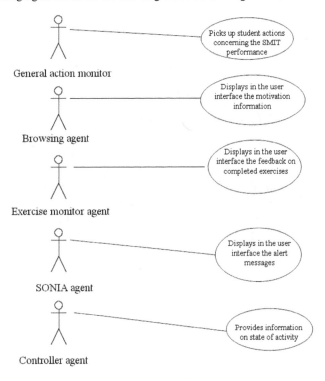

Figure 52.   Use case diagram of the *SMIT* agent

The characteristics of the elements of this diagram are shown in table 23.

Table 23. Characteristics of the SMIT agent use case diagram elements

USE CASE	FUNCTIONALITY	ROLE CONCERNING THE STUDENT ACTIVITY	ACTORS	PRECONDITION	POST-CONDITION
Picks up student actions concerning the *SMIT* performance	Allows users to manage the *SMIT* agent behavior in particular situations.	The student is able to interact with the *SMIT* agent in order to consult the history of displayed messages.	The *Monitor* agent which collects the student actions on the *SMIT* interface.	The *SMIT* agent should have displayed the agent message on the user history.	The student may check the agent message history.
Displays in the user interface the motivation information	Displays to the student the motivation information sent by the *Browsing* agent.	The student is able to get advice on ways to do things if he/she has demonstrated particular behaviors when learning tasks are carried out.	The *Browsing* agent.	The *SMIT* agent should have received from the *Browsing* agent, a request to display a motivation message.	The *SMIT* agent selects from its internal knowledge base an action script to display the message using a life-like character.
Displays in the user interface the feedback on completed exercises	Displays the student the feedback information sent by the *Exercise Monitor* agent concerning aspects of completed exercises	The student is able to receive feedback information concerning exercises he/she has completed.	The *Exercise Monitor* agent	The student should have completed an exercise.	The *SMIT* agent selects from its internal knowledge base an action script to display the message using a life-like character.
Displays in the user interface the alert messages	Displays the student the alert messages prepared by *SONIA* agent when the tasks for which it was programmed have been completed.	The student is able to receive the alert messages that he/she has programmed by means of the *SONIA* agent.	The *SONIA* agent	The tasks for which *SONIA* agent was programmed should have been completed.	The *SMIT* agent selects from its internal knowledge base an action script to display the message using a life-like character.
Provides information on state of activity	Provides information on state of activity (test of survival).	There is no role concerning the student activity. This case is just for the agent *Controller* agent activity control	The information is requested by the *Controller* agent.	The *SMIT* agent should have received a control test message.	The *SMIT* agent response should be coded using the corresponding agent ontology and should be sent to the *Controller* agent.

(Please refer to Annex 3.7 for more complete information about the *SMIT* agent behavior)

Figures 53 and 54 show some mimics used by the SMIT agent to represent messages at the student interface. When it is idle, this agent lives in the navigation tool bar as an icon (see Figure 55) waiting for more messages to display or for students' requests to review the history of the messages displayed.

Figure 53.   Some examples of the *SMIT* agent displaying messages to a student called clarenes

d. Multicast message announcing a chatroom discussion

Figure 54.   Examples of the *SMIT* agent displaying a message programmed by the teacher

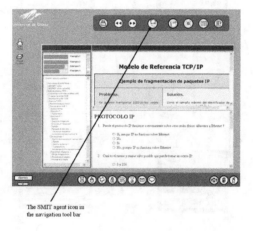

The SMIT agent icon in
the navigation tool bar

Figure 55.   The *SMIT* agent icon in the navigation tool bar

6.11   Analysis and Design of the *Controller* Agent

6.11.1   Introduction

This agent was designed to control the operation of the agents assigned to a connected user during a session. In addition to creating and destroying the suitable interfaces and information agents, the *Controller* agent maintains an individual list of the agent registrations and is willing to receive other agents' queries concerning system events. Figure 56 shows the communication flow (blue and red arrows) in which this agent is involved.

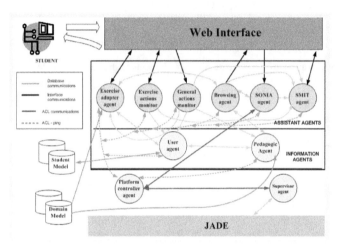

Figure 56.   Agent communication flow of the *Controller* agent

6.11.2   Requirements: Use Case Diagram

The following figure shows the use case diagram of the *Controller* agent.

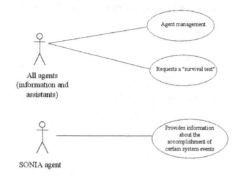

Figure 57.   Use case diagram of the *Controller* agent

The description of the use case diagram elements is shown in Table 24.

Table 24. Controller agent use case diagram elements

USE CASE	FUNCTIONALITY	ROLE CONCERNING STUDENT ACTIVITY	ACTORS	PRECONDITION	POSTCONDITION
Agent management	Starts, re-starts, controls and kills the information and interface agents for each student in a session (see Figure 58).	The student may work comfortably in a personalized and assisted learning environment.	MASPLANG agents	The MASPLANG *Supervisor* agent should have been started	The *Supervisor* agent starts a *Controller* agent for each student that accesses the MASPLANG.
Requests a survival test	Requests a survival test from each of the MASPLANG agents in order to know about their states of activity (ping question).	There is no role directly concerning the student activity. This case is just for the agent activity control.	MASPLANG agents	The MASPLANG agents should have been started.	Each agent should respond to the test in order to inform about its state of activity (pong answer).
Provides information about the accomplishment of certain system events	Provides information about the accomplishment of certain system events if such tasks were programmed by the SONIA agent.	The student is able to receive messages about the accomplishment of the tasks concerning the system events that he/she has programmed by means of the SONIA agent.	SONIA agent	The student should have programmed tasks concerning system events by means of the SONIA agent.	If the task concerning some system events has been completed, the *Controller* agent informs the SONIA agent of the fact.

(Please refer to Annex 3.8 for more complete information about the *controller* agent behavior)

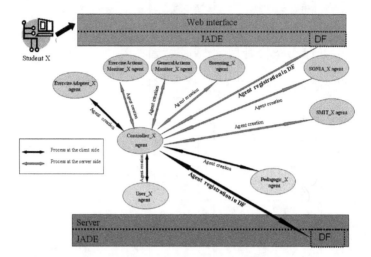

Figure 58.   Creation of the *Information* and *assistant* agents for the student *X*

6.12   Conclusions

In this chapter, the MASPLANG agent design and implementation issues were discussed. We described how agents were designed to carry out flexible and autonomous actions in the environment of the USD platform in order to achieve adaptive presentation and navigation on the learning content using a user-friendly and assisted interface.

Agent flexibility was provided by including features such as reactivity, proactivity, interactivity and learning. The complete ontology for agent communications was also defined (see Annex 3).

Chapter 7.   Experimentation and Evaluation of MASPLANG

7.1   Introduction

The University of Girona had an experimental e-learning platform, a Course Management System, where teachers could perform a managerial role. The objective, which was to participate in a collective project of a group of Catalan universities (supported by the Secretary for the Information Society and the General Direction of Universities) called *Intercampus*, led the BCDS[1] group to test, integrate, redesign and develop the necessary modules to make a functional platform available at operational level [Peñ 2000a]. Because of my experience and expectations of a doctoral degree, I was put in charge of carrying out this task.

Testing the existing platform modules and executing them in operational conditions (current number of students, normal learning procedures, course contents and number of courses) showed that there were some performance drawbacks that needed correcting. It was essential to redesign the existing modules and build new ones (glossary editor, exercise generator by difficulty level and follow-up exercise tools) to improve the technological aspects (independence from network conditions and independence from the browser) and modularity (velocity and ergonomics). These improvements were carried out while I coordinated the development of the e-learning courses in a service department created by the university, called "Unitat de Suport a la Docència Virtual" (Virtual Teaching Support Unit). The experimentation and evaluation was based upon the USD (former PLANG[2]) e-learning platform.

The functionality of the USD platform, together with the projects involved with teaching innovation supported by the UdG, converted the platform into a usable and popular resource for supporting some of the current face-to-face university courses and ODL courses. In this chapter, we discuss reinforcing the experimentation and evaluation of the platform as a mean of improving procedures, the teaching and learning environment, the technological base and

---

[1] BCDS: Broadband Communications and Distributed Systems Group

versatility, as was done when developing the working environment. The experience gained and the methodical evaluation stimulated the planning of either adaptivity (based on learning profiles and student knowledge status,) or assistance (based on affective behavior and significant accompanying). This is the main goal of this work and it is comprised in the MASPLANG prototype.

Systematic evaluation is essential for validating the usefulness of the environment. To this end, the European Union project Galecia[3], when establishing the evaluation guidelines of ODL systems, funded the evaluation of the platform, the materials and the student learning [Mar 2002].

The evaluation should consider the quality and effectiveness of the teaching and learning processes. This is fundamental in the design of distance courses and learner support [Gal 2001]. Items that must be evaluated include the course materials, the support tools, the interaction between teacher and student, the interaction among students, the interaction of the group, the interaction between student and materials, the student's attitude, satisfaction, achievement, persistence, etc., and the interaction between student and tools.

There are two types of evaluation: *formative*, if it is used to improve the materials and the learning process, or *summative*, if it is used to assess the effectiveness of the learning process.

When developing electronic courses, one has to equip the platform with the teachers' perspective; in this way, one has to consider the formal and informal tools he/she uses in face to face education, as Willis in [Wil 1993] says: "*To evaluate classroom learning informally, f2f teachers can pose questions, listen to student questions and comments and monitor body language and facial expressions. Informal, often implicit evaluations permit the teacher to make adjustments in their teaching: to slow down or review material in response to questions, confusion and misunderstandings; or to move on when student performance exceeds expectations*". As distance teachers do not have the face to

[2] The PLANG project was supported by the Spanish Research Council (CICYT) TEL 98-0408-C02-01 and TEL99-0976.
[3] The Galecia Project was supported by the European Union through the program Socrates-Minerva 88089-CP-1-2000-1-PT.

face feedback, they must collect data to determine various aspects[Gal 2001]: Student comfort with the method, appropriateness of assignments, clarity of course contents, quality of time spent, teaching effectiveness and possibilities of course improvements. When developing electronic courses one has to prepare teaching material, which means matching student learning styles. Therefore, it is necessary to know the teacher's approach to the material and the evaluation, and his/her follow up; the student perception about the content format, the instructional strategy, the adaptation of the contents to his/her preferences, the support offered and the permanency and usage of the tools and materials of the platform. The information for this *formative* evaluation was acquired by two surveys; one on the professors and the other on the students.

Summative evaluations aim to assess the overall effectiveness of the finished product or course [Gal 2001]. An analysis of the actions executed by the students when working in the platform, may be used to identify its success.

In the next sections, we describe the organization of the course evaluation, the evaluation of the USD platform and the evaluation of the MASPLANG platform in order to see the drawbacks, the approach used with tools and materials and the working functionality.

7.2   Course Evaluation

Courses were evaluated in the following six areas: *Computer Networks, Statistics, Economy, Criminal Law, Psychology and Education.*

The evaluation of the teaching and learning environments was accomplished in two ways, as follows:

- by surveying teachers and students by means of questionnaires,
- by monitoring the students actions in the system.

We surveyed the teachers using questionnaire 1 which allowed us to evaluate:

- the kind of learning materials offered,
- the teacher's disposition towards producing materials for the platform and

- the characteristics of the processes used to follow up the students' learning activities.

The students were surveyed using questionnaire 2 which allowed us to evaluate:

- the students' opinions about related aspects,
- the means and types of access to the system,
- the importance of the learning environment and learning material that was offered
- the quantity and quality of the interactions with the system,
- the degree of difficulty of the proposed learning activities,
- the instructor's readiness when carrying out consultations,
- the platform technical support,
- the motivation to carry out the learning activities.

7.2.1 Teachers' Survey (Questionnaire 1)

The teachers' questionnaire was as follows:

PROFESSOR

Name:	
Subject for which you have created a teaching unit:	
Academic period:	

COURSE

1. Educational objectives:

2. Type of material offered:	none	low	middle	high
Basic subjects (theoretical - descriptive)	☐	☐	☐	☐
Case studies	☐	☐	☐	☐
Glossaries	☐	☐	☐	☐
Bibliographic references	☐	☐	☐	☐
Links to external web pages	☐	☐	☐	☐
Simulators	☐	☐	☐	☐
Animations	☐	☐	☐	☐

	none	low	middle	high
Exercises	☐	☐	☐	☐
Chats	☐	☐	☐	☐
Discussions	☐	☐	☐	☐
3. Media and formats used:	none	low	middle	high
Graphics	☐	☐	☐	☐
Texts	☐	☐	☐	☐
Hypertexts	☐	☐	☐	☐
Audio	☐	☐	☐	☐
Video	☐	☐	☐	☐
Slide Shows	☐	☐	☐	☐
4. Collaborative work by means of:	none	low	middle	high
Chat	☐	☐	☐	☐
Forum	☐	☐	☐	☐
Electronic mail	☐	☐	☐	☐
5. About the teaching environment:	very low	low	middle	high
It was easy to use the platform ?	☐	☐	☐	☐
It was easy to access the platform?	☐	☐	☐	☐
Did you use the teaching platform tools to create, maintain and evaluate your teaching unit?	☐	☐	☐	☐
Did the technological and administrative platform support work correctly?	☐	☐	☐	☐
Were the system's help tools (user manuals, on-line help tools) sufficient for checking the performance of the teaching environment?	☐	☐	☐	☐
Do you think that the platform offered the support expected for your teaching?	☐	☐	☐	☐
6. Student activities follow-up	very low	low	middle	high
Did you carry out the follow-up of the students' learning activities?	☐	☐	☐	☐
How did you carry out this process?				
Do you think that the students developed the proposed learning activities enjoyably and according to your expectations?	☐	☐	☐	☐
Why?				
Did you assist the students during the evolution of the learning activities?	☐	☐	☐	☐
How did you carry out this assistance?				

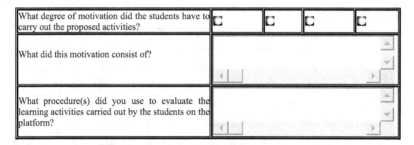

What degree of motivation did the students have to carry out the proposed activities?	☐		☐	☐		☐
What did this motivation consist of?						
What procedure(s) did you use to evaluate the learning activities carried out by the students on the platform?						

In which aspects do you think that the platform should be improved in order to support distance teaching and learning processes?

Thank you very much for your answers.

Submit   Erase data

7.2.2   Students' Survey (Questionnaire 2)

The students' evaluation questionnaire was as follows:

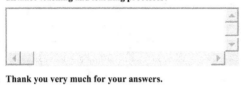

Course:

	Home	Classroom connected to Internet	Other
1. From which place did you usually get access to the platform?	☐	☐	☐
	Not easily	Fairly easily	Easily
2. How did you connect?	☐	☐	☐
Why?			
	Not motivated	Fairly motivated	Very motivated
3. In general, to what degree were you motivated to obtain good results in this course using the learning material offered by the platform?	☐	☐	☐

Could you please extend your answer?			
	Not much	Quite a lot	A lot
4. Did you receive adequate orientation about how to carry out the learning activities proposed and how to get access to the system?	☐	☐	☐
Could you explain how those indications were given and if they were enough?			
	Not much	Quite a lot	A lot
5. Were you satisfied with the presentation of the proposed materials?	☐	☐	☐
Why? / Why not ?			
	Not practical	Practical	Very practical
6. Do you think that the learning material proposed was practical?	☐	☐	☐
Comments:			

If you could choose, what format would you prefer for these materials?

a. Text	☐	
b. Hypertext	☐	
c. Graphics	☐	
d. Simulations	☐	
e. Animations	☐	
f. Slide shows	☐	
g. Exercises	☐	
h. Other	☐	

Could you please explain your answer?

8. Which navigation tool did you use to follow the theoretical subjects?

a. Not applicable	☐
b. Arrows only (to advance, to go back)	☐
c. Navigation tree only	☐
d. Printouts only	☐
e. Arrows and Navigation tree	☐
f. Arrows and Printouts	☐
g. Navigation tree and Printouts	☐
h. Arrows, Navigation tree and Printouts	☐

	Not much	Quite a lot	A lot
9. Did you carry out the learning activities proposed?	☐	☐	☐
10. Do you think that the training carried out by means of the proposed exercises helped you to obtain good results in the exams?	☐	☐	☐
11. Did you benefit from the platform resources?	☐	☐	☐
12. Did you ask your teacher to resolve doubts when you were carrying out the learning activities?	☐	☐	☐

13. Which media did you use to communicate with the teacher?	a Electronic mail ☐ b Chat ☐ c Phone call ☐ d Personal interview ☐ e Other ☐		

	Not much	Quite a lot	A lot
14. Was the professor willing to answer your questions?	☐	☐	☐
15. Did you use the system's help tools?	☐	☐	☐
16. Did you use the forum when carrying out the learning activities?	☐	☐	☐
17. According to your experience, do you consider the work carried out through the forum and the chat sessions to be an important contribution to your learning during the course? Explain.			

	Not much	Usually	Most of the time
18. Did the platform work correctly as you carried out the learning activities?	☐	☐	☐
Why? / Why not ?			

	Not much	Quite a lot	A lot
19. Do you think that the use of the new technologies can make the learning activities easier?	☐	☐	☐
Why?			

Thank you very much for your answers

Submit   Clear data

7.3 USD Evaluation

We evaluated the USD platform in two phases: first, presenting the perceptions of professors and students by means of graphics, using the information obtained through the surveys (questionnaires 1 and 2); and second, recording a summary of the actions taken by the students using the platform.

7.3.1 Teachers' Survey

Questionnaire 1 was answered by fourteen professors (from the six courses) who used the USD teaching environment.

Type of material offered:

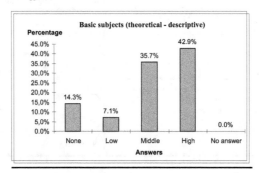

Figure 59.   USD - Contents type

Most professors (85.7%) used theoretical or descriptive contents in their teaching units, as shown in Figure 59. 14.3 percent did not, since they only used the environment to provide materials for assessment (exercises and case studies).

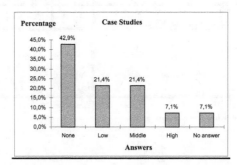

Figure 60.   USD - case studies included in content

Almost half of professors (49.9 %) included case studies to be analyzed with the material, 42.9 percent did not, and 7.1 percent did not answer as shown in Figure 60.

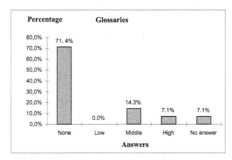

Figure 61.   USD - glossaries included in content

Figure 61 shows that more than 70% of the professors did not include glossaries in their teaching units perhaps because the courses with material limited to exercises and case studies may not require glossaries.

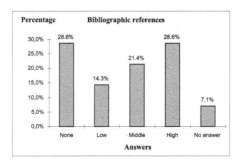

Figure 62.   USD - bibliographical references included in content

The statistics shown in Figure 62 reflect a tendency (64.3%) to include bibliographic references in the teaching material.

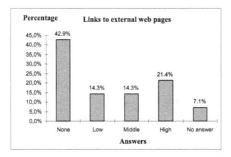

Figure 63.   USD - external web page links included in content

Figure 63 shows that 42% of the professors did not use links to external web pages, perhaps because they considered it unnecessary or because they could not, or did not know how to, include links.

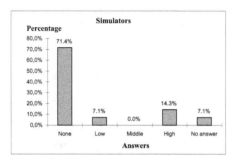

Figure 64.   USD- simulators available in content

Figure 64 shows how few professors used simulators. In general, the use of this type of material was restricted to the Computer Networks courses and to the Economy courses.

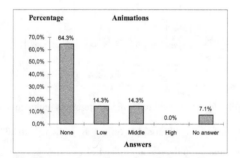

Figure 65.   USD- animations included in content

Animations, as shown in Figure 65, were selected only by those teachers who built their educational units with an emphasis on the theoretical contents, to facilitate the understanding of certain concepts. 28.6% of the reflected usage corresponds to materials created for Computer Networks, World Economy and ICT Resources in Educational Centers.

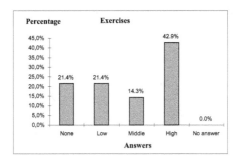

Figure 66.   USD - exercises included in content

Figure 66 shows that almost 80% of the professors included materials for assessment in their teaching units. 42.9% of professors answered "high", this number reflects the answers obtained from professors from the courses on *Basic Concepts in Statistics* and *Case Studies in Criminal Law*, which were developed mostly around multiple choice exercises or case studies.

Media and formats used:

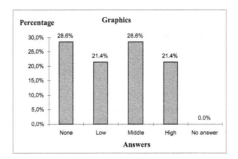

Figure 67.   USD - graphics included in content

The use of graphics depended also on the characteristics of the given course. Courses such as *Case Studies in Criminal Law* or *Instructional Psychology* (because of the nature of the course) did not use them as much as courses with a technical profile such as *Computer Networks* or *Basic Concepts in Statistics*. However, Figure 67 illustrates that 71.4% of the professors included graph material.

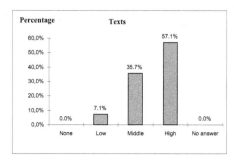

Figure 68. USD - texts included in content

As expected, Figure 68 shows that all the professors used texts to build their Teaching Units. In general, professors re-used the electronic material that had been prepared previously for their face-to-face classes, as it was easy to convert *doc to html* format.

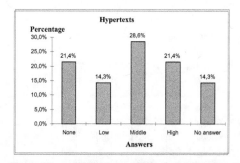

Figure 69. USD - hypertext included in content

According to Figure 69, 64.3% of the professors used the hypertext technique in their didactic materials to make the explanation of the learning topics comprehensible. The professors who constructed the teaching units exclusively around exercises or problems did not consider it necessary to use hypertexts.

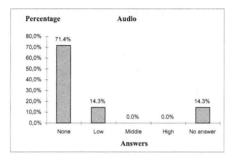

Figure 70.   USD- audio included in content

Audio was scarcely used (Figure 70 shows just 14.3%). Technical difficulties in creating this material may be the major reason.

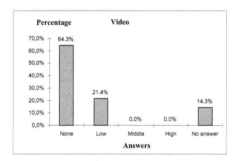

Figure 71.   USD - video included in content

As in the above analysis, video resources were not used very much in the courses (Figure 71 shows 21.4 percent of usage). For the same reasons as for the scarce use of audio: technical difficulties.

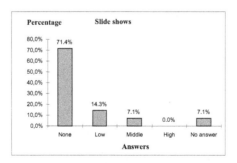

Figure 72.   USD - slide shows included in content

The USD platform offers a meeting-place for traditional educational tools and new technological resources. Slide shows summarize course content and would be very appropriate learning material. However, the professors used them very little, as Figure 72 confirms, showing once again that they need to make more of an effort in using the available resources.

Collaborative work:

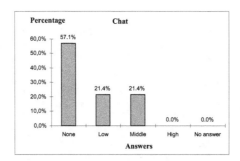

Figure 73.   USD – programmed chat activities

In general, the professors did not use chat facilities and did not encourage their use, either (Figure 73 shows more than 57 percent did not use chats at all). This was because most of the courses carried out in the USD platform were just a complement of the current, traditional, face-to-face courses and the students did not have the need to use it. The 42.8% that did use chats corresponds to the professors of distance courses, where the only way to establish collaborative work was through chats, forums or e-mail.

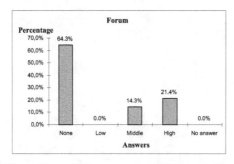

Figure 74.   USD – programmed forum activities

Figure 74 shows that 64.3 percent of the professors did not promote discussions by means of the *forum* tool in their courses. Most of the rest corresponded to the virtual courses.

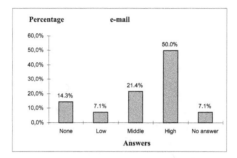

Figure 75.   USD - activities programmed by using the e-mail

Figure 75 shows that e-mail was the most popular tool since the professors encouraged its use when they built the teaching units.

About the teaching environment:

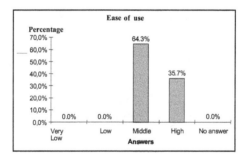

Figure 76.   USD – ease of use

In general, the USD platform offered the professors involved a friendly working environment with different and attractive tools for organizing didactic materials and generating the learning activities according to the nature of their courses. The ease of use of these tools was based on the training and practice the professors had already undertaken. Figure 76 shows 100% of the professors found it easy or very easy to use.

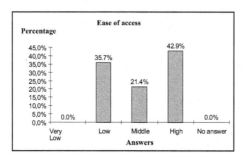

Figure 77.   Easiness for accessing the USD platform

Figure 77 shows that 57.1% of the professors did not access the platform easily (i.e. quickly) when building their teaching materials. This was due to the following factors:

- There were long delay when they connected to the USD platform through a 56 kbps modem.
- Incorrect opening of the session when this was carried out from different browsers or different versions of the same browser.
- Session blocked when it was closed down using an incorrect procedure.

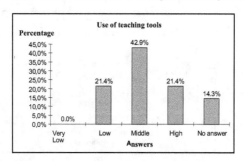

Figure 78.   USD – use of teaching tools

Figure 78 shows that all the professors used the teaching tools on offer. This use depended on the type of the courses prepared.

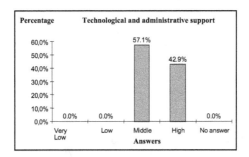

Figure 79.   USD Technological and administrative support

All of the professors felt supported in both the technological and administrative aspects of the platform as shown in Figure 79. 57.1% thought that this support could be further improved.

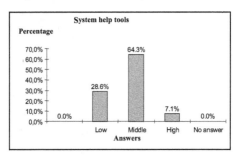

Figure 80.   USD – system help tool usage

Figure 80 shows that the professors worked with the existing help tools but that 28.6% said that they were insufficient.

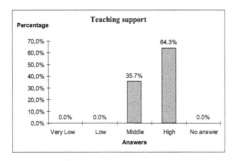

Figure 81.   USD – teaching support

As Figure 81 shows, the USD platform offered the support expected for building particular ODL courses at the University.

Student activities follow-up:

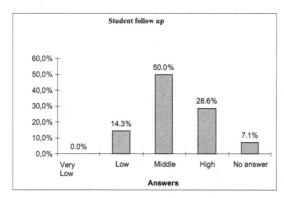

Figure 82.   USD - student follow up

92.9% of the professors followed-up the students' learning activities as shown in Figure 82. Some of the activities carried out by the professors were:

- Checking periodically, if students were accessing the teaching units and checking the exercises solved.
- Assisting the students during problem solving or assessment (synchronously or asynchronously).
- Drawing up evaluation scales that considered both the educational and technical aspects related to the proposed activities. The resolution of the exercises was also commented.
- Commenting on the proposed activities in face-to-face classes.
- Requesting the platform's technical team to provide data collected concerning the students' actions in spreadsheet format.
- Proposing discussions about specific topics of the teaching units.

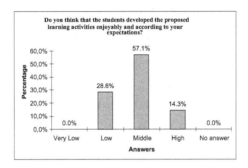

Figure 83.   USD - teachers' perception of student learning activities carried out

All the professors (see Figure 83) agreed the platform may be of some help to students, however, they consider necessary that the following aspects need further analysis:

- Some of the materials were made operational only at the end of the academic period and there was not enough time to study them in depth.
- Some professors found that a large number of students got access to the system just once, with the only objective of printing the teaching contents or the corrected answers for the proposed exercises.
- Problems of infrastructure relating to hardware and software used to access the USD platform. e.g. some students do not have a computer at home; typical incompatibility problems with different versions of the browsers used to navigate through the contents and the low bandwidth of some access devices. However, the problems were clearly more reduced when the students got access through the computer classrooms at University.
- The students were not used to use this type of learning environment and some found it hard to adjust to it.

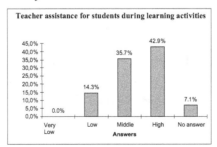

Figure 84.   USD - teacher assistance for students

Figure 84 shows that 92.9% of the professors were interested in assisting the students during the development of their learning activities. Some of the ways to assist students were:

- By e-mail or face-to-face interviews to deal with doubts concerning problem resolution, self-assessment or topic understanding.
- By organizing sessions for small groups of students to give instructions of using the platform and how to work with the proposed materials.
- By encouraging virtual meetings in the chat room in order to resolve various issues on-line.

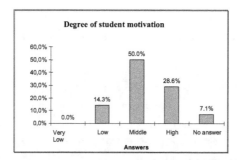

Figure 85.   USD – degree of student motivation

28.6% of the professors said that the students had a high degree of motivation for carrying out the proposed activities; while 14.3% thought the motivation was low, as can be seen in Figure 85. The professors used the following motivation techniques to encourage the students to carry out the learning activities successfully:

- Giving the evaluation exam with the same format of questions as the ones in the self-assessment exercises.
- Evaluating the actions carried out in the learning environment and the solved exercises. Also, the students could test their degree of understanding of the fundamental concepts of the subject through the platform.
- Allowing the testing of real cases using simulators (in some particular courses).
- Developing a specific mechanism to follow up the student's continuous learning progress.

The last two questions of the questionnaire were open questions. Below we summarize their responses.

What procedure(s) did you use to evaluate the learning activities carried out by the students on the USD platform?

- Analyzing the actions carried out by the students in the USD platform as they used teaching units (pages visited, time spent in studying particular pages, participation in programmed chats and forums, etc) and also evaluating the computed answers of the multiple-choice exercises.
- Only by analyzing the marks obtained marks by the students for the exercises.
- Having a regular face-to-face exam using the topics proposed in the teaching units.
- Applying the evaluation ratio proposed at the beginning of the course. For example, for a particular course the following evaluation ratio was computed: 10% of the grade for participation in the programmed chats, 5% for participation in the forums, 5% for answering questions using e-mail, 30% for visiting the all of the web pages of the teaching units and 50% for writing a project related to particular topics of the subjects under study.

In which aspects do you think that the USD platform should be improved to support distance teaching and learning processes?

- Improving the use of some of the teaching tools and especially those related to the follow-up of student activities in the learning environment. At present the system can only generate simple information about the student actions, sessions and visits to particular web pages of the proposed materials, however, it cannot carry out specific statistical analysis of this information (by means of graphics or histograms).
- Improving the process of getting access to the system. Sometimes, the delays are too long.
- Allowing for the use of any desired design in the web pages created to build a teaching unit. Currently this design is subject to particular features of the platform.
- Allowing access to the system by means of any of the common browsers and their related versions. Currently the USD platform is only accessible through recent versions of the MS Internet Explorer.

- Enabling tools for managing information on students.
- Improving the Teaching Unit Editor operation by making it more user-friendly in the graphic environment; in this way adaptive navigation of the proposed materials could be achieved through the establishment of relationships among nodes and through the inclusion of conditions in the arrows.
- Improvements in adapting better the contents according to special characteristics included in the pedagogical strategies.
- Improving the use of the Exercise Generator tool. Currently, it is a little difficult to work with.

Conclusions from the teachers' survey:

- Professors used electronic materials that had been prepared previously in text formats. This was mainly observed in teaching units built exclusively around theoretical contents. It was noticeable that there was a need for more diverse types of material to match student concerns.
- According to the nature of the teaching units offered, different types of media formats were used to explain the learning content.
- The learning activities prepared exclusively for distance students used the collaborative work tools to a very large degree.
- The teaching environment was easy to use for those professors who had the opportunity to practice using the teaching tools sufficiently.
- The tools offered to the professors to follow up student performance were used a great deal and also the enthusiasm of the professors involved in this new teaching modality was very high.

7.3.2   Students' Survey

Questionnaire 2 was answered by 104 students from six different courses at the USD learning environment. The course "Instructional Psychology" used its own questionnaire which is included in the following statistics.

General Statistics

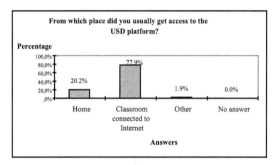

Figure 86.   USD – origin of connection

Most students got access to the platform from the classrooms (see Figure 86). This result was as expected, since the aim of most of the materials was to support face to face classes and therefore the students carried out some of the proposed learning activities during the class itself.

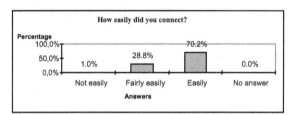

Figure 87.   USD – how easily students connected

In general, the students managed to connect to the USD platform easily (70.2 %, see Figure 87). They sometimes had some problems when they tried to connect via a 56k modem device or when they used versions of browsers different to the recommended browser.

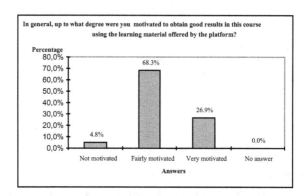

Figure 88.   USD - student motivation during the course

There was a notably positive attitude among the students with this learning approach, as shown in Figure 88. Students were very willing to collaborate, to try for the best results and to take advantage of the USD platform tools.

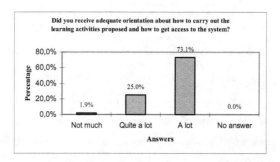

Figure 89.   USD - orientation instructions given to students

As Figure 89 shows, almost the 100 percent of the students received a lot or quite a lot of orientation from the professors in terms of developing the learning activities proposed. The professors used different strategies to offer a clear introduction to USD platform usage such as: sending informative electronic mail messages, doing a complete face to face session to test the system performance by demonstration or handling out a printed copy of the users' manual (which was also available on-line).

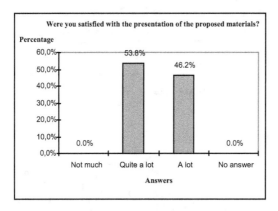

Figure 90.   USD - student satisfaction with the presentation of the material

The responses shown in Figure 90 seem closely related to the nature of the courses. However, almost all of the students benefited from the learning activities proposed and were satisfied with the presentation of the available materials. For instance, for Case studies in Criminal Law they could work on the cases with multiple choice exercises in text format, which is the most appropriate format for this area of knowledge. Course planning and organization carried out by the professors improved the comprehension of subjects presented in any format.

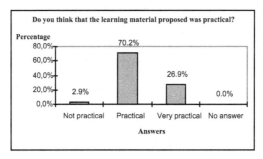

Figure 91.   USD material usefulness for students

The biggest percentage of students, shown in Figure 91, agreed that the material was useful because the professors included what best supported their learning on the course. For instance, students of *Case Studies in Criminal Law* analyzed case studies by means of multiple-choice exercises, students of *Basic Concepts in Statistics* solved problems common selecting questions with different degrees of difficulty and students of *Computer Networks* learned about theoretical subjects on networks and interacted with simulators verifying the performance of certain routing protocols.

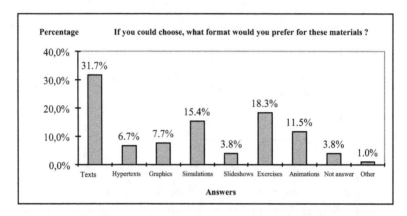

Figure 92.   USD - type of materials preferred by the students

As expected, since most of the answers collected from questionnaires came from students of *Case Studies in Criminal Law*, there was a tendency to prefer materials presented in text format. However, according to the students' remarks at this point, they prefer a combination of formats in order to make the learning process more interesting.

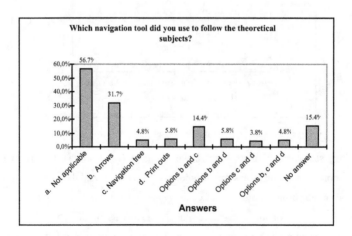

Figure 93.   USD – use of navigation tools

Figure 93 shows how the students chose to navigate through the learning contents. The **not applicable** answers (56.7 percent) corresponded to the students that did not need to navigate through the contents because they entered just to solve cases or do exercises, for example, the students from *Case Studies in Criminal Law* who just had to analyze specific problems outlined in case studies. The rest of the students tended to use all the navigation tools offered. 5.8 percent of the students printed out the learning content, particularly those from courses with a great deal of theoretical content.

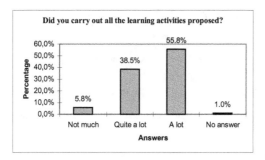

Figure 94.   USD degree of learning activities carried out

The responses shown in Figure 94 were as expected. Each professor made their teaching units with the purpose of allowing the students to assess the knowledge fro themselves and also to permit the system to grade part of the course (obligatory). The 5.8 percent of the students who responded **Not much** may had connection problems.

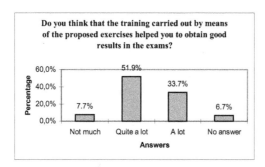

Figure 95.   USD - student perception of improvement in their exam results

The answers shown in the Figure 95 reflected to the learning activities proposed in the teaching units. For example, the students who had self-assessed their acquired knowledge had the advantage of arriving at the exam with more experience and practice than those who had not.

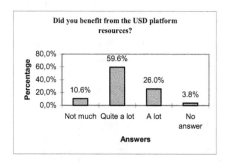

Figure 96.   USD – perceived benefit from the platform

As it may be observed in Figure 96, the students affirmed that they had benefited from the resources offered by the platform while carrying out the learning activities. However, according to student comments, very few of them tried to use different USD resources other than those recommended by the professor (Conductivist behavior).

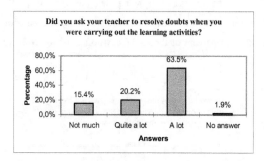

Figure 97.   USD – requests for teacher assistance

The fact that the first contact of the class was via computers ion the Internet was no obstacle to a close relationship forming between the professor and the students, as can be seen in Figure 97. Furthermore, since the professors were always willing to resolve the students' doubts, the students could ask questions more freely using different communication media.

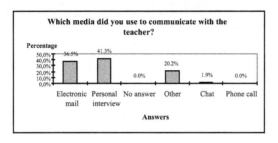

Figure 98.   USD - communication tools used by the students

The responses shown in Figure 98 depended a great deal on the courses that the students were following. For instance, as the approach of several courses was to support face to face classes, the on-line material was accessed from Internet classrooms and in consequence, getting a direct personal interview with the professors was easy. 37 percent of the students used e-mail to communicate with professors and which simply reflects the fact that we think that electronic mail is the most commonly-used Internet service.

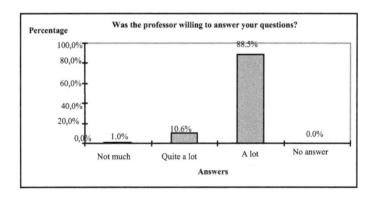

Figure 99.   USD - teachers' willingness to assist students

Almost all of the students were highly satisfied with the attention given to them by the professors during the learning activities. It would be noted that there was a lot of interest and a positive attitude among the students as well.

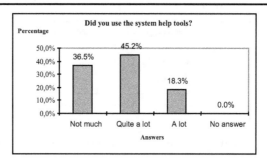

Figure 100.   USD – use of help tools

In this case, the system help tools merely consisted of an on-line user's manual. 36.5 percent of the students carried out their activities using the instructions given by the professors at the beginning of the course (see Figure 100).

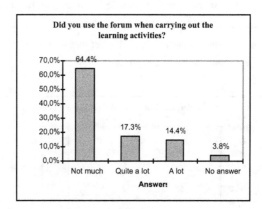

Figure 101.   USD – use of forum

The question involved in Figure 101 was asked to find out how much collaborative work was programmed by the professor during the learning activities. As most of the students who responded to the survey did not have to carry out activities with this tool, the answers show a majority did not use forums much. The 31.7 percent who answered more positively corresponded to the students assigned to the courses programmed to be accessed remotely (i.e. Intercampus courses).

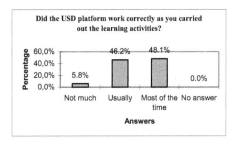

Figure 102.   USD – student perception of technical performance

Figure 102 shows that the performance of the USD platform was acceptable. In general the platform performance was adequate. 94.3 percent of the students could carry out the proposed activities without many problems, excepting the incompatibilities of different versions of the web browsers or when using low bandwidth connections to access the network.

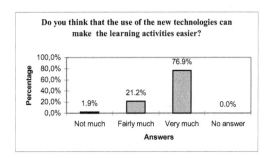

Figure 103.   USD – effect of new technologies on making learning easier

The students agreed (see Figure 103) that the new technologies could help the learning process. They felt, however, that their learning styles should be taken into account when designing the materials.

Conclusions from the students' survey:

- The students felt comfortable carrying out the learning activities proposed in the teaching units even though they would have preferred closer materials and tools.
- The students carried out the learning activities with the motivation of a good final mark.

- We noticed a certain tendency towards Conductivist behavior in the students' learning processes. They tend to use the USD platform resources when strictly necessary and in accordance with the professors guidance.
- The connection problems found and the incompatibilities presented when using different browsers led us to improve the educational framework and to think about redesigning the learning environment from this point of view.
- The students wanted to use more interactive materials with a combination of different media formats.
- There are a few students who do not accept this new method of education at all. They still prefer to study printed materials.

7.3.3 Students' Actions

Commonly carried out actions

The automatic registration of the actions carried out by the students during the sessions on the platform are shown in the following table:

Action Name	Number	Percentage
Click on the **forward** option of the navigation toolbar	16030	30,60
Click on the **back** option of the navigation toolbar	12108	23,11
Click on the **navigation tools** icon of the general tool bar	9039	17,25
Click on the **forum** icon	2090	3,99
Click on the **available destinations** option of the navigation toolbar	1921	3,67
Click on the **exercises** icon of the navigation toolbar	1731	3,30
Click on the **statistics** icon	1312	2,50
Click on the **navigation tree link** of the navigation toolbar	1297	2,48
Click on the **chat** icon	1278	2,44
Click on the icon to select the **type of exercises** to do	1102	2,10
Click on the button to check the personal **solved exercises**	911	1,74
Click on the **rectify** icon of the **current exercise** to check its result	735	1,40
Click on the **e-mail** icon	690	1,32
Click on the **solved exercises history** icon from the access statistics window	584	1,11
Click on the **bibliography** icon of the navigation toolbar	376	0,72
Click on the **glossary** word search icon	371	0,71
Click on the **help** icon	304	0,58
Click on the **print all unit pages** option of the teaching unit window menu	223	0,43
Click on the **glossary** displaying **all terms** icon	195	0,37
Click on the **print page** option of the teaching unit window menu	95	0,18
Total	52392	100,0%

It appears that most students went through the course sequentially since 70.96 percent of their actions involved the forward and backward arrows and the button to activate or deactivate the navigation tool bar. However, in terms of taking advantage of the possibilities of the platform, we expected higher percentages for actions such as the use of the glossary, bibliography, exercises and e-mail tools.

Students of ICT Resources in Educational Centers were carrying out the course in the platform as a requirement of their graduate studies. These students took advantage of the flexibility of the system, since they could log in anywhere and at any time.

Courses such as *Computer Networks*, *World Economy* and *Basic Concepts in Statistics* showed similar behavior whether connecting from home or from the classroom. These were complementary courses, for which part of the material was only to be found on the platform.

Study Cases in Criminal Law and *Instructional Psychology* consisted of exercises to be done in class time, which were evaluated immediately.

7.4   MASPLANG Evaluation

The evaluation of the USD platform revealed the existence of equal contents and navigation structure for all the students, even though they wanted a teaching environment more adapted to their individual interests. The results suggested that the learning outcomes might have been improved if designers of hypermedia courseware provided different presentations of materials, more dynamic tools, non sequential navigation and diverse instructional strategies to accommodate differences in individual learning styles.

The experience gained when setting up the USD platform and the methodical evaluation, led to the design and implementation of the MASPLANG platform. This was spurred on by the requests made by students either for learning procedures that took into account their learning profiles and starting from their current knowledge state, or significant assistance with affective behavior.

When the MASPLANG platform was available, the professors were trained to prepare the material in accordance with the learning profiles. They set up the materials and organized their courses and followed up the students' progress with the platform.

As the students used the new platform, they were categorized according to their ability to process, perceive, input, organize and understand the available information. With this classification, the platform was able to adapt the content and presentation of materials to the students' learning style and prepare it so that the students could follow the courses in a personalized way.

We will therefore describe how the MASPLANG platform was tested in three phases: first of all, the classification of the students' learning styles by the ILS[4] questionnaire; then we will give the results of questionnaires 1 and 2 (teachers' and students' perceptions) in the same way as we did for the USD platform; and finally, we provide a summary of the actions carried out by the students on the MASPLANG platform. The statistics shown correspond to 3 courses involving 5 professors and 25 students.

7.4.1   Students' Learning Styles

The FSLSM model is a synthesis of a great deal of research work that distinguishes four dichotomous dimensions to learning styles:

- The **processing** of information dimension differentiates **active** or **reflective** learners,

- The **perception** of information dimension differentiates **sensitive** or **intuitive** learners,

- The **input** of information dimension differentiates **visual** or **verbal** learners and

- The **progress of learning** dimension differentiates **sequential** or **global** learners.

---

[4] ILS: Index of Learning Style, a diagnostic tool of the FSLSM learning style model.

Information Processing

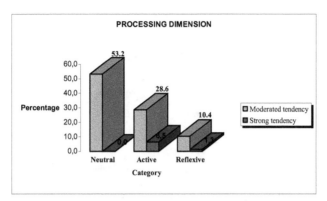

Figure 104.   How the student processes the information

The data from the above figure allows us to infer that 53.2 percent of the students process the information as it comes, 35.1 are active (6.5 strongly); i.e. they retain and understand better if they discuss or apply the knowledge, and 11.7 are reflective (1.3 strongly), i.e. they prefer to think about it calmly.

Information Perception

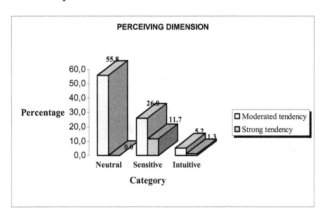

Figure 105.   How the student perceives the information

Figure 105 shows how the students perceive the information. 55.8 percent are neutral, 37.7 perceive the knowledge (better) when it is linked to reality (11.7 strongly) while 6.5 percent perceive it while looking for new concepts and feel comfortable with abstract ideas (1.3 strongly).

Information Input

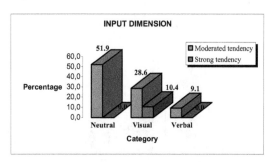

Figure 106.   How the student receives the information

How the information is received allows the students to be classified as *visual*, if they remember better when the information is given by means of drawings, diagrams, etc. (39 percent are visual, 10.4 strongly, as shown in Figure 106); or *verbal*, if they remember better when the information is given by means of texts and verbal explanations (9.1 percent are verbal), or neutral if they can receive information equally well, one way or the other (51.9 percent are neutral).

Student Progress

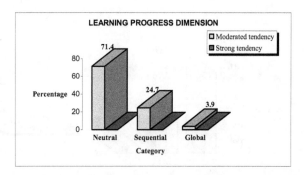

Figure 107.   How the student understands the information

Figure 107 shows that 3.9 percent of the students tend to understand the whole, 24.7 percent tend to understand step by step while 71.4 percent are neutral in this respect.

7.4.2   Teachers' Survey

Questionnaire 1 was answered by five professors, from 3 courses who used the MASPLANG teaching environment. The number of courses was small since the available time to test the prototype was just a couple of months.

Type of material offered:

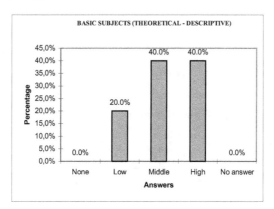

Figure 108.   MASPLANG - content type

The figure shows an increase in the amount of text included, since the same content as for the USD teaching units was used here, but further new content was added.

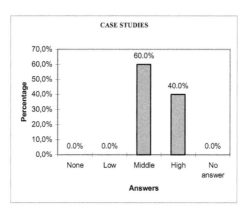

Figure 109.   MASPLANG – case studies included in content

As figure shows, all professors included case studies in the teaching units.

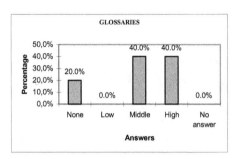

Figure 110.   MASPLANG - glossaries included in content

Taking the learning profile into account meant that the professors prepared more glossaries to facilitate learning for *global students*. Figure 110 shows that 80 percent of the professors included glossaries.

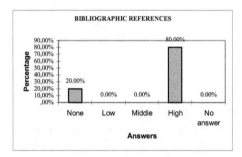

Figure 111.   MASPLANG - bibliographical references included in content

Figure shows that 80 percent of the professors used bibliography, since the courses were highly theoretical.

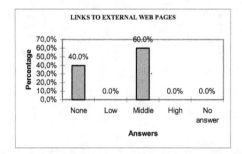

Figure 112.   MASPLANG - external web page links included in content

Figure 112 shows 60 percent included external links to provide additional information.

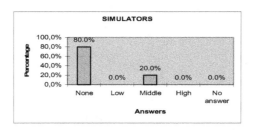

Figure 113. MASPLANG - simulators available in content

Figure 113 shows levels of simulator use for the MASPLANG platform, which was similar to the levels for the USD (see Figure 64).

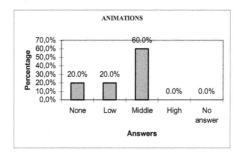

Figure 114. MASPLANG animations included in contents

The animations were used much more in MASPLANG (see Figure 114), perhaps in order to take advantage of the learning profile presentation format.

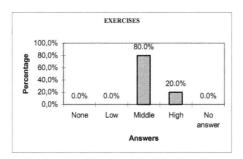

Figure 115. MASPLANG - exercises included in content

Figure 115 shows an increase in the number of exercises included in the courses with respect to USD courses, since, in MASPLANG, there is an agent which adapts the exercises to the student knowledge level.

Media and formats used:

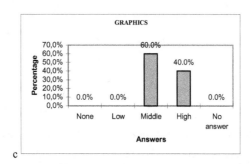

Figure 116.   MASPLANG - graphics included in content

The professors felt much more motivated to include graphics in the new platform. In fact, Figure 116 shows that all professors included this kind of material.

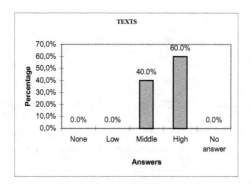

Figure 117.   MASPLANG - texts included in content

As expected and as a logical result, all the professors used texts on a large scale to build their Teaching Units for the MASPLANG platform, as was the case with the USD platform.

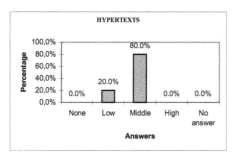

Figure 118.   MASPLANG - hypertext included in content

The use of hypertexts in MASPLANG was similar to that in USD, as shown in Figure 118.

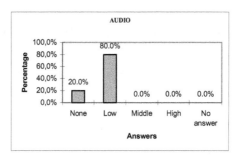

Figure 119.   MASPLANG - audio included in content

This kind of material was used very little in both platforms as indicated in Figure 119 for MASPLANG and Figure 70 for USD. It is possible that in the future its use will increase, especially in language courses.

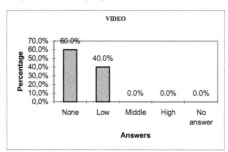

Figure 120.   MASPLANG - video included in content

Similarly, Figure 120 shows that video was introduced very little in the courses in MASPLANG (as was the case for USD). It is expected that in the future all areas of virtual teaching would take advantage of this resource especially since the MASPLANG system can give support for different learning styles.

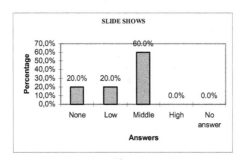

Figure 121.   MASPLANG - slides shows included in content

The MASPLANG platform offers a meeting-place for the traditional educational tools and education that makes use of new technological resources. Slide shows are a good alternative for providing students with a synopsis of the different course subjects. The professors took greater advantage of this resource in MASPLANG than in USD, as shown in Figure 121.

Collaborative work:

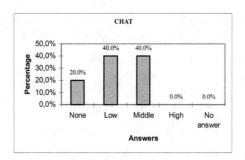

Figure 122.   MASPLANG – programmed chat activities

Figure 122 shows an increase in number of chat sessions programmed by professors compared to the USD platform, perhaps because the professors had more confidence in the new platform.

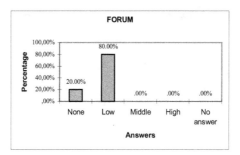

Figure 123.   MASPLANG – programmed forum activities

Figure 123 shows an increase in the use of discussions in MASPLANG courses compared to USD despite facilities for forums being similar in both platforms.

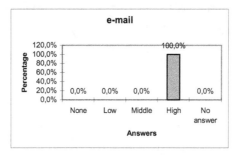

Figure 124.   MASPLANG – programmed e-mail activities

As can be seen in Figure 124, all the professors encouraged the use of e-mail more than any other collaborative work tool. The confidence they had in using e-mail meant they concentrated on this means of intercommunication with students.

About the teaching environment:

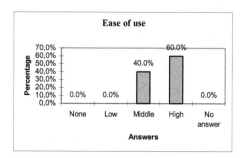

Figure 125.   MASPLANG - ease of use

The MASPLANG platform offered a similar working environment to the USD platform. There was a slight improvement in how professors rated ease of use which may have been due to the need to prepare more material to adapt to each student learning profile and hence more experience and practice with the platform.

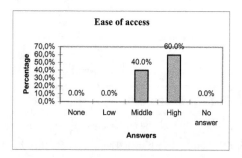

Figure 126.   Ease of access into the MASPLANG platform

Figure 126 shows that all the professors found it easier to access the MASPLANG platform (compared to the USD platform – see Figure 77). This was because MASPLANG uses faster access technology.

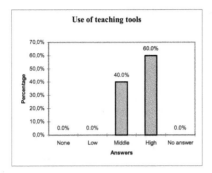

Figure 127.   MASPLANG – use of teaching tools

Figure 127 shows all the professors used the teaching tools; moreover, professors were more motivated to offer courses adapted to the student.

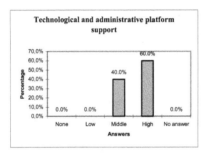

Figure 128.   MASPLANG - technological and administrative support

All the professors felt supported by the managers of the platform.

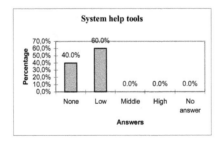

Figure 129.   MASPLANG – system help tools

The professors thought that the system help tools could be improved, as Figure 129 shows.

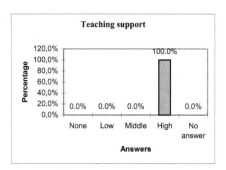

Figure 130.　MASPLANG – teaching support

According to the figure, all the professors consider that the MASPLANG platform was good (excellent, "100% high") for building ODL courses.

Student activities follow-up:

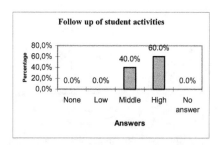

Figure 131.　MASPLANG - student follow up

The behavior of professors in following up on students' learning activities through the teaching units for the MASPLANG platform, was similar to that of the USD.

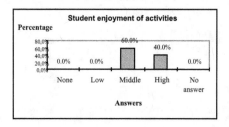

Figure 132.　MASPLANG - teachers' perception of student enjoyment of activities

The professors considered, as shown in Figure 132, that the students enjoyed the learning activities.

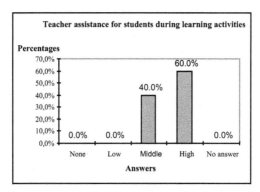

Figure 133.   MASPLANG - teacher assistance for students

The professors provided more assistance for the students during the development of their learning activities when using MASPLANG, as shown in Figure 133.

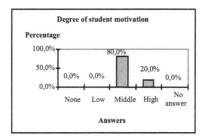

Figure 134.   MASPLANG – degree of student motivation

All the professors considered that the students had a higher degree of motivation to carry out the proposed activities. The results shown in Figure 134 were expected since the MASPLANG platform takes the student profile into account when offering course contents.

The answers to the last two questions from Questionnaire 1 are summarized below:

What procedure(s) did you use to evaluate the learning activities carried out by the students on the MASPLANG platform?

The professors reproduced evaluation strategies used in the USD platform in order to motivate the use of the new platform.

In which aspects do you think that the MASPLANG platform should be improved to support distance teaching and learning processes?

- The flexibility of the teacher's desktop needs to be improved.
- Tools need to be enabled to follow up students automatically. In this case, the idea is to implement assistant agents for the teacher in the MASPLANG platform.

Conclusions from the teachers' survey:

- Professors re-used the electronic materials prepared previously for the course web pages and for the USD platform and prepared additional material for students aimed at building up the teaching units on the MASPLANG platform.
- The teaching environment may be improved by providing additional help for the professors.
- The professors had to prepare varied material to allow the platform to adapt to the students' profile.
- The professors were notably enthusiastic about constructing more teaching units to match student learning styles.

7.4.3 Students' Survey

Questionnaire 2 was answered by twenty five students, from three courses, who used the MASPLANG teaching environment.

General Statistics

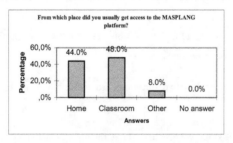

Figure 135.   MASPLANG – origin of connection

Figure 135 shows that students accessed the platform in similar proportions from home and from the classroom.

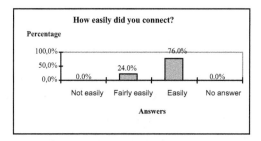

Figure 136.   MASPLANG – how easily students connected

In general and as Figure 136 shows, the students managed to connect easily. Access to the MASPLANG platform was slightly better with respect to that of the USD platform (99 percent found it easy or fairly easy with USD).

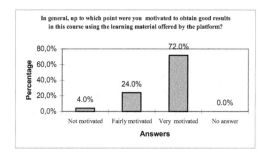

Figure 137.   MASPLANG - student motivation during the course

Figure 137 shows the students were highly motivated to collaborate. This was expected since most of the new developments were aimed at adapting the platform to the students' profile.

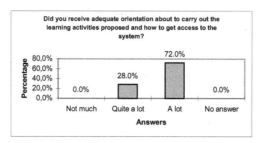

Figure 138.   MASPLANG - orientation given to students

As Figure 138 shows, the students were satisfied with the instructions from professors about how to use the new platform.

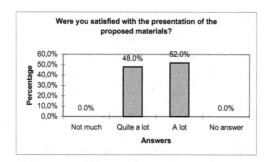

Figure 139.   MASPLANG - student satisfaction with the presentation of the material

In general (see Figure 139)) the students benefited from the materials offered, as they did when using the USD platform.

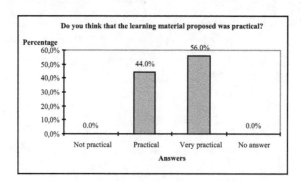

Figure 140.   MASPLANG material usefulness for students

As the students had better, more dynamic access to the material, which was more orientated toward them, they felt it was much more useful, as shown in Figure 140.

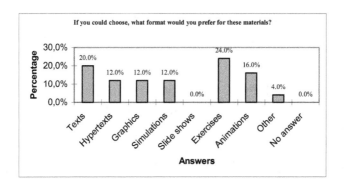

Figure 141.   MASPLANG - type of materials preferred by the students

The students felt more at home and more confident with the flexibility and variety of materials available in the teaching units of MASPLANG (see Figure 141). The results are consistent with the tendency showed by the students in the **receive** dimension of the FSLSM model (detected by means of the ILS questionnaire).

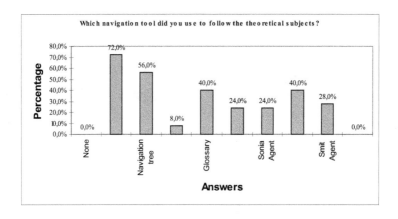

Figure 142.   MASPLANG – use of navigation tools

Figure 142 shows an increase in the use of navigation tools with respect to the USD platform. Noticeably, the students used agents *SONIA*, *SMIT* and *Exercise adapter*, as much as the *glossary*, the *search tool* and the more classical *arrows* and *navigation tree* tools. As may be observed from the graph, many students used several different navigation tools.

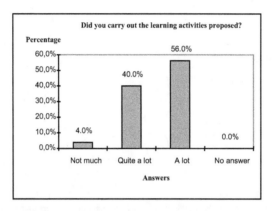

Figure 143.   MASPLANG – degree to which learning activities were carried out

The responses shown in Figure 143 were as expected, because the MASPLANG platform adapted to the student learning model and each professor made their teaching units to allow the students to self-assess their knowledge.

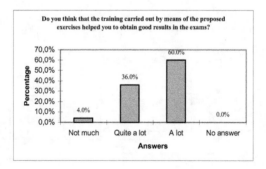

Figure 144.   MASPLANG - student perception of improvement in their exam results

The students thought that the exercises helped them in the learning process, as shown in Figure 144. This might be because the *Exercise Adapter Agent* configured the exercises to match the student needs.

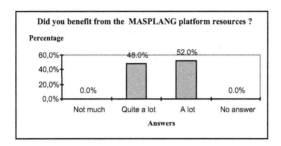

Figure 145.   MASPLANG – perceived benefit from the platform

The students benefited highly from the resources offered by the MASPLANG platform (see Figure 145) perhaps because the platform adapted to their needs.

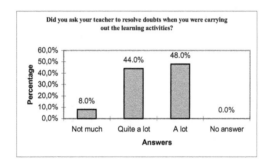

Figure 146.   MASPLANG – requests for teacher assistance

As Figure 146 shows, most of the students asked the teachers for help and since the professors were available in different ways to resolve students' doubts, the students could ask them freely in person or by using different communication media.

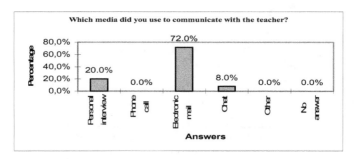

Figure 147.   MASPLANG - communication tools used by the students

The confidence the students had with e-mail, led to them using it to a very high degree (72 percent). Figure 147 shows only 20 percent students communicated by the professors by personal interview and 8 percent by chat.

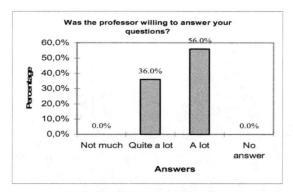

Figure 148.   MASPLANG – teacher willingness to assist students

The students were as satisfied with the attention offered by the professors to them when using the MASPLANG, as they were when using USD.

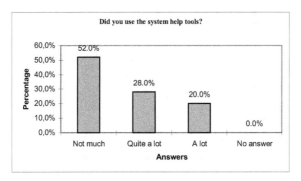

Figure 149.   MASPLANG – use of help tools

As Figure 149 shows, students want more on line help in the platform (or maybe 52.0 percent of them did not need help because the platform was easy to use).

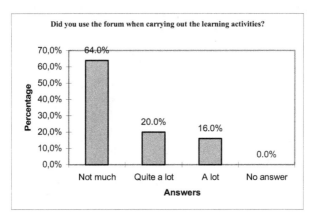

Figure 150.   MASPLANG – use of forum

Figure 150 shows that the use of forum by the students must be encouraged if it is to be considered relevant and beneficial for the course. In this aspect, the two platforms were alike.

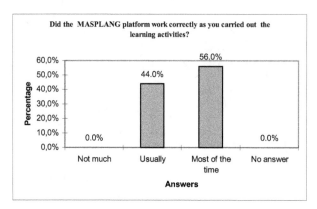

Figure 151. MASPLANG – student perception of technical performance

The students were as confident with the MASPLANG platform as they were with the USD.

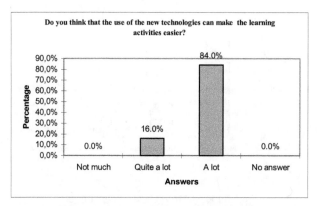

Figure 152. MASPLANG – effect of new technologies on making learning easier

The students think, as shown in Figure 152, that new technologies facilitate the learning process since they may go at any pace and from anywhere they want. With MASPLANG, they come closer to their preferred learning style.

Conclusions from the students' survey:

- The students felt much more comfortable working on MASPLANG.
- The students carried out the learning activities motivated by the adaptivity of the platform.
- The variety of tools and materials used by the students is due to the student learning style detected by the ILS questionnaire.
- The connection problems and the browser incompatibilities presented when using the USD learning environment were corrected in the MASPLANG version.
- The students felt more assisted by the professors through the MASPLANG either because of the design of the course itself or as they carried out the learning activities.
- The students felt more assisted by the platform tools.

7.4.4 Students' Actions

Commonly carried out actions

The actions carried out by the students during the different sessions inside the platform were automatically registered. The most common actions are shown in the following table:

Action Name	Number	Percentage
Click on the **forward** option of the navigation toolbar	3035	11.29
Click on the links of the **navigation tree** window	2712	10.09
Click on the **exercise adapter** icon of the navigation toolbar	2707	10.07
Click on the **glossary** icon of the navigation toolbar	1876	6.98
Click on the link to automatically adapt exercises from the **exercise adapter**	1819	6.77
Click on the **back** option of the navigation toolbar	1554	5.78
Click on the link to configure exercises from the **exercise adapter**	1537	5.72
Click on the **searching word** icon in the **glossary** option	1405	5.23
Click on the **Smit** *agent* icon of the navigation toolbar	1398	5.20
Click on the **alphabetic term list** icon in the **glossary** option	1231	4.58
Click on the **navigation tools** icon	1196	4.45
Click on the icon to check the solved exercise results from the exercise body	1115	4.15
Click on the icon to check the solved exercise solution from the exercise body	1093	4.07
Click on the **Sonia agent** icon	997	3.71
Click on the **printing** icon of the navigation toolbar	904	3.36
Click on the **e-mail** icon	764	2.84
Click on the **statistics** icon	713	2.65
Click on the **forum** icon	209	0.78
Click on the solved exercises' registry icon from the **statistics** window	201	0.75
Click on the **bibliography** icon of the navigation toolbar	165	0.61
Click on the **chat** icon	117	0.44
Click on the **help** icon of the navigation toolbar	84	0.31
Click on the **learning style** icon	53	0.20
Total	**26885**	**100,03%**

7.5 Conclusions

Due to the increasing availability of tools that make it easy and efficient to create hypertext/multimedia documents, a growing community of teachers is experimenting with the use of such facilities to support their learning courses.

Full advantage of teachers efforts can be taken by developing digital platforms such as the USD and the MASPLANG platforms, that avoid the burden of monitoring and provide learning tools the students might use.

We have presented the perceptions of professors and students. The perceived drawbacks of the digital courses when using USD platform were overcome with the MASPLANG platform.

More work needs to be done on increasing flexibility to allow teachers to set up and update their courses. However the interface, adapted to the students' needs is very well set up on MASPLANG. The use of a multiagent platform to adapt the courses (exercises, navigation tools, content presentation, etc.) to the student learning model and knowledge state, with specialized agents to attend the student needs (*Sonia, Smit, Exercise adapter*, etc.), has been shown to be successful despite the fact that this project is still in its early stages.

Conclusions Part 2

In Part 2 we showed the logical and technological solution proposed for the development of the MASPLANG as an adaptive e-learning system. The following schema summarizes the methods and techniques involved:

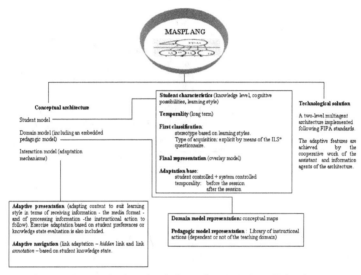

Figure. 153.   Methods and techniques for MASPLANG development

In chapters 5 and 6, the kernel of the conceptual and agent models was described in detail. Figure 154 below shows the global activity of the agents working together to achieve their goals (IA represents the information agents that are closer to databases and PDA represents the assistant agents that are closer to the student). The results of the experimentation carried out by means of the prototype implemented with the proposed multiagent architecture were described in Chapter 7. From this experience, we may conclude that the proposed solution is viable for the e-learning community, who expect a personalized and assisted education with a touch of "humanity".

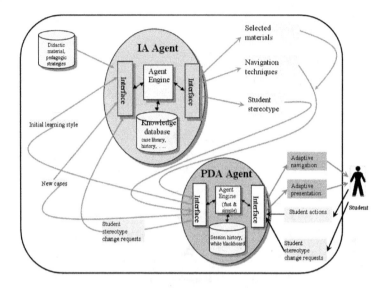

Figure. 154.   MASPLANG activity diagram

General Conclusions

General Conclusions and Future Work

Conclusions

In this book, various aspects concerning e-learning have been presented. They include some pedagogical, psychological and technological aspects which have been investigated deeply. The main motivation in proposing the MASPLANG architecture and methodology was the need to offer students the didactic material best suited to their individual learning profile. This is achieved in combination with a user-friendly style, assisted and customized environment provided by the first implementation of the e-learning platform USD ("Unitats de Suport a la Docència").

In achieving the proposed objectives of adaptivity, Agent Technology has been successfully applied. Working with agents has been highly interesting. Although the proposed architecture is quite complex, the parallelization of the work allowed by such technology was crucial in achieving the desired functionality. The systematic design of the ontology facilitates the overall process. It is also remarkable that the addition of the agent gives a more comfortable feeling for users, in particular the anthropomorphic aspect of the SMIT agent when presenting messages.

The conceptual model of the proposed adaptive hypermedia system is based on a standard architecture; however, the domain, student and interaction models have been designed and added on the basis of previous experience using the USD platform.

There is a prototype MASPLANG system available for some experimentation with reduced groups. This allows us to check some of the desired features of the MASPLANG methodology, in particular the behavior of the agent architecture and its "influence" on this new way of working on the platform, for both teachers and students. The collaborative work of the agent system eventually provided the expected adaptivity.

In conclusion, the main features of the MASPLANG can be summarized as follows:

- The system makes it easier for teachers to design, publish and manage their courses. A set of high level, flexible and ergonomic tools are provided for creating the domain model, to check on student progress and to communicate with them.
- Assistant agents can be set up at the client side (browser). This avoids unnecessary communication with the agents, at the server side, that can result in a degradation of the performance of the overall system.
- Students can access their study material through an adaptable and adaptive environment. In particular, I would like to point out the role of the exercise adapter and the SMIT agents which are closer to the users assisting them during their learning process.

Experimentation results show that teachers tend to re-use the electronic materials prepared previously in text formats to build the new e-learning units, especially units built exclusively around theoretical contents. The learning activities prepared exclusively for distance students used the collaborative work tools a great deal. The teaching environment was easy to use for those professors who were used to working with computers to produce material or who had the opportunity to practice using the teaching tools sufficiently. The effectiveness of the tools offered to the professors to follow up students' performance was appreciated, as the enthusiasm demonstrated by teachers involved in this new teaching modality.

With regard to the students' behavior and attitude, the main conclusions are:

- Students felt comfortable developing the learning activities proposed in the teaching units concerned;
- They carried-out the learning activities, motivated to achieve a good result in the final exams when using self-assessment materials.
- A slight tendency towards behaviorism was detected in the students' learning processes; students still used only those USD platform resources that were strictly necessary. The guidance of teachers or tutors still has a great influence on student activity.

- Some students do not accept this new modality of education at all, preferring to study using printed materials.
- The students wanted to use more interactive materials with a combination of different media formats.

Future work

Based on the theoretical design and experimentation with the MASPLANG, some improvements and new features have been envisaged. Most of them can be carried out with no (or minor) modifications of the proposed system architecture, database design and ontology.

The SONIA agent programmed tasks can be enlarged with new features. For instance, an additional, new function as a notebook allowing students to manage their own notes strongly linked with the system content and structure: let's say an "intelligent notebook". The action library of the SMIT agent could also be enlarged with new and configurable animations and of the chance to change the appearance of the agent (male, female, type of voice, clothes, etc).

Teachers can also be helped with new assistants that can help to keep accurate information about students' progress and behavior. This should be carried out automatically with little or no effort on the part of the teacher. This would include presentation, in graphs, charts, etc., of learning behavior and tendencies, in particular those with no standard parameters.

In the near future, the didactic material should be developed and published following the Instructional Management Systems (IMS) standard. This has to be carried out in a transparent manner by teachers (i.e. without any programming work for the teacher). This can be done by using XML attributes associated with independent didactic objects when edited in the MASPLANG platform.

Students should be updated periodically about changes detected in their behavior, in as far as this implies the format and way in which the lesson material is presented. A continuous assessment of the learning process can also be improved by adding new types of exercises.

As on-line communication tools improve, teachers could provide additional explanations about the most difficult points through a shared whiteboard. A preliminary version of this mechanism was experimented with in the previous USD platform.

In short, it is also desirable to widen the range of experimentation with larger numbers of regular courses, students and didactic units (specifically redesigned for such adaptive environments).

Finally, as an ongoing task, the system should be fine-tuned and improved to provide the best performance with the latest versions of most common browsers. Nevertheless, there has to be a compromise between best performance and the compatibility and the ease with which a system, working with new browser features, can be maintained.

General Bibliography

Personal Publications

[Agu 2002a] Aguilar, M., Peña, C. I., Fabregat, R. SMIT: un agente sintético antropomórfico para un entorno virtual de aprendizaje, Conferencia Internacional sobre Educación, Formación y Nuevas Tecnologías, VirtualEduca 2002, Valencia (España), Junio 12-14, 2002.

[Agu 2002] Aguilar, M., Peña, C. I., Fabregat, R. SMIT: diseño e implementación de un agente sintético de presentación para las Unidades de Soporte a la Docencia del PLAN-G, VIII Jornadas de Enseñanza Universitaria de la Informática, JENUI 2002, Cáceres (España), Julio 10-12, 2002, p.p. 313-320, ISBN: 84-600-9782-X.

[Fab 1999] Fabregat, R., Marzo, J. L. and Peña, C. I. PLAN-G: Plataforma Telemática para la Enseñanza Abierta y a Distancia Utilizando el Web como Soporte, Revista de Enseñanza y Tecnología Nro. 15, Asociación para el Desarrollo de la Informática Educativa, pp. 27 - 41, España, 1999, ISSN 1138-7386.

[Fab 2000] Fabregat, R., Peña, C. I. Teleeducación: la unidad de soporte a la docencia virtual de la UDG, Congreso Latinoamericano de Telecomunicaciones, Universidad Tecnológica de Panamá, Ciudad de Panamá, Panamá, Octubre 2000, Congreso Internacional de Ingeniería de Sistemas, Universidad Industrial de Santander, Bucaramanga, Colombia, Noviembre 2000.

[Fab 2000a] Fabregat, R., Marzo, J. L., Peña, C. I. Teaching Support Units, Kluwer Academic Publishers 2000: *Computers and Education in the 21st Century*, p.p. 163-174, ISBN 0-7923-6577-1.

[Mar 2002] Marzo, J. L., Peña, C. I., Mantilla, C., Carrillo, L. Evaluating distributed learning at the University of Girona, First GALECIA (Group for Advanced Learning Environments using Communication and Information Aids) workshop, IE2002, Vigo (Spain), Noviembre 20-22, 2002, ISBN 848158-227-1.

[Mar 2003] Marzo, J.L., Peña, C.I., Aguilar, M., Palencia, X., Alemany, A., Vallès, M., and Johè, A. Adaptive multiagent system for a web-based tutoring environment, Agentcities.Net project IST-2000-28384 - final report, March 2003.

[Peñ 1999] Peña, C. I. and Marzo, J. L. Adaptive Intelligent Agent Approach to Guide the Web Navigation on the PLAN-G Distance Learning Platform, IEE Colloquium "Lost in the Web - Navigation on the Internet", London, November 1999, UK ISSN 0963-3308.

[Peñ 2000]   Peña, C. I. Guía pedagógica para la generación de contenidos didácticos en sistemas de tutoría inteligente, tutorial de guía al profesor en la plataforma USD de la Universitat de Girona, Julio 2000.

[Peñ 2000a]   Peña, C. I., Fabregat, R., Marzo, J. L. WWW-based Tools to Manage Teaching Units in the PLAN-G Distance Learning Platform,   World Conference on Educational Multimedia, Hypermedia & Telecommunications, Association for the Advancement of Computing in Education, EDMEDIA 2000, Montreal, July 2000, p.p. 1251-1252, ISBN-1-88-00-94-40-1.

[Peñ 2000b]   Peña, C. I., Fabregat, R., Urra, A. and Vallès, M. Gestor de Pizarras Compartidas, Libreta de Notas y Marcas para la Plataforma Telemática del PLAN-G, II Simposio Internacional de Informática Educativa, SIIE2000, Puerto Llano, Ciudad Real, España, Noviembre 2000.

[Peñ 2000c]   Peña, C. I. Sistemas multiagente para el tratamiento de la información en el web: agentes de interfaz, agentes de información, agentes de aprendizaje, agentes intermediarios, I Congreso Internacional de Ingeniería de Sistemas - EISI 30 años, Universidad Industrial de Santander, Bucaramanga, Colombia, Noviembre 2000.

[Peñ 2000d]   Peña, C. I., Fabregat, R., Marzo, J. L. and González, E. Producción y Desarrollo de Material Docente Dinámico, Interactivo y Adaptativo para la Enseñanza de la Familia de Protocolos TCP/IP a través de la Plataforma Telemática Educativa PLAN-G, V Congreso Iberoamericano de Informática Educativa, RIBIE2000, Viña del Mar, Chile, Diciembre 2000.

[Peñ 2001]   Peña, C. I., Fabregat, R., Urra, A., Vallès, M. and Marzo, J. L. Shared Whiteboard Manager and Student Notebook for the PLAN-G Telematic Platform. Kluwer Academic Publishers 2001: Computers and Education - Towards an Interconnected Society, p.p. 283-295, ISBN 0-7923-7188-7.

[Peñ 2002a]   Peña, C. I., Marzo, J. L., De la Rosa, J. Ll. Intelligent Agents in a Teaching and Learning Environment on the Web, 2ond IEEE International Conference on Advanced Learning Technologies (ICALT2002), Kazan (Russia), September 9-12, 2002, p.p. 21-27, ISBN 0-473-08801-0.

[Peñ 2002b]   Peña, C.I., Marzo, J. L., De la Rosa, J. Ll., Fabregat, R. Un sistema de tutoría inteligente adaptativo considerando estilos de aprendizaje, IV congreso iberoamericano de informática educativa, IE2002, Vigo (España), Noviembre 20-22, 2002, ISBN 848158-227-1.

Bibliography

[Aam 1994] Aamodt, A., Plaza, E. Case-Based Reasoning: Foundational Issues, Methodological Variations, and System Approaches, AI Communications, IOS Press, Vol. 7:1, pp. 39-59, 1994.

[Ade 1992] Adelson B. Evocative Agents and Multi-Media Interface Design. In *Proc. of the UIST'92 (ACM SIGGRAPH Symp. on User Interface Software and Technology)*, pages 351–356, Monterey, CA, U.S.A., 1992.

[Aks 1988] Aksscyn, R.M., McCracken, D.L., Yoder, E.A. "KMS: A Distributed Hypermedia System for Managing Knowledge in Organizations". Communications of ACM, Vol.31, No. 7. June 1988.

[And 1983] Anderson, J.R. *The Architecture of Cognition*. Cambridge MA: Harvard University Press, 1983.

[And 1985] Anderson, J.R. and Reiser, B., The LISP tutor, *Byte*, 10(4):159-175, 1985.

[And 1996] André, E. and Rist, T. Copying with temporal constraints in multimedia presentation planning. In Proceedings of the Thirteenth Nacional Conference on Artificial Intelligence, pp. 142-147, 1996.

[And 1997] André, E., Rist, T. and Müller, J. WebPersona: A Life-Like Presentation Agent for Educational Applications on the World Wide Web. Proceedings of the workshop "Intelligent Educational Systems on the World Wide Web", 8th World Conference of the AIED Society, Kobe, Japan, 1997.

[And 1998] André, E., Rist, T., and Müller, J. Integrating reactive and scripted behaviors in a life-like presentation agents. In K.P. Sycara and M. Wooldridge (Eds.), Proc. of the Second International Conference on Autonomous Agents, pp. 261-268, 1998.

[Are 1992] Arents, H., Bogaerts, W. Information Structuring for Intelligent Hypermedia: A Knowledge Engineering Approach., Database and Expert System Applications, DEXA'92, 1992.

[Are 1993] Arens, Y., Hovy, E. and Vossers M. On the Knowledge Underlying Multimedia Presentations, in Maybury M. (ed), Intelligent Multimedia Interfaces, AAAI Press, pp 280-306, 1993.

[Arr 1998] Arruarte, A. Fundamentos y diseño de IRIS: un entorno para la generación de sistemas de enseñanza inteligentes. Tesis doctoral. Euskal Erico Unibertsitatea UPV/EHU. 1998.

[Atk 1995] Atkinson, B. et. al., IBM Intelligent Agents. Unicom Seminar on Agent Software, London, UK, May 25, 1995.

[AAACE1]   AACE, Proceedings of the AACE World Conference on Educational Multimedia/Hypermedia (EDMEDIA 96), (Boston, MA, Jun), 1996.

[AAACE2]   AACE, Proceedings of the Second AACE World Conference on Educational Multimedia/Hypermedia (EDMEDIA 97), (Calgary, Canada, Jun), 1997.

[AIT]   Habitat-Pro^{TM} Environment, Agents Inspired Technologies Corporation, University of Girona, Girona, Spain, 2001, http://www.agentsinspired.com.

[Bac 1996] Bacher, C. and Ottmann, T. Tools and services for authoring on the fly. Proceedings of the AACE World Conference on Educational Multimedia/Hypermedia (EDMEDIA 96), (Boston, MA, Jun), 7-12, 1996.

[Bal 1994] Balasubramanian, V. State of the Art Review on Hypermedia Issues and Applications, Graduate School of Management, Rutgers University, Newark, NJ, 1994.

[Bal 1994a] Balasubramanian, V. and Turoff, M. Incorporating Hypertext Functionality into Software Systems. New Jersey Institute of Technology: Workshop on Incorporating Hypertext Functionality into Software Systems I, Institute for Integrated Systems Research Technical Report #95-10, 1994.

[Bal 2001] Baldoni, M., Baroglio, C. and Patti, V. Structereless, Intention-guided Web Sites: Planning Based Adaptation. In Proc. 1st International Conference on Universal Access in Human-Computer Interaction, a track of HCI International 2001, New Orleans, LA, USA, 2001. Lawrence Erlbaum Associates, 2001.

[Bal 2001a] Baldoni, M., Giordano, L., Martelli, A. and Patti, V. Reasoning about complex actions with incomplete knowledge: a modal approach. In Proc. of the 7th Italian Conference on Theoretical Computer Science, (ICTCS01), volume 2202 of LNCS, Torino, Italy, October 2001.

[Bar 1976] Barr, A., Beard, M., and Atkinson, R. C. The computer as tutorial laboratory: the Stanford BIP project. International Journal on the Man-Machine Studies 8 (5), 567-596, 1976.

[Bar 1990] Barker, J. and Tucker, R. The Interactive Learning Revolution: Multimedia in Education and Training, Kogan-Page, London, 1990.

[Bar 1999] Barra, M., Negro, A. & Scarano, V. When the Teacher learns: a Model for Symmetric Adaptivity. Proceedings of Second Workshop on Adaptive Systems and User Modeling on the World Wide Web, Banff, Canada, 1999.

[Bat 1994]   Bates, J. The role of emotion in believable agents. Commun. ACM
               37, 7 (July), 122-125, 1994.

[Bay 1999]   Baylor, A. Intelligent agents as cognitive tools for education.
               Educational Technology, Volume XXXIX (2), 36-41, 1999.

[Bea 1994]   Beaumont, I. User Modeling in the Interactive Anatomy Tutoring
               System ANATOM-TUTOR. User Modeling and User-Adapted
               Interaction, pp. 21-45, 1994.

[Bec 1996]   Beck, J. Stern, M. and Haugsjaa, E. Applications of AI in education,
               ACM Cross-roads, 1996.

[Bel 1992]   Beltran, T. Educational Hypermedia: from theory to practice,
               EDMEDIA 1993.

[Ben 1987]   Benyon, D.R., Innocent P.R., Murray, D.M. System adaptivity and
               the modeling of stereotypes. In: B. Shackel and H-J. Bullinger
               (Eds.), Proc. INTERACT '87, Second IFIP Conference on Human-
               Computer Interaction (Ámsterdam: Elsevier Science Publishers
               B.V.), 1987.

[Ben 1993]   Benyon D.R. Adaptive systems: A solution to Usability Problems,
               Journal of user modeling and user adapted interaction, Kluwer, 3(1)
               pp. 1-22, 1993.

[Ben 1993b]   Benyon, D.R. Accommodating Individual Differences through an
               Adaptive User Interface. In Schneider-Hufschmidt, M., Kuhme, T.
               and Malinowski, U. (eds.) Adaptive User Interfaces - Results and
               Prospects, Elsvier Science Publications, North-Holland,
               Amsterdam. 1993.

[Ben 1994]   Beynon-Davies, P., Tudhope, D., Taylor, D., and Jones C. A
               Semantic Approach to Knowledge-Based Hypermedia Systems. In
               Information and Software Technology, 36(6), pp 323-329, 1994.

[Ber 1992]   Berners-Lee, T., Cailliau, R., Groff, J.F. and Pollermann B. World-
               Wide Web: The Information Universe. Electronic Networking:
               Research, Applications and Policy, Vol. 1, No. 2, Meckler
               Publishing, 1992.

[Ber 1992a]   Bernsen, N.O. Matching Information and Interface Modalities: An
               Example Study, WPCS-92-1, Roskilde University, Denmark, 1992.

[Ber 1993]   Bernsen, N.O. Modality Theory: Supporting Multimodal Interface
               Design, ERCIM Workshop on Multimodal Human-Computer
               Interaction, 1993.

[Bie 2000]   Bieber, M. Hypertext, Encyclopedia of Computer Science (4th
               Edition), Ralston, A., Edwin Reilly and David Hemmendinger
               (eds.), Nature Publishing Group, 799-805, 2000.

[Bis 1997]   Bishop, A. S., Greer, J. E., and Cooke, J. E., The co-operative peer response system: CPR for students. In: T. Müldner and T. C. Reeves (eds.) Proceedings of ED-MEDIA/ED-TELECOM'97 - World Conference on Educational Multimedia/Hypermedia and World Conference on Educational Telecommunications, Calgary, Canada, June 14-19, AACE, pp. 74-79, 1997.

[Bla 1997]   Blankenhorn, D. Up close and personal, NewMedia, November 24, 1997.

[Blo 1984]   Bloom, B. S. The 2 Sigma Problem: The Search for Methods of Group Instruction as Effective as One-to-One Tutoring. *Educational Researcher*, 13, pp. 3-16, 1984.

[Blo 1995]   Bloom C. P. Roadblocks to Successful ITS Authoring in Industry. In *Proceedings of AI-ED-95 Workshop on Authoring Shells for Intelligent Tutoring Systems*, Washington, DC, 16 August 1995, pp 1-6.

[Bon 1998]   Bonk, C.J. and Cummings, J.A. A dozen recommendations for placing the students at the centre of Web-based learning. Educational Media International, 35(2):82-89, 1998.

[Bon 2001]   Bonk, C.J., Kirkley, J.R., Hara, N. and Dennen, N. Finding the instructor in post-secondary online learning: pedagogical, social, managerial, and technological locations. In: Stephenson, J., Editor, teaching and learning online: pedagogies for new technologies, Kogan Page, London, pp. 76-97, 2001.

[Boy 1994]   Boyle C. & Encarnacion A. O. MetaDoc : An adaptive hypertext Reading System, *Journal of user modeling and user adapted interaction,* 1-19; 1994.

[Bre 1989]   Brecht, B. J., McCalla, G. I., and Greer, J. E. Planning the content of instruction. In: D. Bierman, J. Breuker and J. Sandberg (eds.) Proceedings of 4-th International Conference on AI and Education, Amsterdam, 24-26 May 1989, Amsterdam, IOS, pp. 32-41.

[Bro 1978]   Brown, J. S., and Burton, R. R. Diagnostic models for procedural bugs in basic mathematical skills. *Cognitive Science, 2*, 155-192, 1978.

[Bro 1990]   Brown, S. I. and Walter, M. I. *Problem Posing.* Lawrence Erlbaum: Hillsdale NJ, 1990.

[Bro 1991] Brooks, R. Intelligence without representation, Artificial intelligence 47, pp 139-159, 1991.

[Bro 1993]   Brown, J. S. and Duguid, P. Stolen knowledge. *Educational Technology*, March, 1993.

[Bru 1960]   Bruner, J. The Process of Education. Cambridge, MA: Harvard University Press, 1960.

[Bru 1991]   Brustoloni, J. C. Autonomous Agents: Characterization and Requirements, Carnegie Mellon Technical Report CMU-CS-91-204, Pittsburgh: Carnegie Mellon University, 1991.

[Bru 1992a]   Brusilovsky, P. L. A framework for intelligent knowledge sequencing and task sequencing. In: C. Frasson, G. Gauthier and G. I. McCalla (eds.) Intelligent Tutoring Systems. (Proceedings of Second International Conference on Intelligent Tutoring Systems, ITS'92, Montreal, June 10-12, 1992) Berlin: Springer-Verlag, pp. 499-506.

[Bru 1992b]   Brusilovsky, P. L. Intelligent Tutor, Environment and Manual for Introductory Programming. Educational and Training Technology International 29 (1), 26-34, 1992.

[Bru 1994]   Brusilovsky, P. and Pesin, L., ISIS-Tutor: An adaptive hypertext learning environment. In: H. Ueno and V. Stefanuk (eds.) Proceedings of JCKBSE'94, Japanese-CIS Symposium on knowledge-based software engineering, Pereslavl-Zalesski, Russia, May 10-13, 1994, EIC, pp. 83-87.

[Bru 1995]   Brusilovsky, P., Intelligent Tutoring Systems for World-Wide Web. In: *R. Holzapfel (ed.) Proceedings of Third International WWW Conference*, Darmstadt, Darmstadt, April 10-14, Fraunhofer Institute for Computer Graphics, pp. 42-45, 1995.

[Bru 1996]   Brusilovsky, P., Methods and techniques of adaptive hypermedia, Journal of User Modeling and User Adapted Interaction, 6, (2-3), 87-129, 1996.

[Bru 1996b]   Brusilovsky, P., Schwarz, E., and Weber, G., ELM-ART: An intelligent tutoring system on World Wide Web. In: C. Frasson, G. Gauthier and A. Lesgold (eds.) Intelligent Tutoring Systems. Lecture Notes in Computer Science, Vol. 1086, (Proceedings of Third International Conference on Intelligent Tutoring Systems, ITS-96, Montreal, June 12-14, 1996) Berlin: Springer Verlag, pp. 261-269.

[Bru 1997]   Brusilovsky P., Schwarz E., User as Student: Towards an Adaptive Interface for Advanced Web-Based Applications. In Anthony Jameson, Cécile Paris, and Carlo Tasso (Eds.) *User Modeling: Proceedings of the Sixth International Conference, UM97* (pp. 177-188). Vienna, New York: Springer Wien New York, 1997.

[Bru 1997b]   Brusilovsky, P., Ritter, S., and Schwarz, E., Distributed intelligent tutoring on the Web. In: B. du Boulay and R. Mizoguchi (eds.) (Proceedings of AI-ED'97, 8th World Conference on Artificial

Intelligence in Education, 18-22 August 1997) Amsterdam: IOS, pp. 482-489.

[Bru 1997c] Brusilovsky, P., Eklund, J., and Schwarz, E., Adaptive Navigation Support in Educational Hypermedia on the World Wide Web. In: S. Howard, J. Hammond and G. Lindgaard (eds.) Human-Computer Interaction. (Proceedings of INTERACT97, The 6th IFIP World Conference on Human-Computer Interaction, Sydney, Australia, 14-18 July, 1997) New York: Chapman & Hall, pp. 278-285.

[Bru 2000] P. Brusilovsky. Course sequencing for static courses? Applying ITS techniques in large-scale web-based education. In Proceedings of the fifth International Confer- ence on Intelligent Tutoring Systems ITS 2000, Montreal, Canada, 2000.

[Bue 2001] F. Buendia, J. Sahuquillo, J.V. Benlloch, J.A Gil, M. Agustí, P. Diaz. XEDU, A Framework for Developing XML-Based Didactic Resources, 27th Euromicro Conference 2001: A Net Odyssey (euromicro'01), p. 0427, IEEE Computer Society, Warsaw, Poland, 2001.

[Bul 1997] Bull S. See Yourself Write: A Simple Student Model to Make Students Think. In Anthony Jameson, Cécile Paris, and Carlo Tasso (Eds.) *User Modeling: Proceedings of the Sixth International Conference, UM97* (pp. 315-326). Vienna, New York: Springer Wien New York, 1997.

[Bur 1982] Burton, R. R., Diagnosing Bugs in a Simple Procedural Skill in D. H. Sleeman and J. S. Brown (eds.) Intelligent Tutoring Systems. (Academic Press, New York), 1982.

[Bus 1945] Bush, V. As We May Think, The atlantic monthly, 1945.

[Cag 1997] Caglayan, A. and Harrison, C., Agent Sourcebook, Wiley Computer Publishing, New York, NY, 1997.

[Cal 1997] Calvi, L. and De Bra, P. Using dynamic hypertext to create multi-purpose textbooks. In: T. Müldner and T. C. Reeves (eds.) Proceedings of ED-MEDIA/ED-TELECOM'97 - World Conference on Educational Multimedia/Hypermedia and World Conference on Educational Telecommunications, Calgary, Canada, June 14-19, 1997, AACE, pp. 130-135.

[Cam 1988] Campbell, B., Goodman, J. M. HAM: A general purpose Hypertext Abstract Machine, CACM 31:7, July 1988, pp 856-861.

[Car 1970] Carbonell, J. AI in CAI: an Artificial-Intelligence approach to Computer-Assisted Instruction, IEEE Transactions on Man-Machine Systems, Vol. 11(4), pp. 190-202, 1970.

[Car 1977]   Carr, B. and Goldstein, I. "Overlays: A theory of modeling for computer aided instruction", (AI Memo 406), Cambridge, MA: Massachusetts Institute of Technology, AI Laboratory, 1977.

[Car 1989]   Carberry, S., Plan recognition and its use in understanding dialog. In: *W. Wahlster and A. Kobsa* (Eds.) op. Cit, 1989.

[Car 1999]   Carver, C. A., Howard, R. A. and Lane, W. D. Addressing Different Learning Styles Through Course Hypermedia, IEEE Transactions on Education, 42(1), pp. 33-38, February 1999.

[Car 1999b] Carro, R. M., Pulido, E. and Rodríguez., P. TANGOW: Task-based Adaptive learNer Guidance On the WWW, Proceedings of the 2nd Workshop on Adaptive Systems and User Modeling on the WWW, Canada, 1999.

[Cha 1993]   Chappel H., Wilson M. Knowledge-Based Design of Graphical Responses, 1993 International Workshop on Intelligent User Interfaces, pp 29-36.

[Cla 1979]   Clancey, W. J. Tutoring rules for guiding a case method dialogue, *International Journal of Man-Machine Studies*, Vol. 11, pp. 25-49, 1979.

[Cog 1998]   Cogburn, D. L. Globalization, Knowledge and Education in the Information Age. Paper presentation at the UNESCO InfoEthics Conference, Monaco, October 1998.

[Col 1987]   Collins, A., and Brown J. S. The computer as a tool for learning through reflection. In H. Mandl and A. Lesgold (Eds.), *Learning issues for intelligent tutoring systems*. New York: Springer-Verlag, 1987.

[Con 1987]   Conklin, J. Hypertext: An introduction and survey, IEEE Computer, 20: pp. 17-41, 1987.

[Cop 2002]   Coppola, Nancy Walters , Hiltz, Starr Roxanne and Rotter, Naomi R., Becoming a Virtual Professor: Pedagogical Roles and Asynchronous Learning Networks, Journal of Management Information Systems, Vol. 18 No. 4, Spring 2002 pp. 169 – 190.

[Cor 1992]   Corbett, A. T. and Anderson, J. A. Knowledge tracing in the ACT programming tutor. In: Proceedings of 14-th Annual Conference of the Cognitive Science Society, 1992.

[Cos 1994]   Cossel, R. J. Mosaic-HyperMedia for HyperKids. Second WWW Conf. Mosaic and the Web, .Chicago, 1994.

[Cro 1977]   Cronbach, L. & Snow, R. Aptitudes and Instructional Methods: A Handbook for Research on Interactions. New York: Irvington, 1977.

[Cro 1993]   Crow, D. & Smith, B. The role of Built in Knowledge in Adaptive Interface Systems, Proceedings of the 1993 International Workshop on Intelligent User Interfaces, Orlando, Florida, USA, 4-7, 1993.

[Cum 2002]   Cummings, J. A., Bonk, C. J., and Jacobs, F. R. Twenty-first century collage syllabi; Options for online communication and interactivity, The Internet and Higher Education, Volume 5, Issue 1, May 2002, pp. 1-19.

[Cur 1987]   Curry, L. Integrating concepts of cognitive or learning style: A review with attention to psychometric standards, ON: Canadian College of Health Service Executives, Ottawa, 1987.

[Cur 1992]   Curtis, P. Mudding: Social phenomena in text-based virtual realities. In Proceedings of DIAC92: Directions and Implications of Advanced Computing (Berkeley, Calif., May). Computer Professionals for Social Responsibility, Palo Alto, Calif., 1-21, 1992.

[Dan 1992]   Dannenberg, R. B., Joseph, R. L., Human-Computer Interaction in the Piano Tutor, in Blattner M.M., Dannenberg R.B. (eds), Multimedia Interface Design, ACM Press, pp 65-78, 1992.

[Dan 2002]   Danchak, M. Bringing Affective Behavior to e-Learning. The Technology Source, September/October 2002.

[Dan 2003]   Danchak, M. Using adaptive hypermedia to match web presentation to learning styles, Computer Science, Rensselaer Polytechnic Institute, Troy, New York, 2003.

[Dav 1977]   Davis, R., Buchanan, B. C., and Shortliffe, E.,H. Production rules as a representation for a knowledge-based consultation program. Artif. In tell. 8, I (Feb. 1977), 15-45.

[Dav 1992]   Davis, H., Hall, W., Heath, I., Hill, G., and Wilkins, R. Towards an integrated information environment with open hypermedia systems. Proceedings of the European Conference on Hypertext 1992 (ECHT 92), (Milano, Italy, Nov), 181-190, 1992.

[Dav 1994]   Davis, H., Knight, S., and Hall, W. Light hypermedia link services: A study of third-party application integration. Proceedings of the European Conference on Hypertext 1994 (ECHT 94), (Edinburgh, Scotland, Sep), 41-50, 1994.

[DeB 1999]   De Bra, P., Brusilovsky, P. and Houben, G. J. Adaptive hypermedia: from systems to framework, *ACM Computing Surveys* 31(4), December 1999.

[DeB 1999a]   De Bra, P. Design Issues in Adaptive Web-Site Development, Proceedings of the 2nd Workshop on Adaptive Systems and User Modeling on the WWW, Canada, 1999.

[DeB 1999b] De Bra, P. Pros and Cons of Adaptive Hypermedia in Web-based Education, Eindhoven University of Technology, 1999.

[DeC 1996] De Corte, E. Changing views of computer supported learning environments for the acquisition of knowledge and thinking skills. In S. Vosniadu, E. De Corte, R. Glaser, H. Mandl (eds.), *International Perspectives on the Design of Technology-Supported Learning Environments*, Lawrence Erlbaum Associates Publishers, 1996.

[DeC 1997] De Carolis, B. and Pizzutilo, S. From Discourse Plans to User-Adapted Hypermedia. In Anthony Jameson, Cécile Paris, and Carlo Tasso (Eds.) *User Modeling: Proceedings of the Sixth International Conference, UM97* (pp. 37-39). Vienna, New York: Springer Wien New York, 1997.

[Ded 1986] Dede, C. A review and synthesis of recent research in intelligent computer-assisted instruction, International Journal of Man-Machine Studies, Vol. 24.

[Dem 2000] Demazeau, Y. Foundations of Multi Agent Systems. 2nd European Agent Systems Summer School, EASSS2000, August 14 – 18, Saarbrucken, Germany, 2000.

[Die 1993] Dieterich, H., Malinowski, U., Kuehme, T. and Schneider-Hufschmidt, M. State of the Art in Adaptive User Interfaces, in Schneider-Hufschmidt M., Kuehme T., Malinowski U (eds), Adaptive User Interfaces, Elsevier, pp 13-48, 1993.

[Dij 1983] Dijk, T. A. and Kintsch, W. Strategies of Discourse Comprehension. Academic Press, New York, 1983.

[Dil 1993] Dillenbourg, P., Hilario, M., Mendehlson, D., Schneider, D. and Borcic, B., Intelligent learning environment, *Technical report: Project "Les systemes explorateurs intelligens"*, TECFA, University of Geneva (Switzerland), 1993.

[Dil 1997] Dillenbourg, P. Jermann, D. Schneider, D. and Buiu, C. The design of MOO agents: Implications from an empirical CSCW study. In proceedings of Eighth World Conference on Artificial Intelligence in Education, pp. 15-22, 1997.

[Dun 1999] Dunn, R. & Dunn, K. The Complete Guide to the Learning Strategies Inservice System. Boston: Allyn & Bacon, 1999.

[Dur 1989] Durfee, E. H. and Lesser, V. Negotiating Task Decomposition and Allocation Using Partial Global Planning. In Distributed Artificial Intelligence, Volume 2, eds. L. Gasser and M. Huhns, 229–244. San Francisco, Calif.: Morgan Kaufmann, 1989.

[Ega 1988]   Egan, D. E. Individual differences in Human-Computer Interaction. In Helander, M. (Ed.) Handbook of Human-Computer Interaction, Amsterdam: Elsevier Science Publishers B.V., 1988.

[Ekl 1998]   Eklund, J., Brusilovsky, P. The value of Adaptivity in Hypermedia Learning Environments: A short review of Empirical Evidence, http://wwwis.win.tue.nl/ah/, 1998.

[Eli 1996]   Eliot, C. and Woolf, B. P. Multiple Agents Acting in Parallel within an Intelligent Real-Time Tutor, In *Proceedings of the National Conference on Artificial Intelligence*, AAAI-96, 1996.

[Eli 1996a]   Eliot, C. and Woolf, B. P. A simulation-based tutor that reasons about multiple agents. In Proceedings of the Thirteenth Nacional Conference on Artificial Intelligence, pp. 409-415, 1996.

[Eli 1997]   Eliot, C., Neiman, D., and Lamar, M. Medtec: A Web-based intelligent tutor for basic anatomy. In: S. Lobodzinski and I. Tomek (eds.) Proceedings of WebNet'97, World Conference of the WWW, Internet and Intranet, Toronto, Canada, November 1-5, AACE, pp. 161-165, 1997.

[Ell 1997]   Elliot, C., Rickel, J. and Lester J. C.   Integrating affective computing into animated tutoring agents, IJCAI workshop on Animated Interface Agents, Nagoya, Japan, August, 1997.

[Els 1989]   Elsom-Cook, M. Guided discovery tutoring and bounded user modeling. In *Artificial Intelligence and Human Learning*; J. Self (ed), pp 65-170, 1989.

[Enc 1995]   Encarnaçao, L. Adaptativity in graphical user interfaces: An experimental Framework, Computers & Graphics, pp. 873-884, 1995.

[Etz 1994]   Etzioni, O. and Weld, D. A Softbot-Based Interface to the Internet, *Communications of the ACM,* 37(7): 72-6, 1994.

[Fel 1996]   Felder, R. M. Matters of Style. In ASEEE Prism, 6(4), 1996, pp. 18-23.

[Fel 2002]   Felder, R. M. and Silverman, L. K. Learning and Teaching Styles in Engineering Education, Engr. Education, 78(7), 674-681. The paper is preceded by a 2002 preface that states and explains changes in the model that have been made since 1988.

[Fer 1989]   Fernandez, I. Estrategias de enseñanza en un sistema de enseñanza asistida por ordenador. Tesis doctoral. Euskal Erico Unibertsitatea UPV/EHU. 1989.

[Fet 1998]   Fetterman, D. M. Webs of meaning: computer and Internet resources for educational research and instruction. Educational Researcher 27(3), pp.22-30, 1998.

[Fid 1988]   Fiderio, J. A grand vision. Byte, 13(10):237-244, October 1988.

[Fin 1989]   Finin, T. W. GUMS - A general user modeling shell. In: W. Wahlster and A. Kobsa (Eds.) op.cit, 1989.

[Fin 1991]   Fink, P. K. The Role of Domain Knowledge in the Design of an Intelligent Tutoring System, In Burns, H., Parlett, J.W. and Luckhardt, C., *Intelligent Tutoring Systems. Evolutions in Design,* Lawrence Erlbaum Associates, pp. 195-224, 1991.

[Fin 1994]   Finin, T., Fritzson, R., McKay, D. and McEntire, R. KQML as an Agent Communication Language. In proceedings of the Third International Conference on Information and Knowledge Management (CIKM94), 456-463, New York: Association of Computing Machinery, 1994.

[FIPA]   Foundation for Intelligent Physical Agents. http://www.fipa.org, 2002.

[Fis 1990]   Fisher, G., Mastaglio, T., Reeves, B. & Rieman, J. Minimalist Explanations in knowledge based systems. 23th Annual Hawaii Internatioanal conference on system sciences, Kailua-kona, HI, pp. 309-317, 1990.

[Fra 1996]   Franklin, S. and Graesser, A. Is it an Agent, or just a Program?: A Taxonomy for Autonomous Agents, Proceedings of the Third International Workshop on Agent Theories, Architectures, and Languages, Springer-Verlag, 1996.

[Fra 1997]   Frasson, C., Mengelle, T. and Aimeur, E. Using pedagogical agents in a multi-strategic intelligent tutoring system. In proceedings of the AI-ED 97 workshop on pedagogical agents, pp. 40-47, 1997.

[Fri 1997]   Friedman, B., Nissenbaum, H. Software agents and user autonomy, Proceedings of the first international conference on Autonomous agents, p.466-469, February 05-08, 1997, Marina del Rey, California, United States.

[Fun 2001]   Fung, A. & Yeung, J. An object model for a web-based adaptive educational system, IEEE LTTF ICALT2001, Madison, USA, 2001.

[Fur 1990]   Furuta R., Stotts, P. D., The Trellis Hypertext Reference Model, NIST Hypertext Standardization Workshop, February 1990, pp 83.

[Gag 1985]   Gagné, R. M. The Conditions of Learning and Theory of Instruction. Holt, Rinehart&Winston, USA, 1985.

[Gag 1992]   Gagne, R., Briggs, L. & Wager, W. Principles of Instructional Design (4th Ed.). Fort Worth, TX: HBJ College Publishers, 1992.

[Gal 2001]   GALECIA Project 88089-CP-2000-1-PT-MINERVA-ODL. Evaluating Distributed Learning, work report July 31, 2001.

[Gam 1990]   Gambetta, D. Can we trust trust ? In *Trust: Making and Breaking Cooperative Relations,* pages 213-237. Gambetta, D (editor). Basil Blackwell. Oxford, 1990.

[Gar 1983]   Gardner, H. Frames of Mind. New York: Basic Books, 1983.

[Gar 1988]   Gargan, R. A., Sullivan, J. W., Tyler, S.W. Multimodal Response Planning: An Adaptive Rule Based Approach, CHI '88, 229-234, 1988.

[Gas 1997]   Gaskin, J. New agents help Web merchants, Interactive Week, December 8, pp. 5, 1997.

[Gen 1994]   Genesereth, M. R. and Ketchpel, S. P. Software Agents. Communications of the ACM 37(7): 48–53, 1994.

[Gil 1999]   Gilbert, J. E. and Han, C. Y. Adapting instruction in search of 'a significant difference', Journal of Network and Computer Applications, 22, 000–000, 1999.

[Gra 1996]   Grasha, A. F. Teaching with style: A practical guide to enhancing learning by understanding teaching and learning styles. Pittsburgh: Alliance Publishers, 1996.

[Gri 2001]   Grigoriadou, M., Papanikolaou, K., Kornilakis, H. Magoulas, G., INSPIRE: An Intelligent System for Personalized Instruction in a Remote Environment. [online] Available at http://wwwis.win.tue.nl/ah2001/papers/papanikolaou.pdf, 2002.

[Grø 1994]   Grønbæk, K. Composites in a Dexter-based hypermedia framework. Proceedings of the ACM European Conference on Hypermedia Technology (ECHT 94) (Edinburgh, Scotland, Sep), 59-69, 1994.

[Grø 1997]   Grønbæk, K. and Wiil U. K. Towards a Common Reference Architecture for Open Hypermedia, Journal of Digital information, volume 1 issue 2, 1997.

[Gru 1993]   Gruber, T. R. A Translation Approach to Portable Ontologies. Knowledge Acquisition 5(2): 199–220, 1993.

[Gui 1967]   Guilford, J. P. The Nature of Human Intelligence. New York: McGraw-Hill, 1967.

[Gut 1994]   Gutierrez, J. INTZA: Un sistema tutor inteligente para entrenamiento en entornos industriales. Tesis doctoral. Euskal Erico Unibertsitatea UPV/EHU. 1994.

[Hal 1987]   Halasz, F. G., Moran, T. P. and Trigg T. H. NoteCards in a nutshell. In SIGCHI-Bulletin, Special Issue, pp 45-52, 1987.

[Hal 1988]   Halasz, F. Reflections on NoteCard: Seven Issues for the Next Generation of Hypermedia Systems. Communications of the ACM, July 1988.

[Hal 1990]   Halasz, F., Schwartz, M. The Dexter Hypertext Reference Model, NIST Hypertext Standardization Workshop, February 1990, pp 95-133.

[Ham 1989]   Hammond, N. Hypermedia and learning: Who guides whom? In Maurer H. (ed.) Computer Assisted Learning. Proceedings of the 2-nd International Conference, ICCAL'89. Springer-Verlag, Berlin. 167-181, 1989.

[Ham 1992]   Hammond, N. Tailoring Hypertext for the Learner. In: P.A.M. Kommers, D.H. Jonassen, J.T. Mayes *Cognitive Tools for Learning.* Berlin, Heidelberg, New York: Springer, 149-160, 1992.

[Ham 1993]   Hammond, N. Learning with hypertext: problems, principles and prospects. In: C. McKnight, Dillon, A. and Richardson, J. (Eds). *Hypertext Psychological Perspective.* New York: Ellis Horwood, 1993.

[Har 1973]   Hartley, J. & Sleeman, D. Towards more intelligent teaching systems. *International Journal of Man-Machine Studies 2*, 215-236, 1973.

[Har 1993]   Hartley, J. R. Interacting with multimedia. In *University Computing* No. 15, pp 129-36, 1993.

[Har 1999]   Harris, M. H. Is the revolution now over, or has it just begun ?. A year of the Internet in higher education. The Internet & Higher Education 1(4), pp. 243-251, 1999.

[Hen 1996]   Hendler, J. A. Intelligent Agents: Where AI meets Information Technology. IEEE Expert, pp. 20-22, 1996.

[Hen 1999]   Henze, N., Wolfgang, N. and Wolpers, N. Modeling Constructivist Teaching Functionality and Structure in the KBS Hyperbook System. In *Proceedings of Computer Suppoort for Collaborative Learning (CSCL)*, pp. 223-231, 1999.

[Hen 2000]   Henze, N. and Wolfgang, N. Extendible adaptive hypermedia courseware: Integrating different courses and web material. In Proceedings of the International Conference on Adaptive Hypermedia and Adaptive Web-Based Systems (AH 2000), Trento, Italy, 2000.

[Hen 2001]   Henze, N. and Wolfgang, N. Adaptation in open corpus hypermedia. IJAIED Special Issue on Adaptive and Intelligent Web-Based Systems, 12, 2001.

[Hen 2002]   Henze, N. and Wolfgang, N. Knowledge modeling for open adaptive hypermedia. In Proceedings of the 2nd International Conference on Adaptive Hypermedia and Adaptive Web-Based Systems (AH 2002), Malaga, Spain, 2002.

[Hof 1997]   Hofstetter, F. T. Cognitive Versus Behavioral Psychology, http://www.udel.edu/fth/pbs/webmodel.htm.

[Hoh 1996]   Hohl, H., Böcker, H.-D., and Gunzenhäuser, R. Hypadapter: An adaptive hypertext system for exploratory learning and programming. In P. Brusilovsky and J. Vassileva (eds.), Spec. Iss. on Adaptive Hypertext and Hypermedia, User Modeling and User-Adapted Interaction 6 (2-3), 131-156, 1996.

[Hol 1994]   Holt, P., Dubs, S. Jones, M. and Creer, J. The state of student modeling. In J. Creer and G. McCall (Eds.), Student Models: The key to individualized Educational Systems, Springer Verlag, pp. 3-35, 1994.

[Höö 1996]   Höök, K., Karlgren, J., Waern, A., Dahlback, N., Jansson, C., Karlgren, K. & Lemaire, B. A glass box approach to adaptive hypermedia. User Models and User Adapted Interaction. Vol. 6 p. 157-184. 1996.

[Hop 1995]   Hoppe, U. Use of multiple student modeling to parametrize group learning. In: J. Greer (ed.) Proceedings of AI-ED'95, 7th World Conference on Artificial Intelligence in Education, Washington, DC, 16-19 August 1995, AACE, pp. 234-249.

[Hos 1996]   Hoschka, P. Computers as Assistants: A New Generation of Support Systems. Lawrence Erlbaum Associates Publishers, Mahwah, NJ, New Jersey, pp. 336-340, 1996.

[Hui 1997]   Huitt,   W.   Methods   of   study. http://teach.valdosta.edu/whuitt/col/cogsys/sq4r.html, 1997.

[Hui 1999]   Huitt, W. Implementing effective school achievement reform: Four principles. Paper presented at the School Counseling Summit, Valdosta State University, Valdosta, GA, April 20, 1999.

[Hui 2000]   Huitt,   W.   Taxonomy   of   the   Cognitive   Domain. http://teach.valdosta.edu/whuitt/col/cogsys/bloom.html, 2000.

[HyTime]   Hypermedia/Time-based Structuring Language (HyTime), http://www.ornl.gov/sgml/wg8/docs/n1920/html/n1920.html.

[Iac 1993]   Iaccino, J. F. Left Brain/Right Brain differences, Inquires, Evidence, and New Approaches, Lawrence Erlbaum Associates, Hillsdale, NJ, 1993.

[ILS]   Diagnostic   instrument   for   the   FSLSM   model.
             http://www2.ncsu.edu/unity/lockers/users/f/felder/public/ILSdir/ils
             web.html.

[Ike 1997]   Ikeda, M., Go, S., and Mizoguchi, R. Opportunistic group
             formation. In: B. d. Boulay and R. Mizoguchi (eds.) Artificial
             Intelligence in Education: Knowledge and Media in Learning
             Systems. (Proceedings of AI-ED'97, 8th World Conference on
             Artificial Intelligence in Education, Kobe, Japan, 18-22 August
             1997) Amsterdam: IOS, pp.167-174, 1997.

[JADE]   Java   Agent   Development   Framework.
             http://sharon.cselt.it/projects/jade.

[Jan 1993]   Janssen C., Weisbecker A., Ziegler J. Generating User Interfaces
             from Data Models and Dialogue Net Specifications, INTERCHI
             '93, pp. 418-423, 1993.

[Jen 1992]   Jennings, F. and Benyon, D. R. Database Systems: Different
             Interfaces for different users, in press, 1992.

[Jes 2000]   Jesshope, C., Heinrich, E. & Kinshuk. Technology Integrated
             Learning Environments for Education at a Distance. DEANZ 2000
             Conference, 26-29, April 2000, Dunedin, New Zealand, online
             publication.

[Jiy 2002]   Jiyong, M., Jie, Y. and Cole, R. CUAnimate: Tools for Enabling
             Conversations with Animated Characters, International Conference
             on Spoken Language Processing (ICSLP), vol. 1, pp. 197-200,
             Denver, CO USA, September 2002.

[Joh 1986]   Johnson, W. L. Intention-based diagnosis of novice programming
             errors. Pitman: Morgan Kaufmann, 1986.

[Joh 1998]   Johnson, W. L. and Hayes-Roth, B. The First Autonomous Agents
             Conference. The Knowledge Engineering Review 13(2), pp. 1-6,
             1998.

[Joh 1998a] Johnson W. L., Shaw, E. and Ganeshan, R. Pedagogical Agents on
             the Web. Workshop on WWW-based Tutoring, ITS '98, San
             Antonio, Texas, 1998.

[Jon 1990]   Jonassen, D., Grabinger R. S. Problems and issues in designing
             hypertext/hypermedia for learning. In Hypermedia for Learning, pp
             3-25, D. Jonassen (ed). Springer-Verlag, 1990.

[Jon 1993-1] Jonassen, D., Mayes, I. T. & Mcaleese, R. A Manifesto for a
             Constructivist Approach to Technology in Higher Education. In T.
             Duffy, D. Jonassen, & J. Lowyck (Eds), Designing constructivist
             learning environments. Heidelberg, FRG: Springer-Verlag, 1993.

[Jon 1993-2] Jonassen, D. H., Wang, S. Acquiring Structural Knowledge from Semantically Structured Hypertext. In *Journal of Computer-Based Instruction*; Vol 20 No. 1 pp 1-8, 1993.

[Jon 1996] Jonassen, D. H. Computer in the classroom: Mindtools for critical thinking. Prentice Hall, Inc, 1996.

[Jun 1921] Jung, C. G. Psychological Types. In J. Campbell (Ed.), The portable Jung (pp. 178-269). New York: Viking Press, 1921.

[Kaf 1996] Kafai, Y. and Resnick, M. eds. *Constructionism in Practice: Designing, Thinking, and Learning in a Digital World.* Mahwah, NJ: Lawrence Erlbaum, 1996.

[Kal 1997] Kalyuga, S., Chandler P. and Sweller J. Levels of Expertise and User-Adapted Formats of Instructional Presentations: A Cognitive Load Approach. In Anthony Jameson, Cécile Paris, and Carlo Tasso (Eds.) *User Modeling: Proceedings of the Sixth International Conference, UM97* (pp. 261-272). Vienna, New York: Springer Wien New York, 1997.

[Kas 1989] Kass, R. and Finin, T., The role of user models in co-operative interactive systems, International Journal of Intelligent Systems , Vol. 4(1), 1989.

[Kas 1991] Kass, R. and Finin, T. General user modeling: A facility to support intelligent interaction. In J.W. Sullivan and S.W. Tylor (Eds.), Intelligent User Interfaces, pp. 111-128, 1991.

[Kau 1995] Kautz, H., Milewski, A. and Selman, B. Agent amplified communication. In Information Gathering from Heterogeneous, Distributed Environments: Papers from the 1995 AAAI Spring Symposium (Menlo Park, Calif., March), C. Knoblock and A. Levy, Eds. AAAI Press, Menlo Park, Calif., 78-84, 1995.

[Kay 1994] Kay, J. and Kummerfeld, R. J. An individualised course for the C programming language. In: Proceedings of Second International WWW Conference, Chicago, IL, 17-20 October, 1994.

[Kav 2001] Kavcic, A. Adaptation in Web-Based Educational Hypermedia With Regard to the Uncertainty of User Knowledge, Ph.D. Thesis, University of Ljubljana, Slovenia, June 2001.

[Kea 1993] Kearsley, G. Intelligent agents and instructional systems: implications of a new paradigm, Journal of Artificial Intelligence in Education, Vol. 4 No. 4, pp. 295-304, 1993.

[Kib 1989] Kibby, M. R. and Mayes, J. T. Towards intelligent hypertext. In R. McAleese (ed.) *Hypertext: Theory into Practic* . Oxford: Intellect, 1989.

[Kib 1990]   Kibby, M. and Mayes, T. Learning about Learning from Hypertext. In Hypermedia for Learning; D. Jonassen (ed), pp 135-143. Springer-Verlag, 1990.

[Kin 1995]   King, J. A. Intelligent Agents: Bringing Good Things to Life. AI Expert, February 1995, pp.17-19.

[Kin 1999]   Kinshuk, Oppermann, R., Patel, A. & Kashihara, A. Multiple Representation Approach in Multimedia based Intelligent Educational Systems. Artificial Intelligence in Education, Amsterdam: IOS Press, 259-266, 1999.

[Kin 1997]   Kinshuk, Patel, A. A Conceptual Framework for Internet based Intelligent Tutoring Systems. In *Knowledge Transfer* (Volume II), pp 117-124, Behrooz A (ed); Pace, London, 1997.

[Klu 2000]   Klusch, M. Information agents, 2nd European Agent Systems Summer School, EASSS2000. August 14 – 18. Saarbrucken, Germany, 2000.

[KM]   http://www.km-forum.org/what_is.htm

[Kob 1993] Kobsa, A. User Modeling: Recent work, prospects and Hazards, In Adaptive User Interfaces: Principles and Practice Schneider-Hufschmidt, M. Kühme, T. Malinowski, U. (ed) North-Holland, 1993.

[Kol 1984]   Kolb, D. Learning Styles Inventory, McBer & Co, Boston, 1984.

[Kok 1991]   Kok A. J. A review and Sintesis of user Modeling in intelligent systems. The knowledge Engineering Review, vol. 6(1), pp. 131-183, 1991.

[Koz 1993]   Kozierok, R., and Maes, P., A learning interface agent for scheduling meetings. In Proceedings of the ACM-SIGCHI International Workshop on Intelligent User Interfaces (Orlando, Fla., Jan.). ACM Press, New York, N.Y., 81-88, 1993.

[Lai 1995]   Lai, M.-C., Chen, B.-H., and Yuan, S.-M. Toward a new educational environment, In: Proceedings of 4th International World Wide Web Conference, Boston, USA, December 11-14, 1995.

[Laj 1992]   Lajoie, S. and Lesgold, A. Apprenticeship training in the workplace: Computer-coached practice environment as a new form of apprenticeship in Farr and Psotka, editors, *Intelligent Instruction by Computer*, pp. 15-36, Taylor and Francis, 1992.

[Laj 1993]   Lajoie, S. Computer environments as cognitive tools for enhancing learning. IN S.P. Lajoie and S.J. Derry, editors, *Computers and cognitive tools*, pp. 261-288, N.J. Lawrence Erlbaum Associates, 1993.

[Lak 1994]   Lakin, F. A visual agent for performance graphics. In Software
             Agents: Papers from the 1994 AAAI Spring Symposium (Menlo
             Park, Calif., March). AAAI Press, Menlo Park, Calif., 103-106,
             1994.

[Lan 1992]   Landow, G. P. Hypertext - The Convergence of Contemporary
             Critical Theory and Technology. Baltimore and London: The John
             Hopkins University Press, 1992.

[Lan 1993]   Lange, D. Object-Oriented Hypermodeling of Hypertext Supported
             Information Systems, Proceedings of the Twenty-Sixth Hawaii
             International Conference on System Sciences, January 1993.

[LaR 2000]   LaRose, R. & Whitten, P. Re-thinking instructional immediacy for
             Web courses: A social cognitive exploration. Communication
             Education, 49(4), 320-338, 2000.

[Lar 2001]   Laroussi, M. Conception et réalisation d'un système didactique
             hypermédia adaptatif: CAMELEON, PhD Thesis, Université
             MANOUBA, Université EL MANAR, 2001.

[Lau 1990]   Laurel, B. Interface agents: Metaphors with character. In The Art of
             Human-Computer Interface Design, Brenda Laurel, Ed. Addison-
             Wesley, Reading, Mass., 355-365, 1990.

[Lei 1989]   Leinhardt, G. Math lessons: A contrast of novice and expert
             competence. *Journal for Research in Mathematics Education*,
             20(1), 52-75, 1989.

[Len 1996]   Lennon, J. and Maurer, H. Flexible link architectures in hypermedia
             systems. Proceedings of the AACE World Conference on
             Educational Multimedia/Hypermedia (EDMEDIA 96), (Boston,
             MA, Jun), 384-389, 1996.

[Les 1997]   Lester, J. C., Converse, S. A., Kahler, S. E., Barlow, S. T., Stone, B.
             A. and Bhogal, R. S. The persona effect: Affective impact of
             animated pedagogical agents. In Proceedings of CHI '97, pp. 359-
             366, ACM Press, 1997.

[Les 1997a] Lester, J. and Stone, B. Increasing Believability in Animated
             Pedagogical Agents, Proceedings of the First International
             Conference on Autonomous Agents, pp. 16-21, California, February
             1997.

[Les 1997b] Lester, J., Sharolyn, A., Converse, B., Stone, A., Kahler, S. and
             Todd, S. Animated pedagogical agents and problem-solving
             effectiveness: A large-scale empirical evaluation. In Proceedings of
             Eighth Works Conference on Artificial Intelligence in Education,
             pp. 23-30, Kobe, Japan, 1997.

[Lew 1992]   Lewis, M., McArthur, D., Bishay, M., and Chou, J. Object-Oriented
             Microworlds   for   Learning   Mathematics   through   Inquiry:

Preliminary Results and Directions. Proceedings of the *East-West Conference on Emerging Computer Technologies in Education*, Moscow, April, 1992.

[Lie 1996]   Lieberman, H. Maulsby, D. "Instructible agents: Software that just keeps getting better", IBM systems journal 35(3&4), 1996.

[Low 1999]   Lowe, D., Hall, E. Hypermedia and The Web: An Engineering Approach, Wiley; 1999.

[LSN]   Learning-styles network website. "http://www.learningstyles.net".

[Mac 1986]   Mackinlay, J. D. Automating the Design of Graphical Presentations of Relational Information, ACM Transactions on Graphics, 5(2), pp 110-141, 1986.

[Mae 1994]   Maes, P. Agents that reduce work and information overload, Communications of the ACM 37(7), July 1994.

[Mae 1995]   Maes, P. Artificial life meets entertainment: lifelike autonomous agents, Communications of the ACM, Vol. 38 No. 11, pp. 108-14, 1995.

[Mag 1997]   Maglio, P. P., Barreto, R. How to Build Modeling Agents to Support Web Searchers. In Anthony Jameson, Cécile Paris, and Carlo Tasso (Eds.) *User Modeling: Proceedings of the Sixth International Conference, UM97* (pp. 5-16). Vienna, New York: Springer Wien New York, 1997.

[Maj 1995]   Major, N. How Generic can Authoring Shells Become? In Integrating Hypermedia and Intelligent Tutoring Technologies: From Systems to Authoring Tools. Proceedings of AI-ED-95 Workshop on Authoring Shells for Intelligent Tutoring Systems, Washington, DC, pp 75-82, 1995.

[MARC]   http://www.loc.gov/marc/

[Mas 1970]   Maslow, A. Motivation and Personality (2nd ed.). New York: Harper & Row. 1970.

[Mat 1982]   Matz, M. Towards a process model for high school algebra errors, In D. H. Sleeman & J. S. Brown (Eds.), *Intelligent Tutoring Systems* New York: Academic Press, 1982.

[Mal 1991]   Malcolm, K. C., Poltrock, S. E., and Schuler, D. Industrial Strength Hypermedia: Requirements for a Large Engineering Enterprise, Proceedings of Hypertext '91, ACM Press, December 1991.

[Mau 1994]   Mauldin, M. Chatterbots, Tinymuds, and the Turing test: Entering the Loebner Prize competition. In Proceedings of the Twelfth National Conference on Artificial Intelligence (AAAI '94) (Seattle, Wash., August). AAAI Press, Menlo Park, Calif., 16-21, 1994.

[Mau 1996]   Maurer, H. Hyper-G now Hyperwave: The Next Generation Web Solution. Addison-Wesley, 1996.

[Mau 1997]   Maurer, H. Necessary ingredients of integrated network based learning environments. Proceedings of the AACE World Conference on Educational Multimedia/Hypermedia (EDMEDIA 97), (Calgary, Canada, Jun), 25-32, 1997.

[Mau 1997a] Maule, W. R. Cognitive maps, AI agents and personalized virtual environments in Internet learning experiences. Internet Research – Electronic Networking Applications and Policy, Vol. 8, Issue 4, 347-358, 1998.

[May 1992]   Mayes, T. Cognitive Tools: A Suitable Case for Learning. In: P.A.M. Kommers, D. H. Jonassen, J. T. Mayes: *Cognitive Tools for Learning.* Berlin, Heidelberg, New York: Springer, 7-18, 1992.

[McA 1990]   McArthur, D., Stasz, C., and Zmuidzinas, M. Tutoring techniques in algebra. *Cognition and Instruction*, 7(3), 197-244, 1990.

[McC 1997]   McCalla, G. I., Greer, J. E., Kumar, V. S., Meagher, P., Collins, J. A., Tkatch, R., and Parkinson, B. A peer help sytem for workplace training. In: B. d. Boulay and R. Mizoguchi (eds.) Artificial Intelligence in Education: Knowledge and Media in Learning Systems. (Proceedings of AI-ED'97, 8th World Conference on Artificial Intelligence in Education, Kobe, Japan, 18-22 August 1997) Amsterdam: IOS, pp. 183-190.

[McK 1992]   McKendree, J., Radlinski, B., and Atwood, M. E. The Grace Tutor: a qualified success. In: C. Frasson, G. Gauthier and G. I. McCalla (eds.) Proceedings of Second International Conference, ITS'92, Berlin, Montreal, June 10-12, 1992, Springer-Verlag, pp. 677-684, 1992.

[MER 1993] Merriam-Webster's Collegiate Dictionary, 10th ed., p.22, 1993.

[Mer 1996]   Mergendoller, J. R. Moving from technological possibility to richer student learning: revitalized infrastructure and reconstructed pedagogy. Educational Researcher 25(8), pp. 43-46, 1996.

[Mes 1976]   Messick, S. (editor). Individuality in learning, 1st edition, San Francisco: Jossey-Bass. xiv, 382 pages, 1976.

[MET]   http://www.w3.org/Metadata/.

[MHEG   A Multimedia Presentation Standard (MHEG), http://www.doc.ic.ac.uk/~nd/surprise_96/journal/vol2/srd2/article2.html.

[Mid 2001]   Middleton, S. E. Interface agents: a review of the field. Technical report number: ECSTR-IAM01-001, University of Southampton, UK, 2001.

[Min 1986] Minsky, M. The society of mind, Simon & Schuster editors, New York, 1986.

[Mil 1996] Milne, S., Shiu, E. & Cook, J. Development of a model of user attributes and its implementation within an adaptive tutoring system. User Modeling and User-Adapted Interaction, 6, pp303-335, 1996.

[Mit 1997] Mitchell, T. M. Machine Learning, McGraw-Hill, 1997.

[Mon 2002] Montaner, M., López, B., de la Rosa, J. Ll., "Opinion-Based Filtering Through Trust". In Proceedings of the 6th International Workshop on Cooperative Information Agents (CIA'02). Matthias Klusch, Sascha Ossowski and Onn Shehory (Eds.), Lecture Notes in AI N°2446. Springer-Verlag Berlin Heidelberg, pp. 164-178, Madrid (Spain). 18-20 September, 2002.

[Mon 2003] Montaner, M., López, B., de la Rosa, J. Ll. A Taxonomy of Recommender Agents on the Internet, Artificial Intelligence Review, Kluwer Academic Publishers. Volume 19, Issue 4, pp. 285-330. June, 2003.

[Mor 1989] Morik, K. User models and conversational settings: Modeling the user's wants. In: W. Wahlster and A. Kobsa (Eds.) op. Cit, 1989.

[Mou 1997] Moukas, A. User modelling in a Multi-Agent Evolving System, In International Conference on User Modelling '97, Machine Learning in User Modelling Workshop Notes, Chia Laguna, Sardinia, 1997.

[Mur 1989] Murray, D. M. Modeling for adaptivity, Proceedings of 8th Interdisciplinary Workshop, Informatics and Psychology, Scharding, Austria, May 1989 (Amsterdam: North Holland).

[Nan 1993] Nanard, J., Nanard, M. Should Anchors Be Typed Too? An Experiment with MacWeb ACM HYPERTEXT '93 Conf. Proc., pp. 51-62, Nov 1993.

[NCTM] National Council of Teachers of Mathematics. Curriculum and Evaluation Standards for School Mathematics. Reston, VA: NCTM, 1989.

[Nea 1991] Neal, J. G., Shapiro, S. C. Intelligent Multi-Media Interface Technology, in Sullivan J.W., Tyler S.W. (eds), Intelligent User Interfaces, ACM Press, pp 11-43, 1991.

[Nel 1971] Nelson, T. Computers in instruction: Their future to higher education. Computopia and Cybercrud, R.E. Levien, (ed.), Rand Publishers, Santa Monica, CA., 185-199, 1971.

[Nel 1972] Nelson, T. As we will think. Online 72: Conference Proceedings of the International Conference on Online Interactive Computing, (Uxbridge, England, Sep), 439-454, 1972.

[Nel 1987]   Nelson, T. Literary Machines, Edition 87.1. Available from the distributors, 702 South Michigan, South Bend, IN 46618, 1987.

[New 1972]   Newell, A. and Simon, H. A. Human Problem Solving. Engelwood Cliffs, NJ: Prentice-Hall, 1972.

[Nie 1990]   Nielsen, J. Hypertext and Hypermedia, Academic Press, Boston, MA, 1990.

[Nik 1999]   Nikov, A. & Pohl, W. Combining User and User Modeling for User-Adaptivity Systems. Human Computer Interaction - Ergonomics and User Interfaces (Eds. H.-J. Bullinger & J. Ziegler), 1999.

[NINEVEH]   Nineveh: interactive e-learning knowledge base, Istituto Superiore Mario   Boella,   2002, http://www.nineveh.polito.it/nineveh/index.jsp?page=map.

[Nor 1994]   Norman, D. A. How might people interact with agents, Communications of the ACM 37(7) July 1994, 68-71.

[Nür 1996]   Nürnberg, P., Leggett, J., Schneider, E., and Schnase, J. Hypermedia operating systems: A new paradigm for computing. Proceedings of the Seventh ACM Conference on Hypertext (Hypertext 96), (Bethesda, MD, Mar), 194-202, 1996.

[Nür 1998]   Nürnberg P. J., Tochtermann, K. A comparison of hypermedia architectures for educational applications, Proceedings of the AACE World Conference on Educational Multimedia/Hypermedia (EDMEDIA 98), (Freiburg, Germany, Jun), 1998.

[Nwa 1990]   Nwana, H. S. Intelligent Tutoring Systems: an overview. Artificial Intelligence Review, 4, 251-277, 1990.

[Nwa 1996]   Nwana, H. Software agents: an overview, In The Knowledge Engineering Review, Vol 11:3, 205-244, 1996.

[Nwa 1997]   Nwana, H. S. and Azarmi, N. Software Agents and Soft Computing: Towards enhancing machine intelligence, Springer, 1997.

[ODA]   Open Document Architecture and Interchange Format (ODA) http://www.diffuse.org/docs.html#ODA.

[Ohl 1991]   Ohlsson, S. System hacking meets learning theory: Reflections on the goals and standards of research in Artificial Intelligence and Education. *Journal of Artificial Intelligence and Education*, 2 (3), 5-18, 1991.

[Oka 1997]   Okazaki, Y., Watanabe, K., and Kondo, H. An Implementation of the WWW Based ITS for Guiding Differential Calculations. In: *P. Brusilovsky, K. Nakabayashi and S. Ritter (eds.) Proceedings of Workshop "Intelligent Educational Systems on the World Wide*

Web" at AI-ED'97, 8th World Conference on Artificial Intelligence in Education, Kobe, Japan, 18 August 1997, ISIR, pp. 18-25, 1997.

[Opp 1994]   Oppermann R. Introduction: Adaptive User Support (Ed. Oppermann R.), Lawrence Erlbaum Associates, Hillsdale, New Jersey, pp1-13, 1994.

[Opp 1997]   Oppermann, R., Rashev, R. and Kinshuk. Adaptability and Adaptivity in Learning Systems, Knowledge Transfer (Volume II) (Ed. A. Behrooz), pAce, London, UK, pp173-179, 1997.

[Par 1997]   Paranagama, P., Burstein F., and Arnott, D. Modeling the Personality of Decision Makers for Active Decision Support. In Anthony Jameson, Cécile Paris, and Carlo Tasso (Eds.) *User Modeling: Proceedings of the Sixth International Conference, UM97* (pp. 79-81). Vienna, New York: Springer Wien New York, 1997.

[Par 2000]   Parunak, V. Synthetic Ecosystems: A perspective for Multi-Agent Systems. 2nd European Agent Systems Summer School, EASSS2000. August 14 – 18. Saarbrucken, Germany, 2000.

[Pap 1990]   Papert, S. Introduction: Constructionist Learning. Idit Harel (ed.), Cambridge, MA: MIT Media Laboratory, 1990.

[Pap 1991]   Papert, S. and Harel I. *Constructionism*, Norwood NJ: Ablex Publishing, 1991.

[Par 1989]   Paris, C. L. The use of explicit user models in a generation system. In: *W. Wahlster and A. Kobsa* (Eds.) op. Cit, 1989.

[Pas 1975]   Pask, G. Conversation, Cognition, and Learning. New York: Elsevier, 1975.

[Per 1991]   Pereira, D. C., de Oliveira A., Vaz, J. C. Hypermedia and ITS, *In Intelligent Systems in Education.* Micarelli, Belastra (eds), pp 207-223, 1991.

[Per 1995]   Pérez, T., Lopistéguy, P., Gutiérrez, J. & Usandizaga, I. HyperTutor: From hypermedia to intelligent adaptive hypermedia, InH. Maurer (Eds.), Proceedings of ED-MEDIA'95, World conference on educational multimedia and hypermedia . Graz, Austria: AACE. p. 529-534. 1995.

[Pet 1990]   Petoud I., Pigneur Y. An Automatic and Visual Approach for User Interface Design, in Engineering for Human-Computer Interaction, North-Holland, pp 403-420, 1990.

[Pey 2000]   Peylo, C., Thelen, T., Rollinger, C. and Gust, H. A web-based intelligent educational system for PROLOG, Institute for Semantic Information Processing, University of Osnabrück, April 2000.

[Pia 1969]   Piaget, J. The Mechanisms of Perception. London: Rutledge & Kegan Paul, 1969.

[Pso 1988]   Psotka, J., Massey, D. and Mutter, S. Intelligent Tutoring Systems: Lessons Learned. Hillsdale NJ: Lawrence Erlbaum, 1988.

[Ram 1992]   Ramaiah, C. An Overview of Hypertext and Hypermedia, *International Information, Communication & Education Vol. 11*, No. 1, 1992.

[Rao 1991]   Rao, A. S. and Georgeff, M. P. Modeling rational agents whithin a bdi-architecture. In Proc. of KR'91, pp. 473-484, 1991.

[Rau 1995]   Rauterberg, M. Human information processing in man-machine interaction. *Work with display units 94,* A. Grieco, G. Molteni, B. Piccoli and E. Occhipinti (Editors), 221-226, 1995.

[Rho 2000]   Rhodes, B. J. Margin Notes: building a contextually aware associative memory, In IUI 2000: 2000 International Conference on Intelligent User Interfaces, New Orleans, Louisiana, January 9-12, ACM, 2000.

[Ric 1983]   Rich, E. A. Learning Strategies: A tradicional Perspectiva, In O'Neil, H.F. (Eds.), Learning Strategies, Academia Press, pp. 165-205, 1983.

[Ric 1983a]   Rich, E. Users are individuals: individualizing user models, *International Journal of Man Machine Studies*, Vol. 18, pp.199-214, 1983.

[Ric 1989]   Rich, E. Stereotypes and user Modeling, In: W. Wahlster and A. Kobsa (Eds.) op. cit., 1989.

[Ric 1997]   Rickel, J. and Jonson, L. Integrating pedagogical capabilities in a virtual environment agent. In Proceedings of the First Internacional Conference on Autonomous agents, pp. 30-38, 1997.

[Rid 1989]   Ridgeway J. Of course ICAI is impossible...worse though, it might be seditious. In *Artificial Intelligence and Human Learning;* J.Self (ed), pp 28-48, 1989.

[Rit 1997]   Ritter, S. Communication, cooperation, and competition among multiple tutor agents. In proceedings of Eight World conference on Artificial INtelligence in Education, pp. 31-38, 1997.

[Rob 1970]   Robinson, F. P. *Effective study* (4th ed.). New York: Harper & Row, 1970.

[Rob 1995]   Robotham, D. Self-Directed Learning: The Ultimate Learning Style?, In *Journal of European Industrial Training*, Vol. 19, No. 7, pp. 3-7, 1995.

[Rog 1969]   Rogers, C. R. Freedom to learn: a view of what education might become. Columbus, OH, Charles E. Merrill, 1969.

[Ros 1992]   Roschelle, J. Learning by collaborating: Convergent conceptual change. The *Journal of the Learning Sciences*, 2(3), 235-276, 1992.

[Ros 1999]   Roschelle, J. and Pea, R. Trajectories from today's' WWW to a powerful educational infrastructure. Educational Researcher, 8(5):22-25, 1999.

[Rot 1993]   Roth S., Hefley W. Intelligent Multimedia Presentation Systems: Research and Principles, in Maybury M. (ed), Intelligent Multimedia Interfaces, AAAI Press, pp 13-58, 1993.

[Rus 1997]   Russell, S. and Norvig P. Inteligencia Artificial un Enfoque Moderno. Prentice-Hall, 1997.

[Sag 1997]   Sagula, J. E., Puricelli, M. F., Bobeff, G. J., Martin, G. M. and Carlos, E. P. GALOIS: An Expert-Assistant Model, In Autonomous Agents 97, Marina Del Rey, California USA, 1997.

[Sal 1997]   Salampasis,   M.   Hypermedia. http://aetos.it.teithe.gr/~cs1msa/docs/hypermedia_shortcomings.htm #10.

[San 1993]   Sánchez, J. A. HyperActive: Extending an open hypermedia architecture to support agency. M.S. thesis. Department of Computer Science, Texas A&M University, College Station, Tex., December, 1993.

[San 1997]   Sánchez, J. A. A Taxonomy of Agents, Tech. Rep. No. ICT-97-1, Interactive and Cooperative Technologies, Lab Universidad de las Américas-Puebla Cholula, Puebla, México, 1997.

[San 2000]   Sandip, S. Learning Agents. 2nd European Agent Systems Summer School, EASSS2000. August 14 – 18. Saarbrucken, Germany, 2000.

[Sch 1993]   Schlimmer, J. and Hermens, L. Software agents: Completing patterns and constructing user interfaces. Journal of Artificial Intelligence Research 1 (Nov.), 61-89, 1993.

[Sch 1994]   Schnase, J., Leggett, J., Hicks, D., Nürnberg, P., and Sanchez, J. Open architectures for integrated, hypermedia-based information systems. Proceedings of the 27th Annual Hawaii International Conference on System Sciences (HICSS-27), (Weilea, HI, Jan), 386-395, 1994.

[Sel 1987]   Self, J. *User modelling in open learning systems*. In: J. Whiting and D. Bell (Eds.), Tutoring and Monitoring Facilities for European Open Learning (Amsterdam: Elsevier Science Publishers B.V.), 1987.

[Sel 1991]   Seligmann, D. D., Feiner, S. F. Automated Generation of Intent-based 3D Illustrations, ACM SIGGRAPH '91, pp 123-132, 1991.

[Sel 1994]   Selker, T. Coach: A teaching agent that learns. Commun. ACM 37, 7 (July), 92-99, 1994.

[SGML]   Standard   Generalized   Markup   Language   (SGML). http://www.diffuse.org/docs.html#SGML.

[Sha 1987]   Shapiro, S. Encyclopedia of Artificial Intelligence, Vol. 1 and 2, Wiley- Interscience, 1987.

[Sha 1999]   Shaw, E., Johnson, W. L. and Ganeshan, R. Pedagogical Agents on the Web, Proceedings of the Third International Conference On Autonomous Agents, pp. 283-290, May 1999.

[Shn 1997]   Shneiderman, B. Maes, P. Direct manipulation vs interface agents, Interactions: new visions of Human-Computer Interaction Nov-Dec 1997.

[Shu 1990]   Shute, V. J. and Glaser, R. A large-scale evaluation of an intelligent discovery world: Smithtown. *Interactive Learning Environments*, 1(1), 51-77.

[Shu 1995]   Shute, V. Smart evaluation: Cognitive diagnosis, mastery learning and remediation, In *Proceedings of Artificial Intelligence in Education*, pp. 123-130, 1995.

[Sle 1981]   Sleeman, D. H. and Smith, M. J. Modeling Student's Problem Solving. Artificial Intelligence 16(2): 171-188, 1981.

[Sle 1982]   Sleeman, D. H., Brown, J. S. (eds). Intelligent Tutoring Systems. Academic Press; 1982.

[Sle 1985]   Sleeman, D. UMFE: A user Modeling front-end system, *Internacional Journal of Man Machine Studies* , Vol. 23, pp. 71-88, 1985.

[Smi 1996]   Smith I. and Cohen, P. Toward Semantics for an Agent Communication Language Based on Speech Acts. In proceedings of the Fourteenth National Conference on Artificial Intelligence (AAAI-96). Menlo Park, Calif.: American Association for Artificial Intelligence, 1996.

[Spe 1997]   Specht, M., Weber, G., Heitmeyer, S. and Schöch, V. AST: Adaptive WWW-Courseware for Statistics. In: P. Brusilovsky, J. Fink and J. Kay (eds.) Proceedings of Workshop "Adaptive Systems and User Modeling on the World Wide Web" at 6th International Conference on User Modeling, UM97, Chia Laguna, Sardinia, Italy, June   2,   Carnegie   Mellon   Online,   pp.   91-95,

http://www.contrib.andrew.cmu.edu/~plb/UM97_workshop/Specht.
html, 1997.

[Spe 1998]   Specht, M. Empirical Evaluation of Adaptive Annotation in
Hypermedia in Proceedings of Edmedia, 1998.

[Sta 1997]   Staff, C. HyperContext: A Model for Adaptive Hypertext. In
Anthony Jameson, Cécile Paris, and Carlo Tasso (Eds.) *User
Modeling: Proceedings of the Sixth International Conference,
UM97* (pp. 33-35). Vienna, New York: Springer Wien New York,
1997.

[Ste 1983]   Sternberg, R. J. Criteria for intellectual skills training, Educational
Researcher,12, 6-12, 1983.

[Ste 1993]   Stephanidis, C., Galatis, P., Homatas, G., Koumpis, A. and
Sfyrakis, M. A Methodology for selecting interaction techniques for
users with disabilities in the context of the B-ISDN environment,
FORTH-ICS/Technical Report 111, 1993.

[Ste 1997]   Stern, M., Woolf, B. P. and Kuroso, J. Intelligence on the Web?, In:
B. d. Boulay and R. Mizoguchi (eds.) Artificial Intelligence in
Education: Knowledge and Media in Learning Systems.
(Proceedings of AI-ED'97, 8th World Conference on Artificial
Intelligence in Education, Kobe, Japan, 18-22 August 1997)
Amsterdam: IOS, pp. 490-497.

[Ste 1998]   Stern, M. and Woolf, B. P. Curriculum sequencing in a Web-based
tutor. Lecture Notes in Computer Science, 1452, 1998.

[Sto 1989]   Stotts, P. D. and Furuta, R. *Petri-net-based hypertext: Document
structure with browsing semantics*, ACM Transactions on
Information Systems, 7:1, January 1989, pp 3-29.

[Sut 1994]   Sutcliffe, A. and Faraday R. Designing Presentation in Multimedia
Interfaces, CHI '94, pp 92-98, 1994.

[Sut 1997]   Suthers, D. and Jones, D. An architecture for intelligent
collaborative educational systems. In: B. d. Boulay and R.
Mizoguchi (eds.) Artificial Intelligence in Education: Knowledge
and Media in Learning Systems. (Proceedings of AI-ED'97, 8th
World Conference on Artificial Intelligence in Education, Kobe,
Japan, 18-22 August 1997) Amsterdam: IOS, pp. 55-62.

[Szu 1992]   Szuprowicz, B.O. Multimedia in education, DATAPRO, McGraw-
Hill, 1992.

[Syc 1998]   Sycara, K. Multiagent systems. American Association for Artificial
Intelligence, pp. 79 – 92, 1998.

[Tho 1987] Thomas, C. G., Kollormann, G. M., Hein, H. W. X-AiD: An Adaptive and Knowledge-Based Human-Computer Interface, HCI International '87, pp 1075-1080, 1987.

[Toc 1996] Tochtermann, K., Tresp, C., Hiltner, J., Reusch, B., Weidemann, J., Hohn, H. P., Denker, H. W. and Freund, A. HyperMed: A hypermedia system for anatomical education. *Proceedings of the AACE World Conference on Educational Multimedia/Hypermedia (EDMEDIA 96)*, (Boston, MA, Jun), 667-672, 1996.

[Tow 1999] Towns, S. G., FitzGerald, P. J. and Lester, J. C. Visual Emotive Communication in Lifelike Pedagogical Agents, *International Journal of Artificial Intelligence in Education,* 10, 278-291, 1999.

[Tri 1988] Trigg, R. Guided Tours and Tabletops. In Tools for Communicating in a Hypertext *Environment*, ACM Trans. on Office Information Systems, Vol 6, No 4, Oct 1988, pp.398-414.

[Tri 2002] Triantafillou, E., Pomportsis, A. and Georgiadpu, E. AES-CS: Adaptive Educational System based on Cognitive Styles. AH2002 Workshop, Adaptive Systems for Web education, 2nd International Conference, Adaptive Hypermedia and adaptive web based systems, Malaga, Spain, 2002.

[Tun 1999] Tunbridge, N. The Human Touch. In *New Scientist* No 2170, pp 34-37, Reed Business Internacional, 1999.

[Van 1990] Van der Veer, G. C. Human-Computer Interaction. Learning, individual differences and design recommendation, Offsetdrukkerij Haveka B.V., Alblasserdam, 1990.

[Van 1994] Vanneste, P. The use of reverse engineering in novice program analysis (PhD Thesis). Katholieke Universiteit Leuven, 1994.

[Vas 1997] Vassileva, J. Dynamic Course Generation on the WWW. In: B. d. Boulay and R. Mizoguchi (eds.) Artificial Intelligence in Education: Knowledge and Media in Learning Systems. (Proceedings of AI-ED'97, 8th World Conference on Artificial Intelligence in Education, Kobe, Japan, 18-22 August 1997) Amsterdam: IOS, pp. 498-505.

[Vic 1987] Vicente, K. J. and Williges, R. C. Assaying and isolating individual differences in searching a hierarchical file system., Human Factors , Vol. 29, 349-359, 1987.

[Vic 1988] Vicente, K .J. and Williges, R. C. Accommodating individual differences in searching a hierarchical file system, International Journal of Man-Machine Studies, Vol. 29, 1988.

[Vin 2001] Vincent, A. and Ross, D. Personalize training: determine learning styles, personality types and multiple intelligences online, The Learning Organization, 8(1), 36-43, 2001.

[Vir 2001]   Virvou, M. & Tsiriga, V. Web Passive Voice Tutor: an Intelligent Computer Assisted Language Learning System over the WWW, IEEE LTTF, ICALT2001, Madison, USA, 2001.

[Vyg 1978]   Vygotsky, L. S. Mind in Society: The development of higher psychological processes. Cambridge, MA: Harvard University Press, 1978.

[Wan 1997]   Wang, W. and Chan, T. Experience of designing and agent-oriented programming language for developing social learning systems. In proceedings of eight world conference on Artificial Intelligence in Education, pp. 7-14, 1997.

[War 1997]   Warendorf, K. and Tan, C. ADIS - An animated data structure intelligent tutoring system or Putting an interactive tutor on the WWW, In: P. Brusilovsky, K. Nakabayashi and S. Ritter (eds.) Proceedings of Workshop "Intelligent Educational Systems on the World Wide Web" at AI-ED'97, 8th World Conference on Artificial Intelligence in Education, Kobe, Japan, 18 August 1997, ISIR, pp. 54-60.

[Web 1913]   Webster's   Dictionary, http://humanities.uchicago.edu/forms_unrest/webster.form.html.

[Web 1995]   Weber, G. and Möllenberg, A. ELM-Programming-Environment: A Tutoring System for LISP Beginners. In: K. F. Wender, F. Schmalhofer and H.-D. Böcker (eds.): Cognition and Computer Programming. Norwood, NJ: Ablex, pp. 373-408, 1995.

[Web 1997]   Weber, G. and Specht, M. User Modeling and Adaptive Navigation Support in WWW-Based Tutoring Systems. In Anthony Jameson, Cécile Paris, and Carlo Tasso (Eds.) User Modeling: Proceedings of the Sixth International Conference, UM97 (pp. 289-300). Vienna, New York: Springer Wien New York, 1997.

[Wen 1987]   Wenger, E. Artificial Intelligence and Tutoring Systems, Menlo Park, CA Morgan Kaufmann, 1987.

[WHATIS]   http://searchwebservices.techtarget.com/sDefinition/0,,sid26_gci21 2300,00.html

[Whi 1997]   Whitehead, E. An architectural model for application integration in open hypermedia environments. Proceedings of the Eighth ACM Conference on Hypertext (Hypertext 97), (Southampton, England, Apr), 1-11, 1997.

[Wii 1996]   Wiil, U. and Leggett, J. The HyperDisco approach to open hypermedia systems, Proceedings of the Seventh ACM Conference on Hypertext (Hypertext 96), (Washington, DC, Mar), 140-148, 1996.

[Wil 1993]   Willis, B. Strategies for teaching at a distance, ERIC Document Reproduction Service No. ED 351 008, 1993.

[Wil 1996]   Wilson, B. (Ed.). Constructivist learning environments: Case studies in instructional design. New Jersey: Educational Technology Publications, 1996.

[WIND]   Microsoft   Windows®.
http://www.microsoft.com/windows/default.mspx.

[Wol 2002]   Wolf, C. iWeaver: Towards an Interactive Web-Based Adaptive Learning Environment to Address Individual Learning Styles, EURODL 2002.

[Woo 1992]   Woolf, B. AI in Education. *Encyclopedia of Artificial Intelligence*, Shapiro, S., ed., John Wiley & Sons, Inc., New York, pp. 434-444, 1992.

[Woo 1995]   Woods, P. and Warren, J. RApid Prototyping of an Intelligent Tutorial System (RAPITS). Proc. ASCILITE'95, Melbourne, pp. 557-563, 1995.

[Woo 1995a]   Wooldridge, M. and Jennings, N. Agent theories, architectures and languages: A survey. In Intelligent Agents, M. Wooldridge and N. Jennings, Eds. Springer-Verlag, New York, N.Y., 1-39, 1995.

[Woo 1996]   Woolf, B. Intelligent multimedia tutoring systems, Communications of the ACM, Vol. 39, No. 4, pp. 30-1, 1996.

[Woo 2000]   Wooldridge, M. Intelligent Agents: Introduction. 2nd European Agent Systems Summer School, EASSS2000. August 14 – 18. Saarbrucken, Germany, 2000.

[WWW]   The World Wide Web consortium. http://www.w3.org

[Yaz 2002]   Yazon, J. M. O., Mayer-Smith, J. A. and Redfield, R. J. Does the medium change the message ?. The impact of a web-based genetics course on university students' perspectives on learning and teaching. Computers & Education, Volume 38, Issues 1-3, January-April 2002, pp. 267-285, 2002.

[4MAT]   ®4MAT is a registered trademark of About Learning, Inc. http://www.aboutlearning.com.

Annexes

Qüestionari ILS - Index of Learning Styles

Barbara A. Soloman
First-Year College
North Carolina State University
Raleigh, North Carolina 27695

Richard M. Felder
Department of Chemical Engineering
North Carolina State University
Raleigh, NC 27695-7905

Per a cada una de les 44 preguntes següents, seleccioni la primera o la segona per a indicar la seva resposta.
Trie només una resposta per cada pregunta, si us plau.
Si les dos respostes pareixen aplicar-se a vosté, trie només la que se aplic mes freqüentment.
Quan hagi acabat de seleccionar les respostes per a cada pregunta, fa a clic al botó "enviar" per a enviar el formulari.

1.

   Entenc millor qualsevol cosa desprès de:

   ○ experimentar amb això.
   ○ pensar en això.

2. **Em considere:**

   ○ Realista.
   ○ Innovador.

3. **Quan penso sobre el que vaig fer ahir, el descric millor amb:**

   ○ Imatges.
   ○ Paraules.

4. **Tracte de:**

○ entendre els detalls d'un contingut però sentint-me confús sobre la seva estructura general.

○ entendre l'estructura general d'un contingut però sentint-me confús pels seus detalls.

5. **Quan estic aprenent alguna cosa nova, m'ajuda:**

○ Parlar-ne.

○ Pensar en això.

6. **Si fora professor, preferiria donar un curs:**

○ que tracte amb fets i situacions de la vida real.

○ que tracte amb idees i teories.

7. **Preferisc buscar informació nova en:**

○ imatges, diagrames, gràfics, o mapes.

○ Instruccions escrites o informació verbal.

8. **Una vegada que entenc:**

○ Totes les parts, l'enten tot.

○ Tot, veig les parts que el formen.

9. **En un grup d'estudi sobre un material difícil, em sent més a gust:**

○ Participant activament i contribuint amb ideas.

○ Només escoltant.

10. **Em pareix més fàcil:**

○ Aprendre amb fets.

○ Aprendre amb conceptes.

11. **En un llibre amb moltes imatges i quadros, és probable que:**

○ Examine les imatges i els quadros acuradament.
○ Em centre en el text escrit.

12. **Quan resolc problemes matemàtics:**

○ Normalment treball pas a pas fins a arribar a la solució.
○ Veig la solució però se'm dificulta després imaginar-me els passos per a arribar a ella.

13. **En les classes que he pres:**

○ Normalment he arribat a conéixer various dels estudiants.
○ Rara vegada he aconseguit conéixer a various dels estudiants.

14. **Quan no llig ficció, preferisc:**

○ Qualsevol cosa que m'ensenye nous fets o em diga com fer coses
○ Qualsevol cosa que em de noves idees en què pensar.

15. **Preferisc els professors que:**

○ fan molts diagrames en la pissarra.
○ passen molt de temps explicant.

16. **Quan estic analitzant una història o una novel·la:**

○ Penso en els esdeveniments i tracte d'ajuntar-los tots per a figurar-me els temes.
○ Només conec els temes quan acabe de llegir i després he de tornar darrera per a trobar els esdeveniments que els demostren.

17. **Quan estic resolent un problema m'agrada mes:**

○ Començar treballant immediatament en la solució.
○ Tractar primer d'entendre completament el problema.

18. **Preferisc la idea de:**

○ Certesa.
○ Teoría.

19. **Record millor:**

○ El que veig.
○ El que escolte.

20. **És més important per a mi que un professor:**

○ Organitze el material en passos seqüencials clars.
○ Em d'una visió general i relacione el material amb altres continguts.

21. **Preferisc estudiar:**

○ En un grup d'estudi.
○ Ùnicament jo.

22. **Em considere:**

○ Acurat amb els detalls del meu treball.
○ Creatiu en la forma de fer el meu treball.

23. **Quan demane indicacions sobre un nou lloc, preferisc:**

○ Un mapa.
○ Instruccions escrites.

24. **Aprent:**

○ A un ritme més o menys regular. Si m'esforce, l'aconseguisc.

○ En forma intermitent. Sòl estar totalment confós i "de repent" tot se m'aclareix.

25. **Preferiria:**

○ Experimentar amb les coses.
○ Pensar sobre com fer les coses.

26. **Quan llig per diversió, m'agraden els escriptors que:**

○ Diuen clarament els significats.
○ Diuen les coses en forma creativa i interessant.

27. **Quan veig un diagrama o un esbós en classe, el mes probable és que recorde:**

○ La imatge.
○ Lo que l'instructor diu sobre el.

28. **Quan considere un cos d'informació és més probable que:**

○ Aprofundisca en detalls ometent l'idea general.
○ Tracte d'entendre l'idea general abans d'entrar en els detalls.

29. **Record més fàcilment:**

○ Qualsevol cosa que haja fet.
○ Qualsevol cosa sobre la que haja pensat molt.

30. **Quan he de fer un treball, preferisc:**

○ fer-lo de la manera que m'han ensenyat.
○ Proposar noves maneres de fer-lo.

31. **Quan algú em mostra dades, preferisc:**

○ gràfics.
○ resums amb textos.

32. **Quan escric un treball, és més probable que:**

○ Ho faça (pensi i escrigui) des del principi i avanç progressivament.
○ Ho faça (pense i escriga) en diferents parts i després les ordene.

33. **Quan he de treballar en un projecte de grup, primer vull:**

○ Proposar una "pluja d'idees" i que cada un contribuïsca amb les seves.
○ Realitzar una "pluja d'idees" de forma personal i després ajuntar-me amb el grup per a comparar les idees.

34. **Considere que és millor elogi anomenar a algú:**

○ Sensat.
○ Imaginatiu.

35. **Quan conec gent en una festa, és més probable que recorde:**

○ Com és la seva aparença.
○ El que diuen de si mateixos.

36. **Quan estic aprenent un tema nou, preferisc:**

○ Mantindre'm concentrat en aquell tema, aprenent el que més puga d'ell
○ Fer connexions entre eixe tema i els temes relacionats.

37. **Em considere:**

○ Obert.
○ Reservat.

38. **Preferisc els cursos que donen mes importància a:**

○ Material concret (fets, dades).
○ Material abstracte (conceptes, teories).

39. **Per diversió preferisc:**

○ Veure television.
○ Llegir un llibre.

40. **Alguns professors inicien les seves classes fent un esbós o resum del que ensenyaran, eixos esbossos són:**

○ Poc útils per a mi.
○ Prou útils per a mi.

41. **La idea de fer una tasca en grup amb una sola qualificació per a tots:**

○ Em pareix bé.
○ No em pareix bé.

42. **Quan faig grans càlculs:**

○ Tendisc a repetir tots els meus passos i a revisar acuradament el meu treball.
○ Em cansa fer la seva revisió i he d'esforçar-me per a fer-lo.

43. **Tendisc a recordar llocs en què he estat:**

○ Fàcilment i amb prou exactitud.
○ Amb dificultat i sense molt de detall.

44. **Quan resolc problemes en grup, és mes probable que jo:**

○ Pense en els passos per a la solució dels problemes.
○ Pense en les possibles conseqüències o aplicacions de la solución en un ampli rang de camps.

Cuestionario ILS - Index of Learning Styles

Barbara A. Soloman
First-Year College
North Carolina State University
Raleigh, North Carolina 27695

Richard M. Felder
Department of Chemical Engineering
North Carolina State University
Raleigh, NC 27695-7905

Por favor seleccione solamente una respuesta para cada pregunta. Si más de una respuesta parecen aplicarse a usted, seleccione solo aquella que se aplique más frecuentemente.

1. **Entiendo mejor algo:**

   ○ Si lo practico.
   ○ Si pienso en ello.

2. **Me considero:**

   ○ Realista.
   ○ Innovador.

3. **Cuando pienso acerca de lo que hice ayer, es más probable que lo haga con base en:**

   ○ Imágenes
   ○ Palabras.

4. **Tengo tendencia a:**

   ○ Entender los detalles de un tema pero no ver claramente su estructura completa.
   ○ Entender la estructura completa de un tema pero no ver claramente los detalles.

5. **Cuando estoy aprendiendo algo nuevo, me ayuda:**

   ○ Hablar de ello.
   ○ Pensar en ello.

6. **Si yo fuera profesor, preferiría dar un curso:**

   ○ Que trate sobre hechos y situaciones reales de la vida.
   ○ Que trate ideas y teorías.

7. **Prefiero obtener información nueva en:**

   ○ Imágenes, diagramas, gráficos o mapas.
   ○ Instrucciones escritas o información verbal.

8. **Una vez que entiendo:**

   ○ Todas las partes, entiendo el total.
   ○ El total de algo, entiendo como encajan las partes.

9. **En un grupo de estudio que trabaja con un material difícil, es más probable que:**

   ○ Participe y contribuya con ideas.
   ○ No participe y solo escuche.

10. **Es más fácil para mi:**

    ○ Aprender hechos.
    ○ Aprender conceptos.

11. **En un libro con muchas imágenes y gráficos es más probable que:**

    ○ Revise cuidadosamente las imágenes y los gráficos.
    ○ Me concentre en el texto escrito.

12. **Cuando resuelvo problemas de matemáticas:**

    ○ Generalmente trabajo paso a paso hasta llegar a la solución.
    ○ Frecuentemente sé cuales son las soluciones, pero luego tengo dificultad para imaginarme los pasos para llegar a ellas.

13. **En las clases a las que he asistido:**

    ○ He llegado a saber como son muchos de los estudiantes.
    ○ Raramente he llegado a saber como son muchos de los estudiantes.

14. **Cuando leo temas que no son de ficción, prefiero:**

    ○ Algo que me enseñe nuevos hechos o me diga como hacer algo.
    ○ Algo que me de nuevas ideas en que pensar.

5. **Me gustan los profesores:**

   ○ Que hacen muchos esquemas en la pizarra.
   ○ Que invierten mucho tiempo en explicar.

6. **Cuando estoy analizando un cuento o una novela:**

   ○ Pienso en los incidentes y trato de acomodarlos para figurarme las tramas.
   ○ Me doy cuenta de las tramas cuando termino de leer y luego tengo que regresar y encontrar los incidentes que las demuestran.

7. **Cuando comienzo a resolver un problema de tarea, lo más probable es que:**

   ○ Comience a trabajar en la solución inmediatamente.
   ○ Primero trate de entender completamente el problema.

8. **Prefiero la idea de:**

   ○ Certeza.
   ○ Teoría.

9. **Recuerdo mejor:**

   ○ Lo que veo.
   ○ Lo que oigo.

0. **Es mas importante para mi que un profesor:**

   ○ Exponga el material mediante pasos secuenciales claros.
   ○ Me de un panorama general y relacione el material con otros temas.

1. **Prefiero estudiar:**

   ○ En un grupo de estudio.
   ○ Solo.

2. **Me considero:**

   ○ Cuidadoso en los detalles de mi trabajo.
   ○ Creativo en la forma de realizar mi trabajo.

3. **Cuando busco la dirección de un nuevo sitio, prefiero:**

○ Un mapa.
○ Instrucciones escritas.

24. **Aprendo:**

○ Progresivamente, estudiando paso a paso las distintas partes de un tema.
○ Leyendo primero todo el tema y centrándome después en cada una de sus partes.

25. **Prefiero primero:**

○ Hacer algo y ver que sucede.
○ Pensar bien como voy a hacer algo y luego hacerlo.

26. **Cuando leo por diversión, me gustan los escritores que:**

○ Dicen claramente lo que desean dar a entender.
○ Dicen las cosas de forma creativa e interesante.

27. **Cuando veo un diagrama o esquema en clase, es más probable que recuerde:**

○ La imagen.
○ Lo que el profesor dijo acerca de él.

28. **Cuando me enfrento a una información:**

○ Me concentro en los detalles antes de prestar atención a la idea general.
○ Trato de comprender la idea general antes de entrar en los detalles.

29. **Recuerdo más fácilmente:**

○ Algo que he hecho.
○ Algo en lo que he pensado mucho.

30. **Cuando tengo que hacer un trabajo, prefiero:**

○ Hacerlo de una sola manera.
○ Proponer nuevas maneras de hacerlo.

31. **Cuando alguien me muestra datos, prefiero:**

○ Gráficos.
○ Resúmenes con textos.

2. **Cuando escribo un trabajo, es más probable que:**

     ○ Lo haga (piense y escriba) desde el principio y avance progresivamente.

     ○ Lo haga (piense y escriba) en diferentes partes y luego las ordene.

3. **Cuando tengo que trabajar en un proyecto de grupo, primero quiero:**

     ○ Proponer una "lluvia de ideas" y que cada uno contribuya con las suyas.

     ○ Realizar una "lluvia de ideas" de forma personal y luego juntarme con el grupo para comparar las ideas.

4. **Considero que es mejor elogio llamar a alguien:**

     ○ Sensato.

     ○ Imaginativo.

5. **Cuando conozco gente en una fiesta, es más probable que recuerde:**

     ○ Cómo es su apariencia.

     ○ Lo que dicen de si mismos.

6. **Cuando estoy aprendiendo un tema nuevo, prefiero:**

     ○ Mantenerme concentrado en ese tema, aprendiendo lo que más pueda de él.

     ○ Hacer conexiones entre ese tema y los temas relacionados.

7. **Me considero:**

     ○ Abierto.

     ○ Reservado.

8. **Prefiero los cursos que dan mas importancia a:**

     ○ Material concreto (hechos, datos).

     ○ Material abstracto (conceptos, teorías).

9. **Por diversión prefiero:**

     ○ Ver televisión.

     ○ Leer un libro.

0. **Algunos profesores inician sus clases haciendo un bosquejo o resumen**

de lo que enseñarán, esos bosquejos son:

- ○ Poco útiles para mi.
- ○ Bastante útiles para mi.

41. **La idea de hacer una tarea en grupo con una sola calificación para todos**

- ○ Me parece bien.
- ○ No me parece bien.

42. **Cuando hago grandes cálculos:**

- ○ Tiendo a repetir todos mis pasos y a revisar cuidadosamente mi trabajo.
- ○ Me cansa hacer su revisión y tengo que esforzarme para hacerlo.

43. **Tiendo a recordar lugares en los que he estado:**

- ○ Fácilmente y con bastante exactitud.
- ○ Con dificultad y sin mucho detalle.

44. **Cuando resuelvo problemas en grupo, es mas probable que yo:**

- ○ Piense en los pasos para la solución de los problemas.
- ○ Piense en las posibles consecuencias o aplicaciones de la solución en un amplio rango de campos.

(Enviar)

Questionnaire ILS - Index of Learning Styles

Barbara A. Soloman
First-Year College
North Carolina State University
Raleigh, North Carolina 27695

Richard M. Felder
Department of Chemical Engineering
North Carolina State University
Raleigh, NC 27695-7905

For each of the 44 questions below select either the first or de second one to indicate your answer.
Please choose only one answer for each question.
If both first or second seem to apply to you, choose the one that applies habite frequently.
When you have finished selecting answers to each question please select the submit button at the end of the form to send it.

1. **I understand something better after I:**

   ○ try it out.
   ○ think it through.

2. **I would rather be considered:**

   ○ realistic.
   ○ innovative.

3. **When I think about what I did yesterday, I am most likely to get:**

   ○ a picture.
   ○ words.

4. **I tend to:**

   ○ understand details of a subject but may be fuzzy about its overall structure.
   ○ understand the overall structure but may be fuzzy about details.

5. **When I am learning something new, it helps me to:**

   ○ talk about it.
   ○ think about it.

6. **If I were a teacher, I would rather teach a course:**

   ○ that deals with facts and real life situations.
   ○ that deals with ideas and theories.

7. **I prefer to get new information in:**

   ○ pictures, diagrams, graphs, or maps.
   ○ written directions or verbal information.

8. **Once I understand:**

   ○ all the parts, I understand the whole thing.
   ○ the whole thing, I see how the parts fit.

9. **In a study group working on difficult material, I am more likely to:**

   ○ jump in and contribute ideas.
   ○ sit back and listen.

10. **I find it easier:**

    ○ to learn facts.
    ○ to learn concepts .

11. **In a book with lots of pictures and charts, I am likely to:**

    ○ look over the pictures and charts carefully.
    ○ focus on the written text.

12. **When I solve math problems:**

    ○ I usually work my way to the solutions one step at a time.
    ○ I often just see the solutions but then have to struggle to figure out the steps to get to them.

13. **In classes I have taken:**

    ○ I have usually gotten to know many of the students.

○ I have rarely gotten to know many of the students.

4. In reading nonfiction, I prefer:

○ something that teaches me new facts or tells me how to do something.
○ something that gives me new ideas to think about.

5. I like teachers:

○ who put a lot of diagrams on the board.
○ who spend a lot of time explaining.

6. When I'm analyzing a story or a novel:

○ I think of the incidents and try to put them together to figure out the themes.
○ I just know what the themes are when I finish reading and then I have to go back and find the incidents that demonstrate them.

7. When I start a homework problem, I am more likely to:

○ start working on the solution immediately.
○ try to fully understand the problem first.

8. I prefer the idea of:

○ certainty.
○ theory.

9. I remember best:

○ what I see.
○ what I hear.

0. It is more important to me that an instructor:

○ lay out the material in clear sequential steps.
○ give me an overall picture and relate the material to other subjects.

1. I prefer to study:

○ in a study group.
○ alone.

22. **I am more likely to be considered:**

○ careful about the details of my work.
○ creative about how to do my work.

23. **When I get directions to a new place, I prefer:**

○ a map.
○ written instructions.

24. **I learn:**

○ at a fairly regular pace. If I study hard, I'll "get it".
○ in fits and starts. I'll be totally confused and then suddenly it all "clicks"

25. **I would rather first:**

○ try things out.
○ think about how I'm going to do it.

26. **When I am reading for enjoyment, I like writers to:**

○ clearly say what they mean.
○ say things in creative, interesting ways.

27. **When I see a diagram or sketch in class, I am most likely to remember:**

○ the picture.
○ what the instructor said about it.

28. **When considering a body of information, I am more likely to:**

○ focus on details and miss the big picture.
○ try to understand the big picture before getting into the details.

29. **I more easily remember:**

○ something I have done.
○ something I have thought a lot about.

0. When I have to perform a task, I prefer to:

- ○ master one way of doing it.
- ○ come up with new ways of doing it.

1. When someone is showing me data, I prefer:

- ○ charts or graphs.
- ○ text summarizing the results.

2. When writing a paper, I am more likely to:

- ○ work on (think about or write) the beginning of the paper and progress forward.
- ○ work on (think about or write) different parts of the paper and then order them.

3. When I have to work on a group project, I first want to:

- ○ have "group brainstorming" where everyone contributes ideas.
- ○ brainstorm individually and then come together as a group to compare ideas.

4. I consider it higher praise to call someone:

- ○ sensible.
- ○ imaginative.

5. When I meet people at a party, I am more likely to remember:

- ○ what they looked like.
- ○ what they said about themselves.

6. When I am learning a new subject, I prefer to:

- ○ stay focused on that subject, learning as much about it as I can.
- ○ try to make connections between that subject and related subjects.

7. I am more likely to be considered:

- ○ outgoing.
- ○ reserved.

38. **I prefer courses that emphasize:**

   ○ concrete material (facts, data).
   ○ abstract material (concepts, theories).

39. **For entertainment, I would rather:**

   ○ watch television.
   ○ read a book.

40. **Some teachers start their lectures with an outline of what they will cover. Such outlines are:**

   ○ somewhat helpful to me.
   ○ very helpful to me.

41. **The idea of doing homework in groups, with one grade for the entire group:**

   ○ appeals to me.
   ○ does not appeal to me.

42. **When I am doing long calculations:**

   ○ I tend to repeat all my steps and check my work carefully.
   ○ I find checking my work tiresome and have to force myself to do it.

43. **I tend to picture places I have been:**

   ○ easily and fairly accurately.
   ○ with difficulty and without much detail.

44. **When solving problems in a group, I would be more likely to:**

   ○ think of the steps in the solution process.
   ○ think of possible consequences or applications of the solution in a wide range of areas.

(Submit)

Annex 2: Curriculum of the Computer Networks course

PARTNER	
INSTITUTION	University of Girona - Spain
DEPARTMENT	Departament d'Informàtica i Aplicacions (Computer Science Department)
COURSE	
TOPIC	Computer networks
EDUCATIONAL OBJECTIVE	To describe the diverse protocols that allow providing quality of service in Internet and the necessary technologies for the creation of applications that achieve these requirements.
CONTENTS	Computer networks • Current state of the TCP/IP protocols: • Part I • Part II • Introduction to the new protocols of Internet with guarantee of quality of service: • Client-server applications • Quality of Service • The new Internet Protocols • Multicast routing
COURSE	
DATE	2001 - 2002
SCOPE	This course was carrying out as a 1 credit complement of the f2f Computer Networks course program.

COURSE PRESENTATION ISSUES

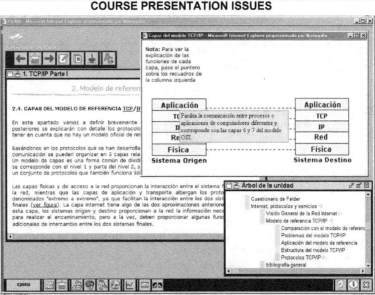

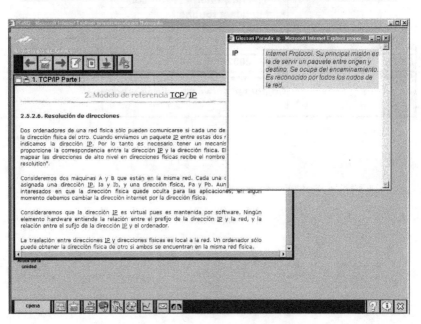

338

COURSE PRESENTATION ISSUES

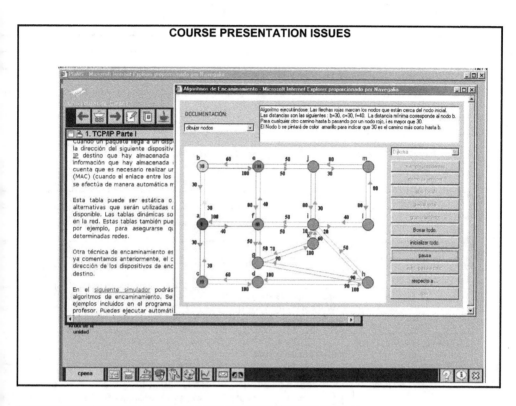

COURSE	
TARGET AUDIENCE	
TYPE	40 students from the third undergraduate course of Computer Science program
MOTIVATION	To complement their course credits.
PREVIOUS DL EXPERIENCE	Was not considered.
DELIVERY METHODOLOGY	All modules completely by Internet.
STAFF	
RESPONSIBLE	José Luis Marzo Lázaro
TEACHERS	José Luis Marzo Lázaro
INSTRUCTIONAL DESIGNER	Ramón Fabregat – Clara Inés Peña de Carrillo – Jose Luis Marzo

COURSE	
SUPPORT STAFF	
TECHNICAL	Clara Inés Peña de Carrillo, Carles Coll Madrenas
PEDAGOGICAL	José Luis Marzo – Ramón Fabregat – Clara Inés Peña de Carrillo
OTHER (Functions)	Eugenia Luz González – subjects developer

REQUIRED RESOURCES (State if they already exist or will be developed)	
TRADITIONAL RESOURCES	
REFERENCE BOOK	Yes
NOTES	Yes
OTHER	
TECHNOLOGY	
VIRTUAL LEARNING ENVIRONMENT	USD (Unitats de Suport a la Docència): own UdG ODL platform
STUDENT GUIDE	Yes; A guide to help the students in their DL environment is available. Student manual at PDF document and online navigatio help guide.
COURSE GUIDE	Yes; Course activities for students were planned and detailed in the course guide.
ELECTRONIC DOCUMENTATION	Yes; The material was developed specifically for the course. It is composed of about 128 HTML pages distributed in 6 course modules as follows: 58 HTML pages for the first module, 28 HTM pages for the second module, 6 HTML pages for the third and fo modules, 3 HTML pages for the fifth module and 25 HTML pages for the sixth module.
INTERACTIVITY	Yes
ANIMATION	Yes, especially at modules 1 and 2.
SIMULATION	Yes, especially at modules 1 and 2.
EXTERNAL LINKS	Yes, to bibliography references

REQUIRED RESOURCES (State if they already exist or will be developed)	
SOFTWARE APPLICATIONS	Yes
ELECTRONIC MAIL (when and how)	At any time by means of any electronic mail application.
TECHNOLOGY	
INTERACTIVITY	
STUDENT-TEACHER	Yes; students were able to contact directly the teacher; teacher was requested to answer in 24 hours.
STUDENT-STUDENT	Yes
STUDENT-INSTITUTION	Yes; technical support was available for students.
ASSYNCHRONOUS DISCUSSION	
DISCUSSION FORUM	No
NEWSGROUP	No
MAILING LIST	Yes
SYNCHRONOUS DISCUSSION	
CHAT	Yes, by means of the chat module at the USD platform
WHITEBOARD	No

REQUIRED RESOURCES (State if they already exist or will be developed)	
INTELLIGENT TUTORING	No
ASSESSMENT	
SELF-ASSESSMENT	No; asynchronous assessment by means of accomplishing a teacher proposed exercise and sending it back to the teacher via e-mail.
ONLINE ASSESSMENT	Yes; course assessment was based on the following aspects:
	Student's activities carried out during on-line sessions (visited HTML pages, time spent in visited pages, type of actions, etc.)
	Participation on the programmed chat (assistance).
	e-mail comments.
RELEVANCE	Successful students had accomplished a 1 course credit complement.

342

Annex 3. Description of the Agent behaviors

This annex offers a detailed description of the agent design and implementation issues introduced in Chapter 6.

3.1 Monitor Agent

3.1.1 Identification of the necessary behaviors

The operation of an agent is defined according to the executed behaviors. A behavior is an ontology class that an agent may load when needed. A behavior defines a sequence of actions that an agent should carry out.

The use cases presented above for the *Monitor* agent define the following behaviors:

- **CourseStartingAlert:** behavior that informs the *Pedagogic* and the *User* agents that the student has begun to study a lesson.
- **CourseMonitoring:** behavior that allows the students' actions to be collected when the students study a lesson.
- **ExerciseMonitoring:** behavior that allows the students' actions to be collected when the students solve exercises.
- **SessionMonitoring:** behavior that allows the general students' actions of the current learning session to be collected.
- **FelderQuestionnaire:** behavior that allows the answers to the Felder questionnaire to be collected. This behavior is executed only once when the student accesses the system for the first time.
- **ControllerReplies:** behavior that informs to the *Controller* agent, the *Monitor* agent state of activity.

The monitor agent uses some FIPA protocols and some classes of the MASPLANG ontology to communicate with other agents of the system. The next section describes the activity diagrams of the behaviors mentioned above and the ontology used by this *Monitor* agent.

343

3.1.2   Activity diagrams and ontology

CourseStartingAlert: This behavior is executed when the student begins studying a lesson. It is used to inform the *Pedagogic* and the *User* agents of the code that identifies the lesson and the beginning time of the lesson learning activities. The *newUnit* object of the ontology allows the corresponding message to be sent. See the structure of this object in Table 25.

Table 25. Structure of the newUnit object

newUnit			
:code	Integer	O	Code that identifies the lesson
:time	Time	O	Time of the lesson initiation

Figure 155 shows the activity diagram of this behavior.

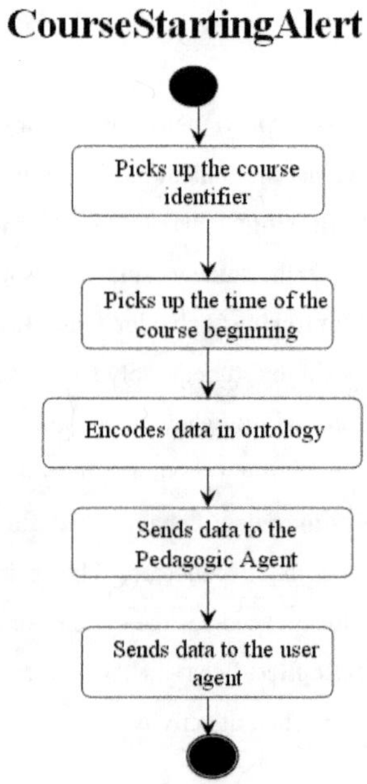

Figure 155.   Activity diagram of the *CourseStartingAlert* behavior

CourseMonitoring: This behavior is executed when the student begins studying a lesson. The student actions from the navigation toolbar or from the navigation tree should be gathered. The navigation toolbar offers tools to consult the bibliographical references or the glossary, to wake up the *SMIT* agent, to search for a particular contents, to execute self assessment exercises, to follow up the course by means of the direct guidance technique (using the backward and forward arrows) or the navigation tree (free navigation between the adapted links of the course). The collected data is coded according to the *Units* object of the MASPLANG ontology (see Table 26) and sent to the *User* agent. The *SMITWakeup* object (that requests the *SMIT* agent to have available the historial of the messages) and the *SMITmessage* object (that requests the *SMIT* agent to display an already displayed message) are used to requests actions on the *SMIT* agent (see Table 27).

Table 26. Structure of the Units object

Units			
:tree_clicks	Integer	O	Number of mouse-clicks on the navigation tree
:arrows_clicks	Instance of arrows_clicks	O	Multiple cardinality: backward arrow, forward arrow
:glossary	Integer	O	Number of mouse-clicks on the glossary button
:bibliography	Integer	O	Number of mouse-clicks on the bibliography button
:searcher	Integer	O	Number of mouse-clicks on the searcher button
:exercises_clicks	Instance of exercises_clicks	O	Multiple cardinality: configured_exercises (according to student preferences), adapted_exercises (according to student knowledge level)
:node_clicks	Instance of node_clicks	O	Multiple cardinality: node_name, number_of_visit, time spent in visit
:smit_clicks	Integer	O	Number of mouse-clicks on the *SMIT* icon
arrows_clicks			
:backward	Integer	O	Number of mouse-clicks on the backward arrow
:forward	Integer	O	Number of mouse-clicks on the forward arrow
exercises_clicks			
:configured_exercises	Integer	O	Number of mouse-clicks on the exercise configuration window
:adapted_exercises	Integer	O	Number of mouse-clicks on the ExerciseAdapter agent button
Node_clicks			
:node_name	Char	O	Name of the visited node
:visit_number	Integer	O	Visit number
:time_spent	Time	O	Time spent in the visit

SmitWakeup			
:wakeup	Boolean	O	Flag to wake up the *SMIT* agent
SMITmessage			
:code	Integer	O	Message code
:type	Integer	O	Message type: 1-user_online_student, 2-user_online_teacher, 3-warning_at_time, 4-Exercises, 5-Bibliography, 6-motivation, 7-reinforcement
:message_time	Time		Time for message of type 3
:user_online	Set of string		List of users for message type =1 or 2
:message_content	String		Message content for message type = 2, 3, 6 or 7

Figure 156 shows the activity diagram of this behavior.

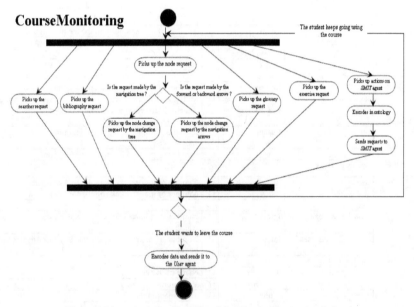

Figure 156.   Activity diagram of the *CourseMonitoring* behavior

ExerciseMonitoring: this behavior is executed when the student begins to solve an exercise. Figure 157 shows the activity diagram of this behavior.

ExerciseMonitoring

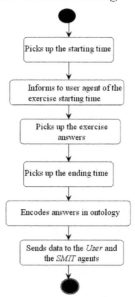

Figure 157.   Activity diagram of the *ExerciseMonitoring* behavior

The monitor agent picks up the beginning time of the exercise execution. At this point and using the *beginExercise* object of the MASPLANG ontology (see Table 28) the monitor agent informs the *User* agent of the characteristics of the exercise that the student will solve.

Table 28. Structure of the object beginExercise

beginExercise			
:exerciseCode	Integer	O	The exercise identifier
:exerciseInstance	Integer	O	The exercise instance identifier
:exerciseType	Integer	O	The exercise type

During the execution of the exercise, the monitor agent picks up the student's answers and, once the student has finished, the time spent solving the exercise is also recorded. By using the *Exercise* object of the MASPLANG ontology (Table 29), this information is coded and sent to the *User* agent.

347

Table 29. Structure of the object Exercise

Exercise			
:exerciseCode	Integer	O	The exercise identifier
:exerciseNode	Integer	O	The exercise instance identifier
:exerciseInstance	Integer	O	The exercise type
:questionResults	Instance of questionResults	O	Multiple cardinality: questions, level of difficulty, answers and feedback
:time_elapsed	Time	O	Time used to solve the exercise
questionResults			
:questionN	Integer	O	Question code
:questionL	Integer	O	Question level of difficulty
:AnswerN	Integer	O	Answer code
:feedback	String		The feedback information that will correct the student performance if necessary

SessionMonitoring: this behavior is executed when the student enters into the learning environment (see the activity diagram in Figure 158). The session beginning and ending times as well as the student mouse-clicks on the chat, forum, e-mail and *SONIA* agent buttons are collected. At the end of the session the monitor agent codes the information using the *Session* object of the ontology (see Table 30) and sends it to the *User* agent.

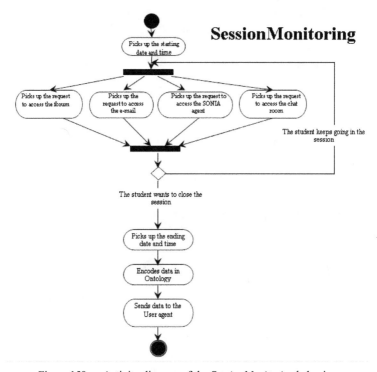

Figure 158.   Activity diagram of the *SessionMonitoring* behavior

Table 30. Structure of the object Session

Session			
:chat_clicks	Integer	O	Number of mouse-clicks on the chat button
:forum_clicks	Integer	O	Number of mouse-clicks on the forum button
:mail_clicks	Integer	O	Number of mouse-clicks on the e-mail button
:sonia	Integer	O	Number of mouse-clicks on the *SONIA* agent button
:begin_time	Time	O	The beginning time of the session
:end_time	Time	O	The ending time of the session

ControllerReplies: this behavior is executed when the monitor agent receives a message from the *Controller* agent with a Query-if performative. The possible answers that the monitor agent may give are: *refuse*, if it does not want to respond, *inform* with a *true* or *false* value if it has a stable or unstable state respectively, or *not-understood* if it does not understand the message.

The activity diagram of this behavior is shown in the next figure.

349

ControllerReplies

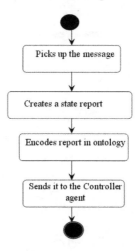

Figure 159.   Activity diagram of the *ControllerReplies* behavior

FelderQuestionnaire: this behavior is executed when a student enters the system for the first time or when the student does not have a learning profile assigned yet. The *Monitor* agent receives a request (using the *FIPA-request* protocol) from the *User* agent to evaluate the student learning profile from the Felder Questionnaire (ILS). The *Monitor* agent should respond to this request using a *not-understood*, a *refuse* or an *agree* message. Once the student has responded to the questionnaire, the *Monitor* agent evaluates his/her learning profile and sends it to the *User* agent (using the *Profile_rp* object of the ontology whose structure is shown in Table 31).

Table 31. Structure of the object Profile_rp

Profile_rp			
:profile	Instance of profile	O	Multiple cardinality: dimension, learning style
profile			
:dimension	Integer	O	Felder learning style dimension
:learningStyle	Integer	O	Learning style in Felder dimension

Figure 160 shows the activity diagram of this behavior.

350

FelderQuestionnaire

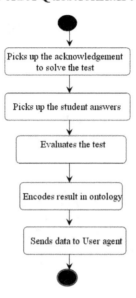

Figure 160. Activity diagram of the *FelderQuestionnaire* behavior

3.1.3 Protocol diagram

The Protocol diagram of the *Monitor* agent is shown in figures 161 and 162. Since the *Monitor* agent is mainly limited to informing the *User* agent of what it perceives of the student's learning environment and the *SMIT* agent the actions that students want to carry out, the use of the performative *inform* dominates this agent communication exchange. However, an exception is presented when the *User* agent requests the assignment and evaluation of the ILS questionnaire from the *Monitor* agent in which case the *FIPA-request* protocol is used. Finally, the *FIPA_query* protocol is used by the *Controller* agent to request a survival test from the *Monitor* agent.

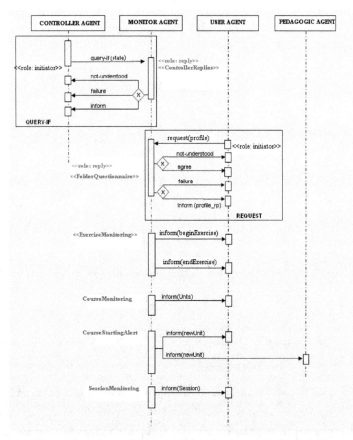

Figure 161.   Protocol diagram of the *Monitor* agent behaviors (1)

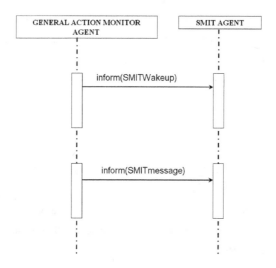

```
GENERAL ACTION MONITOR        SMIT AGENT
        AGENT

                inform(SMITWakeup)


                inform(SMITmessage)
```

Figure 162.   Protocol diagram of the *Monitor* agent behaviors (2)

3.2   Exercise Adapter Agent

3.2.1   Identification of the necessary behaviors

The use cases presented above for the *Exercise Adapter* agent define the following behaviors:

- **MountExercise**: behavior that allows the construction and presentation of an exercise.
- **AdaptExercise:** behavior that builds an exercise adapted to the progress of student knowledge.
- **ConfigureExercise:** behavior that allows the student to configure the exercise characteristics according to his/her preferences.
- **ControllerReplies**: behavior that informs the *Controller* agent of the state of activity of the *Exercise Adapter* agent.

3.2.2   Activity diagrams and ontology

MountExercise: this behavior is executed when the *Browsing* agent sends an ACL message (FIPA-request) to the *Exercise Adapter* agent requesting the construction of an exercise instance. The behavior is partially executed when the

353

student makes a request to build an exercise using his/her preferences or the characteristics that the Exercise Adapter agent considers appropriate to the student's knowledge level. In this case, the message is built using the *MakeExercise* object of the ontology as shown in Table 32.

Table 32. *Structure of the object MakeExercise*

MakeExercise			
:code	Integer	O	The exercise identifier
:instance	Integer	O	The identifier of the exercise instance

The properties of the exercise are obtained from the exercise instance stored in the database. The questions are randomly chosen following the directions of the exercise instance.

The following figure shows the activity diagram of this *Exercise Adapter* agent.

Figure 163.   Activity diagram of the *MountExercise* behavior

AdaptExercise: this behavior is executed when the student requests that the *Exercise Adapter* agent builds an adapted exercise. In this case, the exercises are not provided a priori; they depend on the navigation domain and on the ability demonstrated by the student up until that moment (stored in the student model). The system contains a base of questions organized by levels of difficulty that are associated with each concept and the student is evaluated in those concepts that he/she has previously seen. The criteria applied for adapting exercises is based on some of the Gagné learning principles mentioned previously in the domain model description (see Chapter 5).

Figure 164 shows the activity diagram of this behavior.

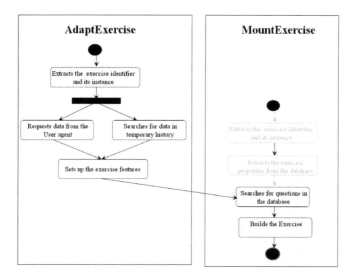

Figure 164.   Activity diagram of the *AdaptExercise* behavior

According to the activity diagram shown above, the *User* agent is requested (by means of the *ExerciseInfo_rq* object of the ontology) to provide information concerning the exercises in the student model. This information is necessary for the *Exercise Adapter* agent to apply the adaptation mechanisms based on the evolution of student knowledge in past sessions.

The structure of the *ExerciseInfo_rq* object is shown in Table 33. The *User* agent responds to this request using the *ExerciseInfo_rp* object shown in Table 34.

Table 33. Structure of the ExerciseInfo_rq object

ExerciseInfo_rq			
:code	Integer	O	The exercise identifier
:instance	Integer	O	The identifier of the exercise instance

Table 34. Structure of the ExerciseInfo_rp object

ExerciseInfo_rp			
:code	Integer	O	The exercise identifier
:instance	Integer	O	The identifier of the exercise instance
:BestQualEx	Float	O	Qualification of the best execution of the exercise
:NEasyok	Integer	O	Number of correct answers at the *Easy* level of difficulty
:NNormalok	Integer	O	Number of correct answers at the *Normal* level of difficulty
:NDifficultok	Integer	O	Number of correct answers at the *Difficult* level
:NEasyna	Integer	O	Number of unanswered questions at the *Easy* level
:NNormalna	Integer	O	Number of unanswered questions at the *Normal* level
:NDifficultna	Integer	O	Number of unanswered questions at the *Difficult* level
:NEasyin	Integer	O	Number of incorrect answers at the *Easy* level
:NNormalin	Integer	O	Number of incorrect answers at the *Normal* level
:NDifficultin	Integer	O	Number of incorrect answers at the *Difficult* level

ConfigureExercise: this behavior is executed when the student requests the *Exercise Adapter* agent to build a configured exercise. In this case, the student provides the basic characteristics of the exercise that he/she wants to solve. The Exercise Adapter agent builds the exercise selecting the questions randomly from a set of possible questions.

Figure 165 shows the activity diagram of this behavior.

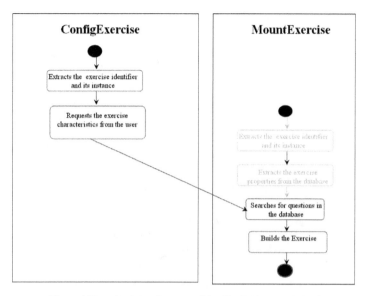

Figure 165.   Activity diagram of the *ConfigExercise* behavior

ControllerReplies: this behavior is executed when the *Exercise Adapter* agent receives a message with a Query-if performative from the *Controller* agent. The possible answers that the Exercise Adapter agent may give are: *refuse* if it does not want to respond, *inform* with a *true* or *false* value if it has a stable or unstable state respectively, or *not-understood* if it does not understand the message. The activity diagram of this behavior is similar to that described for the *Monitor* agent.

3.2.3　Protocol diagram

Figure 166 shows the Protocol diagram of the *Exercise Adapter* agent.

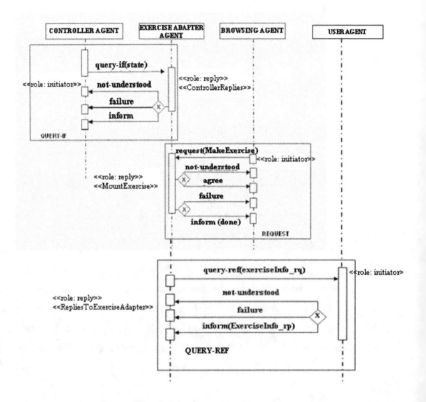

Figure 166.　Protocol diagram of the *Exercise Adapter* agent

3.3　User Agent

3.3.1　Identification of the necessary behaviors

The use cases presented above for the *User* agent define the following behaviors:

- **LearningStyleAssignment**: behavior that allows the initialization of
  the student learning profile.

- **MonitorSends**: behavior that allows the updating of the temporary or permanent student model using the data sent by the monitor agent (the information of the use case diagram is grouped in compound behaviors that call on different functions according to the message sent).
- **RepliesToPedagogic:** behavior that receives and interprets the *Pedagogic* agent requests. A message with the requested information is sent to the *Pedagogic* agent using the corresponding object of the ontology.
- **RepliesToExerciseAdapter:** behavior that receives and interprets the *Exercise Adapter* agent petitions. A message with the requested information is sent to the *Exercise Adapter* agent using the corresponding object of the ontology.
- **ControllerReplies**: behavior that informs the *Controller* agent of the *User* agent state of activity.

The next section describes the activity diagrams of the behaviors mentioned above.

3.3.2   Activity diagrams and ontology

LearningStyleAssignment: if the student begins a learning session for the first time, he/she does not yet have any learning profile assigned. In this case, the *User* agent asks the *Monitor* agent (using a FIPA-request message) to assess the student learning style through the ILS (Index of Learning Styles from the Felder learning style model) questionnaire. This learning profile is later fine-tuned using CBR techniques applied to the analysis of student action in the learning environment. The monitor agent sends the message with the requested information using the *Profile_rp* object of the ontology (see Table 31 mentioned previously when the *Monitor* agent behavior was described).

Figure 167 shows the activity diagram of this behavior.

LearningStyleAssignment

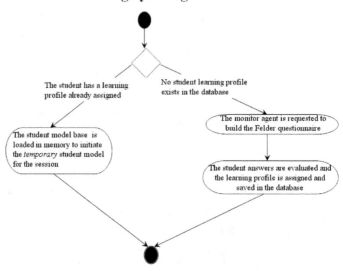

Figure 167.   Activity diagram of the *LearningStyleAssignment* behavior

MonitorSends: this is a complex behavior. It is executed when the *User* agent receives information coming from the *Monitor* agent. To know the content of the message, the corresponding object of the ontology is analyzed. The *Monitor* agent may send information concerning:

- The beginning of a lesson. A message that indicates which lesson the student is going to study (using the *newUnit* object of the ontology described in Table 25).
- The ending of a lesson. A message indicating that the student has finished studying the lesson (using the *Unit* object of the ontology described in Table 26).
- The beginning of the solution of an exercise. Information concerning the type of the exercise that the student will solve (using the *beginExercise* object of the ontology described in Table 28).

- The completion of an exercise. Information concerning the student performance when solving the exercise (using the *Exercise* object of the ontology described in Table 29).
- The ending of the learning session. Information concerning the student performance in the learning session (using the *Session* object of the ontology described in Table 30).

Figure 168 shows the activity diagram of this behavior.

MonitorSends

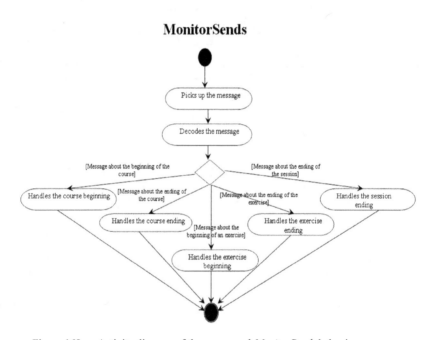

Figure 168.   Activity diagram of the compound *MonitorSends* behavior

RepliesToPedagogic: this behavior is used to send the information requested by the *Pedagogic* agent concerning the student model (information about the student learning profile or information about the student's knowledge state). The *Pedagogic* agent needs information about the student model when it is evaluating the pedagogic decision rules designed in the curriculum sequencing.

The objects of the ontology involved in the communication between the *user* and the *Pedagogic* agents are described globally in Tables 35 and 36.

Table 35. Some objects used in the communication between the User and the Pedagogic agents (_rq means request and _rp means respond)(1)

About the learning style			
Profile_rq			
:dimension	Integer	O	Felder dimension
:profile	Integer	O	learning style
Profile_rp			
:profile	Integer	O	Learning style
About the number of correct or incorrect answers to an exercise			
Results_rq			
:code	Integer	O	The exercise identifier
:instance	Integer	O	The exercise instance identifier
:type	Integer	O	1 if the correct answers are requested
Results_rp			
:code	Integer	O	The exercise identifier
:instance	Integer	O	The exercise instance identifier
:number	Integer	O	The number of answers of the type requested
:type	Integer	O	1 if the number indicates the correct answers or 0 if the number indicates the incorrect answers
About the qualification of the best execution of an exercise			
Qualification_rq			
:code	Integer	O	The exercise identifier
:instance	Integer	O	The exercise instance identifier
Qualification_rp			
:code	Integer	O	The exercise code
:instance	Integer	O	The exercise identifier
:qualification	Real	O	The exercise qualification
About the number of executions of an exercise			
TotalExecutions_rq			
:code	Integer	O	The exercise identifier
:instance	Integer	O	The exercise instance identifier
TotalExecutions_rp			
:code	Integer	O	The exercise identifier
:instance	Integer	O	The exercise instance identifier
:number	Integer	O	The number of the exercise executions
About the total number of questions answered per levels of difficulty throughout the executions of the exercise			
GlobalTotal_rq			
:code	Integer	O	The exercise identifier
:instance	Integer	O	The exercise instance identifier
:level	Integer	O	The level of difficulty requested (1-*Easy*, 2-*Normal*, 3-*Difficult*)
GlobalTotal_rp			
:code	Integer	O	The exercise identifier
:instance	Integer	O	The exercise instance identifier
:level	Integer	O	The level of difficulty responded to (1-*Easy*, 2-*Normal*, 3-*Difficult*)
:number	Integer	O	Number of questions responded to in the corresponding level of difficulty

About the qualification of the best execution of an exercise using questions of a particular level of difficulty			
QualificationDetail_rq			
:code	Integer	O	The exercise identifier
:instance	Integer	O	The exercise instance identifier
:level	Integer	O	The level of difficulty requested (1-*Easy*, 2-*Normal*, 3-*Difficult*)
QualificationDetail_rp			
:code	Integer	O	The exercise code
:instance	Integer	O	The exercise identifier
:level	Integer	O	The exercise level of the qualification
:qualification	Real	O	Qualification
About the visited nodes in a lesson			
NodeVisits_rq			
:codes	Set of string	O	A list of nodes
NodeVisits_rp			
:codes	Set of string	O	A list of nodes
:visited	Boolean	O	True if all the nodes were visited; false if the nodes were not visited

The activity diagram of this behavior is shown in the next figure.

RepliesToPedagogic

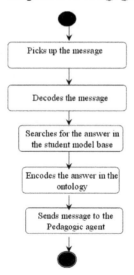

Figure 169.   Activity diagram of the *RepliesToPedagogic* behavior

RepliesToExerciseAdapter: this behavior is used to respond to requests coming from the *Exercise Adapter* agent (using the FIPA-query protocol) about the student performance when solving particular exercises. The exercise adapter agent uses the *ExerciseInfo_rq* object of the ontology described in Table 33 to make the request and the *User* agent responds to this request using the *ExerciseInfo_rp* object of the ontology described in Table 34.

ControllerReplies: this behavior is executed when the *User* agent receives from the *Controller* agent a message with a Query-if performative. The possible answers that the *User* agent may give are: *refuse* if it does not want to respond, *inform* with a *true* or *false* value if it has a stable or unstable state respectively, or *not-understood* if it does not understand the message. The activity diagram of this behavior is similar to that described for all the agents mentioned previously.

3.3.3   Protocol diagram

Figures 170 and 171 show the Protocol diagram of the *user* agent behaviors.

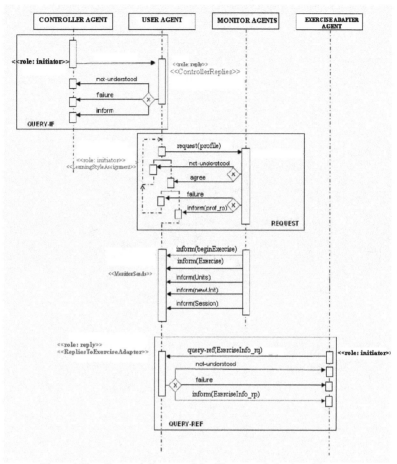

Figure 170.   Protocol diagram of the *User* agent behaviors (1)

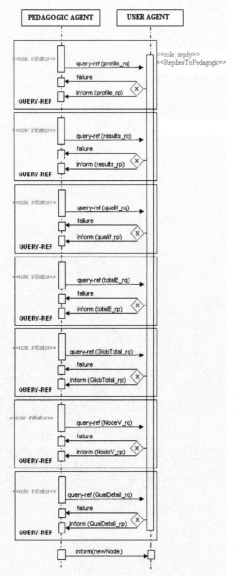

Figure 171.   Protocol diagram of the *User* agent behaviors (2)

3.4   Pedagogic Agent

3.4.1   Identification of the necessary behaviors

Considering the requirements described for this agent in Chapter 6, the following behaviors are identified:

- **HandlesTheCourseBeginning**: behavior that allows the lesson that the student is beginning to study to be identified.
- **BuildsNavigationTree**: behavior that allows the navigation tree of the course adapted to the student model characteristics (student learning profile and student knowledge state) to be built.
- **BuildsConceptStateDiagram**: behavior that allows the concept state diagram of the lesson that the student is learning to be built.
- **ControllerReplies**: behavior that informs the *Controller* agent about the *Pedagogic* agent state of activity.

3.4.2   Activity diagram and ontology

HandlesTheCourseBeginning: in this case, the monitor agent picks up the lesson code from the student action (opens a lesson) at the interface and informs the *Pedagogic* agent using the *newUnit* object of the ontology (see Table 25). The *Pedagogic* agent then proceeds to identify the learning materials for that lesson (see Figure 172).

HandlesTheCourseBeginning

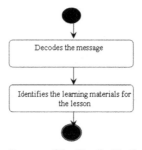

Figure 172.   Activity diagram of the HandlesTheCourseBeginning behavior

BuildsNavigationTree: this behavior works when the *Pedagogic* agent receives a request message from the *Browsing* agent using the *Tree_rq* object of the ontology. The pedagogic agent consequently responds using the *Tree_rp* object of the ontology after having evaluated the pedagogic decision rules proposed in the pedagogic domain of the course. The evaluation of these rules is done by requesting the *User* agent for information concerning the student model. The next figure shows the activity diagram of this behavior. Table 37 shows the structure of the *Tree_rq* and *Tree_rp* objects used in the agent communication (*Browsing* agent – *Pedagogic* agent).

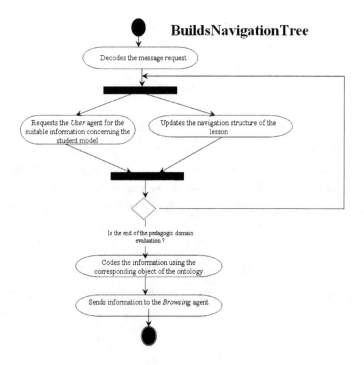

Figure 173.   Activity diagram of the *BuildsNavigationTree* behavior

Table 37. Objects involved in the communication between the Browsing and the Pedagogic agents

Tree_rq			
:code	Integer	O	The lesson identifier

Tree_rp			
:code	Integer	O	The lesson identifier
:node	Instance of node	O	Multiple cardinality: the graph structure (nodes and links)
nodes			
:name	String	O	The node identifier
:type	Integer	O	The type of node (basic content, bibliography, exercise, reinforcement)
:concept	Integer	O	The concept identifier to which the node belongs
::htmlfile	String	O	The learning content
links			
:Source_node	String	O	The source node identifier
:Destination_node	String	O	The destination node identifier
:state	Boolean	O	True if the link should be enabled or false if the link should be hidden

When the *Pedagogic* agent is evaluating the pedagogic decision rules, the communication between the *Pedagogic* and the *User* agents is carried out using the objects of the ontology described in Table 37.

BuildsConceptStateDiagram: this behavior works when the *Pedagogic* agent receives a request message from the *Browsing* agent using the *Concept_rq* object of the ontology. The *Pedagogic* agent then responds using the *Concept_rp* object of the ontology. Figure 174 shows the activity diagram of this behavior. The structure of the *Concept* objects used in the agent communication is shown in Table 38.

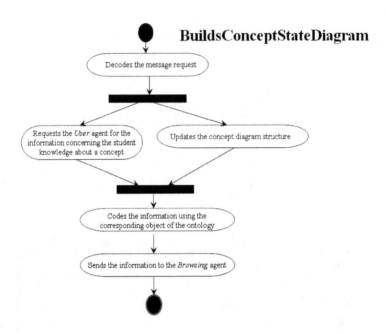

BuildsConceptStateDiagram

Figure 174.   Activity diagram of the *BuildsConceptStateDiagram* behavior

Table 38. Structure of the Concept objects

Concept_rq			
:code	Integer	O	The lesson identifier
Concept_rp			
:concept	Instance of concept	O	Multiple cardinality: concept, knowledge
concept			
:concept_i	String	O	The concept identifier
:knowledge	Float	O	The student knowledge rate for the concept

ControllerReplies: this behavior is executed when the *Pedagogic* agent receives a message with a Query-if performative from the *Controller* agent. The possible answers that the *Pedagogic* agent may give are: *refuse* if it does not want to respond, *inform* with a *true* or *false*, or *not-understood*. The activity diagram of this behavior is similar to that described for all the agents mentioned previously.

Protocol diagram

The Protocol diagram of the *Pedagogic* agent behaviors is shown in Figures 175 to 177.

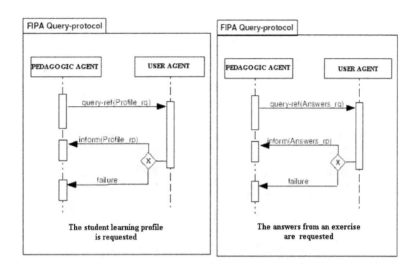

Figure 175.   Protocol diagram of the *Pedagogic* agent behaviors (1)

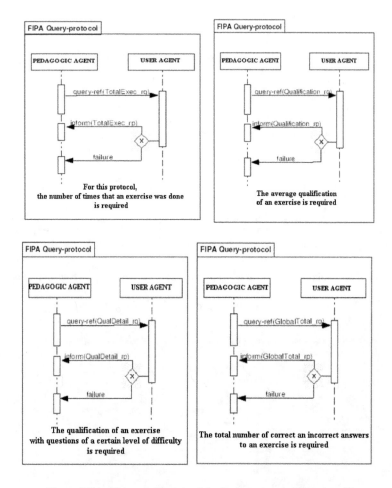

Figure 176.   Protocol diagram of the *Pedagogic* agent behaviors (2)

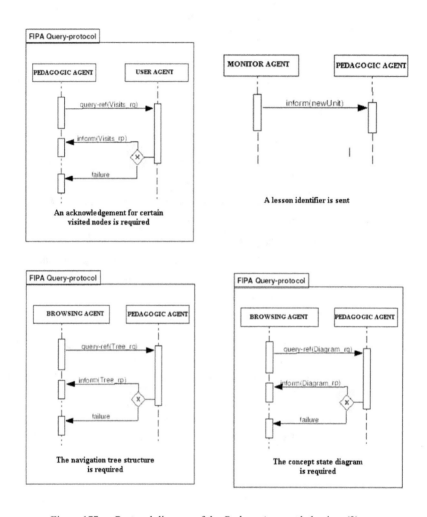

Figure 177.   Protocol diagram of the *Pedagogic* agent behaviors (3)

3.5   Browsing Agent

3.5.1   Identification of the necessary behaviors

Considering the requirements described in the last two tables, the following behaviors are identified:

- **AllowsAdaptiveNavigation:** behavior that allows the implementation of adaptive navigation techniques on the lesson contents by means of the student interface.
- **ShowConceptsDiagram:** behavior that allows the presentation of the state of student knowledge on the concepts of the course by means of the student interface.
- **RequestsExercises:** behavior that allows the construction and the presentation of the exercises proposed in the lesson by means of the student interface.
- **InformsAlerts:** behavior that allows the alert information concerning the existence of bibliographical references or exercises in particular sections of the lesson, to be sent.
- **SendsMotivReinfor:** behavior that allows the motivation or the reinforcement information to be sent to the *SMIT* agent in order to be presented to the user by means of an affective interface.
- **ControllerReplies:** behavior that informs the *Controller* agent about the *Browsing* agent state of activity.

3.5.2   Activity diagram and ontology

AllowsAdaptiveNavigation: in this case, the *Browsing* agent builds, by means of an HTML page, the navigation tree of the course applying the *hidden link* and the *link annotation* techniques of adaptive navigation in hypermedia. The course navigation tree structure is sent and refreshed by the *Pedagogic* agent each time the result of the pedagogic decision rule evaluation changes (cyclic behavior). The objects of the ontology used for this agent communication are the *Tree_rq* and the *Tree_rp* described in Table 37. The next figure shows the activity diagram of this behavior.

374

AllowsAdaptiveNavigation

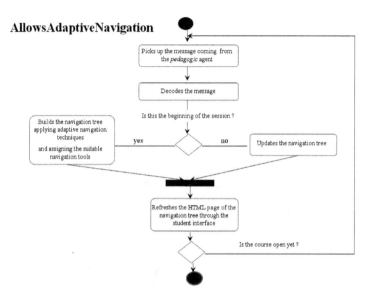

Figure 178.   Activity diagram of the *AllowsAdaptiveNavigation* behavior

ShowConceptsDiagram: by means of this behavior, the *Browsing* agent builds and updates, in the user interface, the diagram that represents the student knowledge state of the learned concepts. The information that allows this diagram to be built and updated is coming from the *Pedagogic* agent each time the student advances in the development of the learning activities (i.e., the student learns more concepts). The objects of the ontology used for this agent communication are the *concept_rq* and the *concept_rp* described in Table 38. Figure 179 shows the activity diagram of this behavior.

ShowsConceptsDiagram

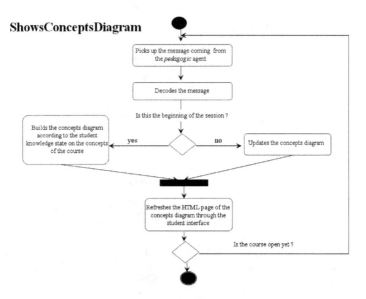

Figure 179.   Activity diagram of the *ShowConceptsDiagram* behavior

RequestsExercises: by means of this behavior, the *Browsing* agent requests that the *Exercise adapter* agent builds and presents the exercises prepared for the lesson. The basic characteristics of the exercises were sent by the *Pedagogic* agent with the structure of the navigation tree of the course. The object of the ontology used for this agent communication is the *makeExercise* described in Table 32. Figure 180 shows the activity diagram of this behavior.

RequestsExercises

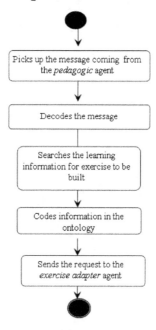

Figure 180.   Activity diagram of the *RequestsExercises* behavior

InformsAlerts: by means of this behavior the *Browsing* agent informs the *SONIA* agent of the accomplishment of an alert task that has been programmed by the student through the *SONIA* agent interface. In this case the programmed task is concerned with warning the student when a section of the lesson has bibliographical references to review or exercises to solve. The objects of the ontology used for this agent communication are shown in Table 39. Figure 181 shows the activity diagram of this behavior.

Table 39. *Structure of the ontology objects used to warn the agent SONIA with the accomplishment of the alert messages*

WarnBibliography_rq			
:need	Boolean	O	False if there is not any bibliography to review
WarnBibliography_rp			
:need	Boolean	O	True if there is a bibliography to review
WarnExercises_rq			
:need	Boolean	O	False if there is not any exercise to solve
WarnExercises_rp			
:need	Boolean	O	True if there is an exercise to solve

InformsAlerts

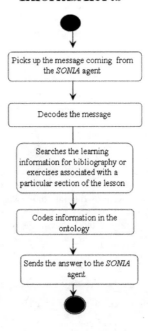

Figure 181.   Activity diagram of the *InformsAlerts* behavior

378

SendsMotivReinfor: this behavior is used by the *Browsing agent* to send the *SMIT* agent the motivation and the reinforcement messages that should be presented to the student by means of an affective interface (i.e., to make the student feel assisted while he/she learns). The *SMITmessage* object of the ontology (see Table 27) is used by the *Browsing* agent to send the information to the *SMIT* agent. Figure 182 shows the activity diagram of this behavior.

SendsMotivReinfor

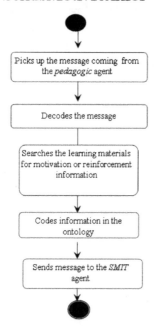

Figure 182.   Activity diagram of the *SendsMotivReinfor* behavior

ControllerReplies: this behavior is executed when the *Browsing* agent receives a message from the *Controller* agent with a Query-if performative. The possible answers that the *Browsing* agent may give are: *refuse* if it does not want to respond, *inform* with a *true* or *false* value if it has a stable or unstable state respectively, or *not-understood* if it does not understand the message.

3.5.3   Protocol diagram

The Protocol diagram for the behaviors described above is shown next in Figures 183 and 184.

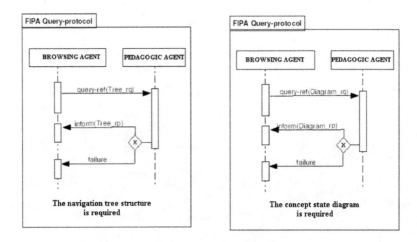

Figure 183.   Protocol diagram for the *Browsing* agent behaviors (1)

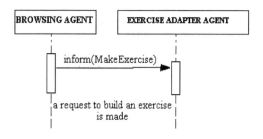

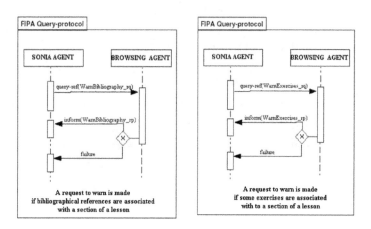

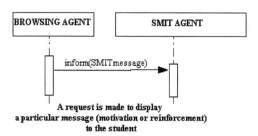

Figure 184.   Protocol diagram for the *Browsing* agent behaviors (2)

3.6 SONIA Agent

3.6.1 Identification of the necessary behaviors

The following behaviors, considering the requirements described in last table, are identified:

- **SONIAProgramming:** behavior that allows the tasks that the user wants the *SONIA* agent to carry out to be collected.
- **SMITRequests**: behavior that allows the messages that *SMIT* agent should display to the user interface to be sent.
- **ControllerReplies:** behavior that informs the *Controller* agent of the *SONIA* agent state of activity.

3.6.2 Activity diagrams and ontology

SONIAProgramming: with this behavior the *SONIA* agent collects the tasks to be programmed from the user interface. The user requests are later coded using the corresponding object of the ontology and sent to the agents working cooperatively to perform the tasks (Table 40). Figure 185 shows the activity diagram of this behavior.

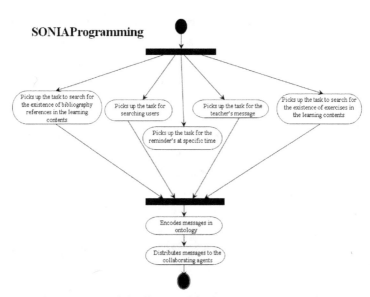

Figure 185.   Activity diagram of the *SONIAProgramming* behavior

Table 40. Structure of the objects involved in the SONIAProgramming behavior

Communications with the Controller agent			
UserOnline_rq			
:user_name	Set of string	O	List of users to search
:type	Integer	O	Message requester (1-teacher, 2-student)
UserOnline_rp			
:user_name	Set of string	O	List of users found
:type	Integer	O	Message requester (1-teacher, 2-student)
:connected	Boolean	O	True (the requested users are connected)
UserWarn_rq			
:time	time	O	Time to reach
UserWarn_rp			
:time	time	O	
:control	Boolean	O	True (the time is reached)
Communications with the Browsing agent			
WarnBibliography_rq			
:need	Boolean	O	False if there is not any bibliography to review
WarnBibliography_rp			
:need	Boolean	O	True if there is a bibliography to review
WarnExercises_rq			
:need	Boolean	O	False if there is not any exercise to solve
WarnExercises_rp			
:need	Boolean	O	True if there is an exercise to solve

SMITRequests: with this behavior the *SONIA* agent requests the *SMIT* agent to display the corresponding messages that inform the student of the accomplishment of the tasks that he/she had programmed. The *SMITmessage* object of the ontology (see Table 27) is used to achieve this goal.

ControllerReplies: this behavior is executed when the *Browsing* agent receives a message with a Query-if performative from the Controller agent. The possible answers that the *Browsing* agent may give are: *refuse* if it does not want to respond, *inform* with a *true* or *false* value if it has a stable or unstable state respectively, or *not-understood* if it does not understand the message.

3.6.3   Protocol diagram

The Protocol diagram for the behaviors described above is shown next in Figure 186.

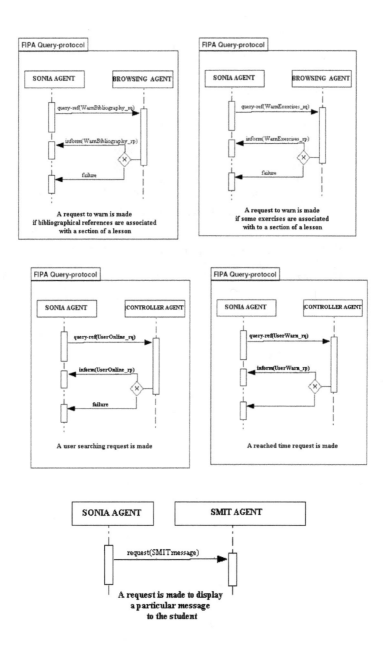

Figure 186.   Protocol diagram of the *SONIA* agent communications

385

3.7   SMIT Agent

3.7.1   Identification of the necessary behaviors

- **MonitorSmit:** allows the student-*SMIT* interaction if the student wants to check the message historial.
- **SmitDisplays:** allows the *SMIT* agent to choose a suitable representation of its behavior (using an animated life-like character) to display messages to the student.
- **ControllerReplies**: behavior that informs the *Controller* agent about the *SMIT* agent state of activity.

3.7.2   Activity diagram and ontology

MonitorSmit: with this behavior the *Monitor* agent allows the student to interact with the *SMIT* agent. The student petitions are coded using the *SMITwakeup* (if the SMIT wake up is requested) or the *SMITmessage* (if the *SMIT* is requested to display a message) objects of the ontology (see Table 27). The following figure shows the activity diagram of this behavior.

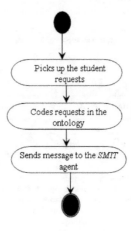

Figure 187.   Activity diagram of the *MonitorSmit* behavior

SmitDisplays: through this behavior the *SMIT* agent assumes its corresponding personality using a pre-stored, life-like character (anthropomorphous) to display the message. Figure 188 shows the activity diagram of this behavior.

SMITDisplays

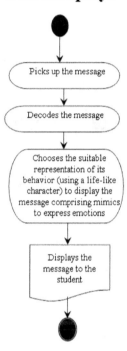

Figure 188.   Activity diagram of the *SMITDisplays* behavior

ControllerReplies: this behavior is executed when the *SMIT* agent a message with a Query-if performative receives from the *Controller* agent. The possible answers that the *SMIT* agent may give are: *refuse* if it does not want to respond, *inform* with a *true* or *false* value if it has a stable or unstable state respectively, or *not-understood* if it does not understand the message.

3.7.3   Protocol diagram

The following figure shows the Protocol diagram of the *SMIT* agent behaviors.

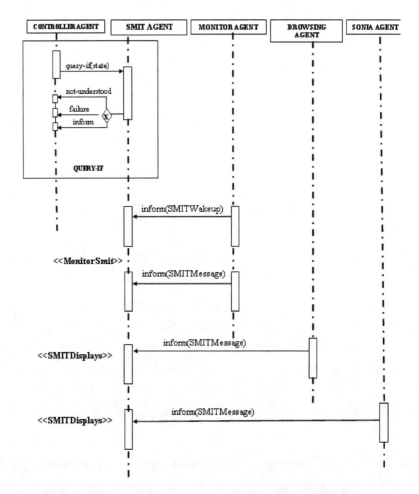

Figure 189.　Protocol diagram of the *SMIT* agent behaviors

3.8   Controller Agent

3.8.1   Identification of the necessary behaviors

The *Controller* agent behaves in a similar way to the AMS (Agent Management System) agent of the *JADE* platform, carrying out tasks for starting, restarting and killing agents in the MASPLANG session. In order to supervise the activity state of the agents, it uses the ping protocol at certain times to request a survival test. For the SONIA agent it carries out tasks concerning the supervision of certain system events.

3.8.2   Protocol diagram

The next figure shows the Protocol diagram of the *Controller* agent behaviors that are directly concerned with the agent control in the learning session.

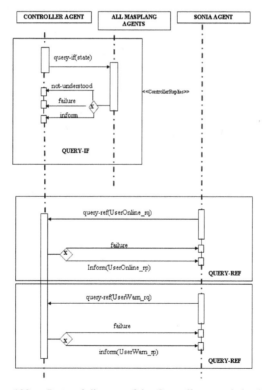

Figure 190.   Protocol diagram of the *Controller* agent behaviors

www.ingramcontent.com/pod-product-compliance
Lightning Source LLC
LaVergne TN
LVHW022259060326
832902LV00020B/3171